Governor

Inside the Maze

William McKee

Gill & Macmillan

Gill & Macmillan Ltd
Hume Avenue, Park West, Dublin 12
with associated companies throughout the world
www.gillmacmillan.ie

© William McKee, 2009
978 07171 4591 1

Type design: Make Communication
Print origination by Carole Lynch
Printed and bound by ColourBooks Ltd, Dublin

This book is typeset in Linotype Minion and Neue Helvetica.

The paper uses in this book comes from the wood pulp of
managed forests. for every tree felled, at least one tree is
planted, thereby renewing natural resources.

A CIP catalogue record for this book is available
from the British Library.

5 4 3 2 1

To my three children —
'You were the light that drew me
from the darkness.'

Contents

Acknowledgments

I would like to thank all the various people involved in assisting me to bring my book to publication. To everyone at Gill & Macmillan, especially Sarah Liddy, Aoife O'Kelly, Neil Ryan and Claire Egan.

To Alfie, Gavin and Ian: Three true friends. Your care and support carried me through the most difficult period of my life. To my brother and sisters: Thank you for being there for me. Your loving words and actions sustained me through the dark days when my illness threatened to overwhelm me. To Mike Radford, my psychotherapist from TMR Health Professionals: Your invaluable, on-going professional support and advice has helped me try to learn to live with and manage my illness. And finally to my partner Joanna: For all your love, support and understanding that kept me sane throughout the three most challenging years of my life.

WILLIAM McKEE
December 2008

Chapter 1
The Road to Silver City

On 12 July 1955 the first son and third child of George and 'Dolly' McKee entered the world. Every generation of the McKees, as far as could be traced back, always had a William, and this generation was to be no different. The boy was named William John Phineas McKee and joined his two elder sisters, Georgina and Barbara, in the McKee household. My brother Alan was to complete the family some four years later.

The name Phineas came from a relation of my father who was a Presbyterian minister. My father had wanted to give me Phineas as my first name but thankfully my mother, who had aspirations that I might have a vocation to the ministry, was sensible enough not to stick that one on me.

Of course my date of birth also played a part in the choice of my first name, 12 July in the Protestant calendar being a significant date in our history. (I was not the first McKee to be born on 12 July: I also had an uncle and cousin born on that date years before me, and why they were not called William I can't imagine.) I recently raised that very question with an uncle and wished that I had let the proverbial 'sleeping dogs lie'. He told me that he had two brothers called William. One however had died at birth and the other had died while a teenager after he was kicked in the head by a horse. Following these two tragic deaths the family had believed that the name William was unlucky and as a result it was not used again for obvious reasons.

Perhaps my father had forgotten this part of the family history or maybe he was not superstitious but as my adult life unfolded there were certainly many occasions when I would have been in total agreement with my grandparents' suspicions with regard to the name William being unlucky. The many life-changing events that will be recalled in these pages may well cause the reader to ponder it too.

I think it's important to explain at this point that being born on 12 July and being named William did not mean that I grew up to be a religious bigot; on the contrary, my parents raised me to be both tolerant and respectful of other people's religion and beliefs.

As was typical of most families in the 1950s and 60s, we were anything but affluent. My father was a bus driver and part-time farmer (and that was more by necessity than choice). We were in our third house by the time I was five and this was really the house that became the McKee family home for the remainder of our childhood. The house was in the countryside some three miles from Downpatrick. Although I last lived there some thirty years ago (and although my mother died there), fond memories of the house are ingrained in my mind forever: I still smile when one of those memories slips into my mind. Little did I know that in the future how different, incomprehensible circumstances would dictate the same house-moving scenario for my own children too.

School was Ballytrim Primary, a small two-room school situated in the countryside halfway between Crossgar and Killyleagh. Classes One to Three were taught by Miss Ritchie in one room, and the rest by Miss Morrison next door.

I started school a year early, which meant that I had to stay in Primary Seven for two years. I remember how strange it felt when the friends I had known since first year left and headed to secondary school. Not that the two years in Primary Seven proved any advantage to me: I still failed my Eleven Plus despite spending two years covering the preparation for the exam.

Failing the Eleven Plus had a devastating impact on me, feeding my insecurity and worsening the stammer I had had since early childhood. It became so bad that any stressful situation left me almost speechless. My mother, God rest her, took me to a speech specialist every Tuesday, and by the time I commenced secondary school the problem had become manageable.

I was also a chubby child—in today's terms I would probably be classified as a clinically obese—and as I got older this added to my lack of confidence. My awareness that we were not the richest of families (at one stage we had neither electricity nor a television) also had an effect on me. Little did I realise at the time how these circumstances would drive me towards the top of my profession. It was not until early in my career that some of these problems arose again and the insecurities of my youth returned to haunt me.

I had started Killyleagh Secondary School in September and settled in well. Although my old friends from Primary One were now in second year I was able to renew their acquaintance as well as making new friends among my own classmates.

It would have been hard to believe at the time that the paths of some of the people that I got to know then were to cross with mine in the future, in different, difficult circumstances; circumstances that would put some of us on opposing sides of the law.

Unfortunately my contentment at my new school didn't last. Towards the end of November 1967 things changed for ever. My mother was diagnosed with breast cancer on a Monday, underwent an operation on Tuesday and was dead by the following Wednesday. This was my first experience of bereavement: my father's parents had passed away before I was born and my mother's had died when I was too young to understand. Because I hadn't realised my mother was ill I never had the opportunity to say the words I would have wanted her to hear before she passed away. Neither did I attend her funeral: it seems it was decided that I was too young to go through such a difficult experience.

My one abiding memory from the week of her death is of me and my brother Alan, who was eight years old, hugging each other in the garden and crying over her passing. This was my earliest encounter with grief. Few of the tears I would shed in years to come would be over the death of close relations: they would be an expression of a different sort of grief, a grief that was just as emotionally draining, and that drove me to the brink of suicide.

Two years in Killyleagh Secondary were enough for me. I hadn't really settled following the death of my mother and I decided at the age of thirteen to move schools to Downpatrick Secondary. This turned out to be a mistake: the quality of teaching at Downpatrick was, in my opinion, of a lower standard than at Killyleagh and my education suffered as a result.

After leaving Downpatrick Secondary I went to the local technical college and studied for my O levels. On reflection, 'studied' is a gross exaggeration. I had developed a healthy interest in both football and girls, and this time the blame for my academic failures lay squarely at my own door.

While waiting for my O level results I helped out on a schoolfriend's family's dairy farm for three pounds a day plus meals. I was happy and even managed to scrape enough money together to buy my first car. The novelty soon wore off, however, or perhaps I should say it was soon washed off. One morning after the cows were milked, I was standing in my oilskins washing down the yard, accompanied by an incredible downpour of rain. It was at that moment that I decided that being a farm hand was not a career I would pursue for very much longer.

Within weeks I had secured alternative employment with Harland & Wolff. Despite my own low opinion of my mathematical ability I was selected, on the basis of the results of an aptitude test, to work in the Wages Office.

At the time I began my shipyard career there were ten thousand staff employed there along with five thousand subcontractors. (I wonder where these men are now?) The main belief among the workforce at that time, which was encouraged by the unions, was that 'they will never close the Yard'. Over the years that followed, contract after contract was lost because the strength of the unions and the ever-present threat of strike action meant that completion dates could not be guaranteed.

There was one particular occasion when the then chief executive required a guarantee from the unions not to strike during the duration of a big engine contract. He received the guarantee as requested, but a strike was called just weeks before the engine contract was due to be signed. The chief executive resigned, promptly took up a new position with another ship builder and, needless to say, took the unsigned engine contract with him.

I quickly settled into my new environment in the 'Yard' and soon got used to my duties. The only cloud on my new horizon was the atmosphere in the office. I had noticed that on a couple of occasions the conversation had stopped abruptly when I entered the office. Bearing in mind I was only eighteen years old, and this was my first 'real' job, I had to fight against my old feelings of insecurity. Was I paranoid or was there something about me that my colleagues didn't like? I just wasn't sure.

At the time my office supervisor was Fred Kernahan, a big friendly man, but a man who called a spade a spade. Fred was a Protestant, as was his number two, Roy Lemon. Apart from myself, there were four other staff employed in the office, three of whom were Protestants and one Catholic.

I hadn't thought much about the dichotomy of being called William McKee and coming from Downpatrick, a predominantly Catholic town in County Down, and now I was employed in one of the bastions of Protestantism in East Belfast. This contradiction was what lay at the heart of the uneasiness I had sensed among my colleagues.

Big Fred solved the problem in a flash. 'Look, young McKee, the lads have been talking—no, arguing—about your religion. So are you a Taig or a Prod?'

I was stunned, for two reasons. First, that my religion should be given such a high priority in the context of a busy office. Second, what difference would it make if I were a Catholic or a Protestant? I had had a sheltered upbringing in a religious context, and I couldn't come to terms with the bigotry I was being confronted with in the workplace. But I also annoyed and disappointed myself by my response to Fred's question. I blurted out, 'I am a Protestant!' Almost immediately I had a feeling of great relief followed by a sense of disappointment in myself for joining 'the club': the club that deemed that being a Protestant was somehow 'better' than being of a different faith.

This one incident, more than any other, highlighted the bigotry that existed in the company, a company which was one of Northern Ireland's biggest employers. I often wondered, had I been a Catholic and had the staff taken the time to get to know me, would I have gained the same respect? Maybe it was my old enemy, insecurity, on my shoulder again, but my gut feeling was that I wouldn't have!

The 'Yard' took me into its arms and I spent three of the most enjoyable years of my working life there. I suppose my working experience was enhanced when I fell hopelessly in love for the first time with a beautiful Catherine Zeta-Jones lookalike. The love went unrequited until a few months after I left Harland's, when our paths crossed and we were entwined for a few very special and memorable months.

Around the middle of 1976 there was talk of staff reductions in the 'Yard' and as they worked on a 'last in, first out' system I thought my name would be in the hat. I had enjoyed my time in Harland's, not just because of my Catherine lookalike, but there were little or no further career opportunities. It was literally a case of waiting to fill 'dead men's shoes'. This was brought home to me in the starkest terms possible with the death of 'big Fred' and the subsequent promotion of Roy to Fred's post. Roy was in his late twenties or thereabouts, and a shipyard career man to boot, so this just reinforced my belief that my career opportunities were practically non-existent. I was fed up travelling to Belfast each day and when the cost of fuel, and my five

pounds contribution to the McKee household, was taken from my
£13.50 a week salary there was not a lot left to get excited about. I was
paid fortnightly— £27 each pay day—which meant the first weekend
was great, but it was a struggle until pay day came around again
almost two weeks later.

I decided to look for employment closer to home, which took me
to Richard Kew and Sons, in Downpatrick, as a sub-accountant. I
received a big salary increase, my income progressing to a massive
£35 per week, complemented by a vastly reduced fuel bill. I also sup-
plemented my income by giving the younger girls from the factory a
lift to the local discos, for which I charged £1 a head. I did this on aver-
age three nights a week, so my wallet accepted that further financial
boost with pleasure. There were also hidden benefits in these arrangements, benefits that I had not considered at the inception of my little
scheme.

I was employed with Richard Kew for only about nine months, but
what a nine months! The factory produced belts and braces for the
fashion houses and also had a contract with the army for soldiers'
webbing. The army contract surprised me because Downpatrick,
where the factory was situated, had a strong nationalist community,
and I thought that working for the Armed Forces would have been a
definite no-no.

Ninety per cent of the factory employees were women whose ages
ranged from sixteen years old (the school leavers) to fortyish, the
oldest of the 'housewife' shift. Because of its location the workforce
was also ninety per cent Catholic. I had moved from one extreme to
the other, albeit on a much smaller scale than at Harland & Wolff.

As in most factories the craic was mighty, and I don't believe a
single day passed in the nine months I was there when I didn't laugh
at least once. There were scary moments too—it was hard to anticipate
what tricks the girls were going to pull next. One year, as Christmas
approached, and with the order book full, the Christmas spirit was
well up and running. I had been teasing the girls about my Christmas
present and was close to getting a present that almost frightened the
life out of me. It wasn't the fact that the girls had knitted me a 'willie
warmer' that frightened me the most—it was more the fact that they
threatened to fit it.

During 1976–7 I started to feel undervalued, purely from a
monetary perspective, and while I accepted that the factory was not

awash with money I believed that a little more of it should be making its way into my pocket.

One evening as I was browsing the jobs section of the *Belfast Telegraph* I came across the invitation to 'Earn £80 per week in the Prison Service'. Did I want to join the Prison Service? Could I see myself wearing a uniform and guarding terrorists? The answer to both these questions was a definite 'no'!

But a plan presented itself to me as how I might use that Prison Service advertisement to my advantage, and that very night I posted my request for an application form. A career in the Prison Service? Had I changed my mind? Not at all!

Within a few days the application form arrived, accompanied by brochures that focused more on the £80 a week than anything else. (Maybe that's not fair, though: perhaps since that was the part that caught my eye in the first place it's what's stayed in my mind most strongly.)

In to work I went the following morning having convinced myself that my little scheme would provide me with an increase in income. (No, I still had no intention of joining the Prison Service.) My plan was put into practice around ten o'clock, just as the directors of the company were joining me for coffee, as was the norm each morning. As they followed each other into my office I spread the Prison Service brochures on my desk and focused intently upon them, almost to the point of ignoring the two directors as they entered my office.

'Aha! What's this, young William?' asked Aiden Killen, one of the directors.

'Just looking, Aiden', I replied. 'I don't mean to be disrespectful, but the salary I am on now is not enough for me to be comfortable and I'm just exploring other avenues to see what's out there.'

'So what have you there?' he enquired.

It's working better than I imagined, I thought.

'It's the Prison Service. Eighty pounds a week. Seems to be the best on offer at the moment,' I informed him (hint, hint).

Alan Barnes, the other director, had heard what Aiden had said, and it became a three-way conversation.

'So would you really go into the Prison Service then, young William?' Alan asked. I looked up just in time to catch a wink from Aiden to Alan. They had me rumbled. They knew I was bluffing and was just using the threat of the Prison Service brochure to encourage them to increase my current salary.

They spotted that I had in turn rumbled them. Now we were at an impasse.

Aiden stopped smiling. 'Look, William, you know as well as we do that the company is not the type that can afford to pay big salaries, and with the high unemployment in Downpatrick you also know that if we advertised your position, even at slightly less than the salary that you receive, we would fill your role in a week.'

Of course I knew he was right, but I was still not prepared to resign myself to defeat. I knew they both valued me for the quality and accuracy of my work and I decided to go for broke.

'I understand exactly where you're coming from,' I explained, 'but as I said I can't live comfortably on my current wage, so I will go ahead and apply for the Prison Service and if successful I will give the company a month's notice to allow you time to advertise and appoint someone to fill my position.'

I looked straight into their faces. They were smiling again. They were still calling my bluff. Right there at that very moment I made another of those decisions that a long way down the road would come back to haunt me. If the directors had offered me an extra ten pounds per week at that meeting I would have binned the Prison Service brochures there and then, but I didn't and, as they say, the rest is history.

I completed my application form and posted it, without hesitation, ten minutes later—not because I was afraid I would change my mind; it was more that I had made my decision and that was that.

Within seven days I had my acknowledgement and a date for interview. The interview went well—I could answer all the questions without too much difficulty—and a few days later I was notified of the date to attend a medical. The medical proved straightforward and then the waiting game began. I had been told that no news was good news. If I had been successful at interview, and provided that no problems had arisen at the medical, it would take a number of weeks for the Prison Service to complete background security checks and receive character references and references from previous employers.

Three weeks to the day after the interview I received a letter with the news I had been waiting for. Yes, I had been successful. The last few lines of the letter instructed me to report to Belfast Prison on the morning of 14 July 1977.

When I handed in my letter of resignation to the directors at coffee the following morning, I took satisfaction from the dumbfounded expression that spread across their faces.

'You were serious?' Aiden said in a tone somewhere between surprise and shock. Clearly he still believed I had been bluffing. It hadn't helped, of course, that I had attended the interview and the medical for my new career while on leave.

'We need to get on sorting out a replacement as soon as possible,' he said, directing his concerns to Alan. At that very moment I realised that even if they offered me an extra twenty pounds a week I would not have changed my mind. It was as if I had started a new chapter of a book, and turning back a page was definitely not an option I would have considered.

After coffee I started thinking about what I was going to tell the workers: they would want to know where my career move was going to take me. I was concerned about what to say because Downpatrick was a nationalist town with many known IRA sympathisers. A number of prison officers had been murdered by the Provisional IRA and obviously the factory workers knew all about me, including my home address. Even though I had not yet started my new job, this was the first time I became aware of the security implications that my new career was going to have for me and my family.

I need not have worried—the decision was taken out of my hands. One of the director's wives worked on the shop floor and naturally enough he mentioned to her that 'young William' was leaving for a career in the Prison Service. Of course, by tea break the following morning the whole workforce was aware of my new career direction.

The number of visits to my office from the staff between the time they found out I was leaving and my actual resignation date was both surprising and touching. I had enjoyed a great working relationship with them. (In fact with some of the girls it was more than that!)

I laugh now when I recall the morning Alan Barnes burst into my office, red faced, clearly very angry. 'Can I ask you—no, tell you—to keep your bloody love life outside the gates of this factory?' he shouted at me. I was taken aback. 'What?' I spluttered out in reply.

'For the first time in all my time employed in this factory,' he went on, 'the production lines in both belt and brace packing have ground to a halt, and it's all down to you and your bloody love life!' He was still shouting.

'I'm sorry, Alan, but I honestly don't know what you're getting at,' I protested. My mind was racing. What had I done? Finally the penny dropped. I had been seeing a girl from belt packing on a fairly casual basis and the previous night I had bumped into a girl from braces packing. One thing led to another and I ended up leaving her home. Late—very late!

But I still couldn't understand how that could have impacted on the factory and how, more significantly, it could have brought the factory production line to a halt. Could it really be something to do with that?

Alan saw the look on my face and released that I was halfway to reaching a conclusion. 'You don't know how your little exploits last night impacted on the production line? Let me explain.' He went on sarcastically, 'Karen came in this morning and had a little boast that she was out with you last night. The belt packing got to hear of it and production stopped while they discussed if Rosie should be told. The brace packing has now ceased production to discuss the problem as they think it is nobody else's business and the belt packing should mind their own business. So, as I said, keep your love life outside the factory gates, please!' He turned on his heel and left the office, nearly taking the door of the hinges in the process.

Of course Rosie found out and brought the matter to a close just before lunch that same day. My face still throbs when I remember the slap she landed after her angry outburst!

The rest of the workers must have had a short memory. On my last day there I received a call asking me to go to brace packing. I made my way up the stairs and was surprised to find every single member of staff there, including the directors and the clerk from the store room. Even the driver was there.

My face was scarlet by the time I was led to the centre of the room. What happened next was diametrically opposite to the kind of experience I had endured in my first few weeks in the shipyard.

Aiden opened the proceedings with a short speech, in which he said the kind of things that are said in hundreds of places of work up and down the country when a valued employee is leaving.

'We are sorry to lose William, a valued member of the workforce, liked by all, now leaving us to try to better his career. We wish him luck, but before he leaves, if I could now call Wilma, who wishes to say a few words on behalf of the staff on the shop floor, to come up.'

Everyone clapped in recognition of Aiden's speech, short and all that it was.

Wilma made her way to the front. She clearly had a gift in her hand. I don't know what colour of red is darker than scarlet, but if there was one my face displayed it now!

A thought suddenly struck me but Wilma, always quick on the uptake, started to laugh. 'No,' she said, 'don't worry, it isn't the willie warmer.' The whole place erupted and it took a call from Aiden to bring it back under control.

'William,' Wilma said, 'we are so sorry that you are leaving, some more than most.'

A chorus of 'oooh!' went up from the floor, clearly directed at Jacinta, who, the staff believed, had romantic intentions towards me.

'No, William, seriously, we have really taken you into our hearts and appreciated how helpful you were with any queries during your time with us and also the way you have integrated yourself into the spirit of our wee factory. So we have all clubbed together to show our appreciation.'

A lump formed in my throat and I could feel myself starting to fill up.

Wilma continued, 'We know you are a Protestant and may not believe in or really want to retain these gifts so we have kept the receipt and needless to say we won't be offended if you take the gifts back and change them for something more to your preference.'

Safe to say I didn't have a clue what the small parcel in her left hand contained. Although it did strike a chord that, in contrast to the ship-yard, they were not letting my religion colour their opinion of me.

Wilma handed me the parcel and, judging by the look of antici-pation on everyone's face, they wanted me to open the parcel there and then. I carefully opened the crisp coloured paper and much to my surprise and delight opened first a little statue of St Christopher, closely followed by a sterling silver locket-size St Christopher. I couldn't speak and was grateful that Wilma filled the gap.

'We are all extremely fond of you, William McKee, and because of the new environment that you will soon find yourself in we are worried for you and would hate that you should come to any harm. We have bought you first the statue of St Christopher to keep in your car and would ask you, as long as it is not against your beliefs, to keep the silver one on your person to keep you safe.'

I was so touched by her words that all I managed to get out was a mumbled 'Thanks so very much.' On looking round, I saw a fair number of the audience had tears in their eyes.

Of course I knew that St Christopher was the patron saint of travellers and had already decided that I would not even think about returning either of the presents to the shop.

I left work with a mixture of feelings that last day, initially sad at the thought of leaving the enduring friendships that I had cultivated in my nine months at the factory but also excited by the new challenges that lay ahead. I have to add that the thought of the £80 a week put quite a smile on my face as well.

As I was driving home that day my mind drifted back to about six months earlier, a cold January night when I had left a girl home to Lisburn after a night's entertainment at the Milbrook Lodge in Ballynahinch.

We were parked on the Moira side of Lisburn and as we 'talked' I noticed over her left shoulder a massive glow in the sky. 'What's that over there?' I asked. 'Oh, that's Silver City,' she replied.

'Silver City?' I said, thinking that it looked a bit big for a Chinese restaurant.

'Long Kesh!' she said, seeing the question on my face. 'The Maze Prison.'

'So that's the Maze Prison,' I said.

Little did I know that night that within nine months I would be a serving prison officer in that very prison, the first step in what would start as a challenging career but that ultimately led to unimaginable heartache and pain.

Chapter 2
Millisle to the Maze

A few months before I embarked on my new career, my father was lucky enough to be bequeathed a fairly substantial amount of money. It would have been easy for him to go out and buy a new property and sell our existing house, which we all regarded as our home, but thankfully he felt the same as the rest of us and instead bought a temporary home in Crossgar, where the family moved until our old home had been replaced by a new build.

I never imagined that the night before we moved to our temporary home would be the last night I ever slept there. By the time the new house was built my life had changed unimaginably.

I could not start my new job in the Northern Ireland Prison Service soon enough. Now that my decision had been made the only direction I was looking was forward. I had my letter instructing me to report to Belfast Prison at eight o'clock on the morning of Wednesday 14 July 1977, and my feelings alternated almost constantly between anticipation and concern as I waited for the morning to arrive.

On the Saturday night before my starting date I was at the Millbrook Lodge, Ballynahinch, my usual entertainment spot at the weekend. I rarely missed a Saturday night at the Millbrook: in 1977 it was regarded as one of the better local night spots and I knew many of those who went there. I hadn't been there that long when I was approached by Eugene, an old schoolfriend who had been at the local technical college with me a few years earlier.

'Willie McKee, what are you at these days?' he asked.

I was about to share my new career details with Eugene when suddenly the security implications of being a prison officer kicked in for a second time. I realised that I couldn't just go shooting my mouth off to any Tom, Dick or, in this case, Eugene that I was about to embark on a career in a section of the security forces in Northern Ireland, members of which were identified as legitimate targets for murder by the Provisional IRA.

I couldn't say that I was still working in the factory because two of the girls from the factory lived in the same village as Eugene and I wasn't even sure if he didn't already know that I was no longer employed there.

'Not a lot,' was the best answer I could come up with and I tried to move the conversation on to another subject as quickly as possible.

'You still at Jordanstown University then?' I inquired.

'Well, no, actually,' he said. 'A few weeks ago I wrecked one of my mates' cars and I've had to get a job to pay him back. No insurance!'

'So where are you working, then?' I asked.

Before answering he looked around as if he didn't want to say anything within earshot of anyone else; which was all but impossible in the Millbrook on a Saturday night. He leaned close to my ear and whispered, 'I am starting work in the Prison Service next Wednesday morning.'

I couldn't speak. The hairs were raised on the back of my neck. My mind was struggling with a jumble of emotions—disbelief, concern, fear, astonishment. My first thought was that it was a wind-up. It was too much of a coincidence to be true. One of the girls from the factory must have told him.

'Are you really?' I asked suspiciously.

'Yes, and I'm still not sure if I've made the correct decision,' came the answer.

He then went on to explain that after writing off his friend's car he was desperate to get a decent paying job so that his friend could be reimbursed as soon as possible. He had spotted the same advertisement I had, had applied and had been successful, just like me.

Suddenly another paranoid thought struck me. Eugene was a Catholic and lived in Drumaness, a small nationalist village on the outskirts of Ballynahinch. Was he a republican sympathiser? I didn't know. Had PIRA already found out about my joining the Prison Service?

We made our way outside the main function room and found an area where we could discuss the matter without yelling in each other's ear. I had already decided not to share my new career details with Eugene, at least not until I had satisfied myself that he was genuine and that my personal security was not about to be compromised. 'God!', I thought, 'I haven't even got to my first day and already paranoia is taking its toll on me.'

Eugene talked. I listened. He described his experience at the interview and the medical and as he spoke I began to relax and gradually came to accept that he was actually joining me on Wednesday morning at the gates of HMP Belfast. I laughed and Eugene looked puzzled until I started to share my new career details with him. Now it was his turn to look shocked and to wonder whether I was winding him up.

Once each accepted that the other was actually telling the truth we felt relieved to know we each had the support of a colleague in the same position and with the same fears and concerns.

Eugene knew well that the Prison Service, like the RUC, was ninety-odd per cent made up of men and women from the Protestant community. This naturally took me back to the shipyard and the way Catholic employees were perceived there. I felt for him, but there was nothing that I could say to allay Eugene's fears for the simple reason that I didn't know what either of us could expect.

My family was as supportive as ever, especially my father, who added the proviso that I should be careful. He used one of his favourite phrases when we spoke: 'Good care cuts the head of bad luck.'

It was hard to get to sleep on Tuesday night. The excitement was immense, but tempered to a degree by the concerns about stepping into the unknown.

On the morning of Wednesday 14 July, two days after my twenty-second birthday, I arrived at the gates of HMP Belfast. I was directed to the secure car park at the side of the prison and then made my way to the training room.

There were about thirty of us, all strangers to each other except Eugene and me. The roll was called—'McBride, Condon, Smith, Schofield, O'Hare . . .' — and as Eugene's name was called he leaned across to me and whispered, 'Spot the Fenian.'

The first few days were a blur. We reported to the stores and were fitted out with our uniforms, had the security talk, listened to a brief history of the Prison Service, then a history of the 'Crum', as HMP Belfast Crumlin Road was affectionately known.

After a few days we were allowed on the wings. It's fair to say we were apprehensive: this was to be our first encounter with the prisoners, some of whom were on remand for heinous terrorist crimes. But our concerns were groundless: the inmates seemed oblivious to us and just passed by without a word or indeed any form of acknowledgement.

The only time I saw a prisoner speak to an officer was to reply to a question or to ask for a light for his cigarette.

The wings were the long three-tier-high units that ran from a central point in the prison known as the Circle. The 'Crum' was an old Victorian-style prison of a design that was shortly to be replaced by the new H Block-style units that were currently under construction at HMP Maze.

My one abiding memory of the 'Crum' was the way the staff treated us new recruits. We were highly motivated individuals with minds like sponges, desperate to soak up whatever knowledge and advice these long-in-the-tooth warders could impart to us. To a man we were unbelievably disappointed.

The staff told us to stay out of their offices and remain on the landings. (The landings were the walkways that ran along the wings past the cell doors.) We assumed that the staff would discuss the wing routine and give us the benefit of their many years of experience. We were totally ignored! There and then I decided that if I had any influence over where I was posted after completing my training it would not be HMP Belfast.

The wings were divided into cells, where the inmates were secured, and various offices—converted cells—that were used for administrative functions. There was also an office for the principal officer in charge of the wing and another office for the wing governor. At the time I thought it strange that there were two grades responsible for the wing, and that one of them, a governor, seemed to be rarely there.

I could not have imagined at that time that it would be some twenty years before I would return on a permanent posting to the 'Crum' as the Governor of A Wing, the biggest wing in the prison.

Another issue that surprised me was that the inmates had to use pots in their cells during lock-up periods if they could not wait to be unlocked to go to the toilet. This was particularly relevant when they were locked up at 8.30 each evening until 8.00 the following morning. An additional embarrassment for the inmates was of course that there were two prisoners in each cell. Some prisoners however had an understandable reluctance to use the pot and then spend the remainder of the night suffocating with the blankets covering their head to avoid the smell that their toileting efforts had produced. It was these prisoners that instead defecated on newspapers and threw the 'mystery parcels' out through the cell window into the yard below. Of course the poor yard orderly had the unenviable task of recovering and disposing of these 'mystery parcels' the following day!

The two weeks at the 'Crum' passed quickly, and we were made very much aware that we were now part of a disciplined service. Along with the 'yes sir, no sir' and, of course, the salutes, we were made aware of the structure in the service, which ran from basic grade officer up to governor with four ranks in between. The highest uniformed rank was chief officer 1 and my initial impression was that although the governor was in charge of the prison, the 'chief' seemed to have greater influence. I arrived at this conclusion on the basis of a few observations, the most significant being the respect that the chief seemed to receive from the staff, which was just not as apparent with the governor. I thought this was probably because a chief officer would have joined the service as an officer and worked his way up through the ranks, while most governors would have joined at a grade equivalent to chief officer 2. The other factor was that the chiefs had a different management style from that of the governor and would bawl out an officer for the slightest indiscretion. I also heard industrial language used on more than one occasion.

Over the two weeks at the 'Crum' I had begun to get to know other members of this latest squad of prison officer trainees, and one particular relationship made in those days of summer 1977 still flourishes some thirty years later.

The officer, an ex-Ulster Defence Regiment soldier, is the most sincere person I have ever had the pleasure of knowing. One of his strengths is the ability to pluck out of thin air just the right phrase to lift the burden of despondency from a friend's shoulder and to give an alternative slant to a situation that another person cannot see. 'Alfie's gift' was to come to my aid many times in the future.

After two weeks at HMP Belfast my training continued at the Prison Service College, Millisle. There had been a rapid increase in the prison population following the introduction of internment, and the Prison Service was unable to meet the additional facilities required, particularly in relation to training, and on arrival at Millisle I discovered that the training facilities amounted to two large Portakabins and not a lot else.

The squad was divided into two for the duration of the six-week training period, during which we covered most aspects of the role of a prison officer. We had two tutors, Dessie Stewart and Harry Forester, highly experienced principal officers who, in addition to covering the course syllabus, passed on to us accounts of real situations that they had experienced during their time at the sharp end.

Our duties in relation to escorting prisoners to court, the use of handcuffs, how we should address judges, the searching of prisoners and their cells, and a general understanding of the Prison Rules and Chief Officers' Orders took up the majority of our time in Millisle.

The other aspect of our training, which was strongly emphasised, was marching. The ex-soldiers in our ranks were given the job of instructors, and one such instructor was John Schofield, an ex-squaddie who relished his role. Definitely a sergeant major in disguise! I really could not understand this emphasis on 'square bashing', as the only time I ever marched in earnest was the day we passed out of the college; and I reckon it was the same for the majority of the class. From that day to the end of my career I never marched again.

While I am not criticising this part of the training, I felt that since the course was condensed into six weeks the time taken up with marching could have been better spent in preparing us for the many difficult situations that lay ahead.

One day halfway through the course, while we were studying some tedious element of the prison officer training, the majority of which was classroom-based, the silence was broken when a very serious-looking Principal Officer Forester cam into the classroom.

He bent over and whispered quietly into Principal Officer Stewart's ear, at which Principal Officer Stewart's face adopted the same serious expression.

'Sorry, lads,' he said. 'Could I have your attention, please?' I didn't like the sound of that. His facial expression, his tone, his body language all spelled bad news.

Bad news didn't come close to describing the terrible stomach-wrenching words that followed. 'Last night a serving prison officer at HMP Magilligan was murdered in a bar between Ballymoney and Ballymena. His name was Graham Fenton.'

You could have heard a pin drop. There was not a sound. I searched for Eugene. I met his gaze and saw the uneasiness in his eyes. My thoughts at that time, I am embarrassed to admit, were not for the murdered officer, but were focused solely on myself. Fear, I suppose, was the excuse I used for my selfishness. Fear for my own life. Whatever had possessed me to even consider becoming part of an organisation that was losing its members through murder by the paramilitaries? I breathed long and slow.

'You okay, Officer McKee?' Principal Officer Stewart interrupted my thoughts.

'Yes, fine, sir,' I answered, a little too quickly. I could feel the sweat trickling down my back. This was the first time I had felt the effects of the stress of the job. The first time, but by no means the last.

Principal Officer Stewart gave us the rest of the day off: he knew that to continue with our studies after the disturbing news would have been futile. Those of us who were living in the college during our period of training returned to our respective houses and strangely enough the subject was not discussed again. Now I was beginning to recognise one of the reasons we were getting paid a salary of £80 a week to be a prison officer. Danger money!

Our training also involved a visit to HMP Maze Compound, which frightened the living daylights out of us. The Maze Compound was like a prisoner of war camp. Internment had been introduced with such speed that there was inadequate time to build a new prison. Long Kesh, the army camp located on an abandoned airfield just outside Lisburn, was an obvious choice. There were old Nissen huts left over from the Second World War, when the airfield had last been used, which were to provide accommodation for the hundreds of suspected paramilitaries who were lifted from our streets following the implementation of internment.

The huts were fenced in, each fence being topped by razor wire to deter the inmates from scaling the fences to partial freedom. Only partial freedom because outside the fences there was a high, purpose-built concrete wall which was designed to prevent prisoners escaping from the compounds.

We listened wide-eyed and half disbelieving as Principal Officer Stewart informed us that although the compounds gave the impression of securing the prisoners, 'temporary containment' was a more apt description. He described how the prisoners could—and indeed had—emptied their respective compound in minutes. They would place a table against the wire fence and throw a mattress over the razor wire. The prisoners would then jump on the table and with a little assistance from their fellow inmates would roll over the wire, using the mattress for protection, before dropping onto the ground on the other side of the fence.

That was frightening enough, but there was worse to come. Part of the routine of the staff allocated to each compound was to enter the compound every hour, two abreast, and patrol!

This first piece of information was closely followed by the second chilling tale of the day, 'the kangaroo court'.

On the most serious occasion an inmate who had been suspected of a certain 'crime' against the organisation was tried in a kangaroo court by his former colleagues. He was found guilty and sentenced to death, and his death was carried out by placing his head in a vice and turning the vice until he died. Such was the pressure applied that his skull had flipped open to reveal his brain.

There were also, of course, the tales of the 'lost prisoners'—prisoners who disappeared and have never been accounted for. The conclusion reached in the majority of these disappearances was that they had resulted from tunnel collapse while the prisoners were trying to escape. The sandy earth under the compounds was easy to dig through, and the ground rapidly became a rabbit warren of tunnels. The downside was of course that it took very little to cause a tunnel collapse and when this happened the inmates were reluctant to call for the authorities' assistance. Looking back, I am not sure whether the prisoners were aware that an army spotter plane regularly flew over the Maze with specialized x-ray equipment which could be used to detect the position of the tunnels.

There was also an occasion when two prisoners attempted to escape in the bin lorry. Unfortunately the bin lorry they choose was the 'corkscrew' variety and they made their escape from the prison straight to a plot in the graveyard.

Another tale—and I say tale because I had no supporting evidence for the stories we heard that day from Principal Officer Stewart (though this did not prevent us listening with rapt attention)—was no doubt meant to highlight the resourcefulness and organisational ability of the prisoners. Principal Officer Stewart explained that they knew that in one of the compounds there was a 'still' which was being used to supply its inmates with 'hooch' (a prison term for illegally distilled alcohol). The prison authorities had proof of this intelligence from observing the inebriated state of some of the prisoners at unlock. The suspect compound had been subject to thorough searches on more than one occasion in an attempt to discover and remove the illegal still.

But it had taken a long-serving warder to make the breakthrough. During yet another of the surprise searches he had been surveying the interior of one of the Nissen huts and realised that there was something just not right. The longer he looked the further he seemed to move away from the solution. Then he decided to count the beds and quickly realised that there were two fewer beds than in the other huts. He also knew that the huts were identical, give or take a few inches lost in the build process. Then the answer hit him like a sledgehammer. Two beds had been removed, one from each side of the hut, and a false wall the width of the two beds had been fitted. Once the false wall was dismantled the still, spare hooch and other prohibited articles were discovered and removed.

Earlier I used the term 'surprise search', but there was really no such thing as a surprise search in the Maze Compound. Before any search was carried out the OC (the prisoners' officer commanding) had to be informed. (Some twenty years later I was shocked to discover that this practice was still alive in the new H Blocks at HMP Maze Cellular.)

As we headed back to the college that evening I remembered the thought I had had after my two weeks' induction training at Belfast— that if I had any say in where I was posted my destination would definitely not be HMP Belfast. After my visit to the Maze, and with the tales of Principal Officer Stewart still going round in my mind, I reckoned that a review of that wish was urgently required.

The last week of our training arrived and we had to sit an examination covering all aspects of the training. But, due to the prison population explosion caused by the introduction of internment, the service was so desperate for staff that failing the examination was not an obstacle to continuing in the job.

We had a passing out parade on our final day, by which time we had all received our postings. The phrase 'Be careful for what you wish for' was never more appropriate than when I received my posting. The thought that I had about not wanting to go to HMP Belfast had come back to haunt me. Most of the group, including me, were posted to HMP Maze Compound; our worst fears were realised.

We reported on Monday to our posting location and underwent a further week's induction training to enable the local training department to fully brief and instruct us on our new roles as serving officers at HMP Maze Compound.

My enthusiasm for my career in the Prison Service had dampened somewhat during the last few weeks in Millisle, no more so than when the assassination of Officer Fenton had been relayed to us. It was some weeks before I allowed myself time to reflect on his murder and give thought to his family and colleagues. After all, I had never known the officer and the feelings of sadness that overcame me would obviously have been nothing in comparison to those who loved him.

This was the first time I experienced the grief associated with the murder of a fellow officer, but it was by no means the last. In fact, many years down the line and on at least two occasions that I am aware of, I came close to joining Officer Fenton; another name on the roll of honour that recorded the names of prison staff murdered during the course of the Troubles.

Chapter 3
Welcome to the Prison Service

That was the end of training, thank God. I certainly couldn't have coped with much more. My initial excitement and enthusiasm had now long gone, replaced by worry about the unknown situations that lay ahead.

I was detailed to general duties, which was normal for a new officer. This was used as a further development tool in that it ensured, first, that new officers became familiar with the geography of the jail; and second, that they began to familiarise themselves with the officers' various roles and the procedures involved in each of these roles.

Within a few weeks our group had found its feet and our combined fears started to drift to the back of our mind. Even when patrolling the compounds we discovered that we had lost some of our initial apprehension. The prisoners didn't actually bother that much with us. They had been there long enough to settle into the regime as detailed not just by the prison authorities but also by their own military-type regime as dictated by the officer commanding (oc).

Occasionally I would be detailed to the search team and deployed to assist in searching one of the compounds: I didn't mind this duty as it broke the monotony of manning gates and Towers. On one particular day I was detailed to a search that was to take place in the uvf compound in the prison. This was the first time I had been involved in a search of this particular compound. Gusty Spence was the oc of the uvf and could regularly be seen heading off to meetings with the governor, his little baton tucked neatly under his arm. I never spoke to the man as it appeared that the principal officer in charge of the staff was the lowest rank that Gusty dealt with. But I can honestly say that I never heard any staff complain about Gusty. They just did their job, and I suppose Gusty just did his too!

The way the lead-up to the search was handled was almost laughable. The principal officer in charge of the search would speak to the oc of the prisoners in the compound that was to be searched, who would then agree to the search and inform his men. Some twenty years later, to my surprise, I found the same procedures and worse were happening in the supposedly top-security prison known as Maze Cellular. (On one occasion there the prisoners were given time to dispose of their 'hooch' before the search went ahead.)

The searches always followed more or less the same routine, with little variation, so there were few or no surprises for the prisoners. Illegal items were sometimes discovered, but on most occasions nothing untoward was found. I firmly believed that the prisoners deliberately left irrelevant items to be discovered so as to minimise the effectiveness of the search, because when items were discovered I believe staff subconsciously felt 'job done'.

Imagine my surprise on one particular day as we drew towards the end of the search and were just coming into contact with the inmates, when suddenly I was looking straight at two prisoners whose identity I knew well. They were two brothers from Killyleagh, two ex-pupils of the school I had attended. I was shocked, to say the least. I hadn't even been aware that they were in the prison, which shows how much attention I paid to the local media. Initially I froze, not knowing what to do; but thanks to my uniform, I suspect, and the fact that the last contact I had had with them was when I was thirteen years old, there was no sign of recognition from either of the brothers.

A short time later I came across another inmate I knew from Killyleagh, a young man from a wealthy middle-class family on the outskirts of the town who had somehow found himself sucked into the murky world of the uvf, but again I could tell from his demeanour and body language that he had no recollection of me.

There is nothing to be gained from mentioning the names of the individuals concerned now: one is dead and the other two have reintegrated themselves back into the community. I would imagine that if I were to meet the brothers today their reaction would be the same as it was that day in the compounds.

Of course it wasn't just schoolfriends on the opposite side of the law I came across during my early days in the service. The day I started in the prison Visits section I met a guy who had been the head boy of one of the two schools I had attended as a teenager. He was just one of dozens of officers I knew from my youth. Funny thing, all of them came from Killyleagh!

There were many experienced officers employed at Maze Compound but internment had meant that additional staff were recruited from the Scottish and English prison services. In addition to their salaries these staff received a subsistence allowance, which often amounted to a considerable sum of money. Because of the level of staff shortages, some of these officers, who actually lived in the Long Kesh Complex, worked back-to-back day and night shifts. I was amazed at how they were able to stay awake during the day after a full twenty-four-hour shift the previous day/night. I discovered the answer to this on one occasion when I was detailed to cover a night guard (as night shifts were called).

On night guard there was a post to cover for each hour of the shift apart from one hour when the officer was stood down for a break. It was when I went to relieve one of the English 'detached duty' officers, who was supposed to be patrolling a compound, that I discovered the 'coat hanger shift'. The officer I was relieving appeared to be standing still against the wire fence of the compound and as I approached him I was amazed to realise that he was sleeping while standing up. I couldn't believe my eyes. How could anyone sleep standing up? I woke the officer, who laughed at my mystified expression as he drifted back into the world of the living and promptly unhooked himself from the wire. What he had done was to place a coat hanger inside his jacket as if to hang the jacket up, and keeping the jacket on he attached himself by the hanger to the wire that surrounded the compound. This was just one of the methods staff used to help them cope with the tiredness that threatened to engulf them in the course of the demanding role of prison officer in the Maze Compound in the late 1970s.

After about four months in the job I had progressed from general duties and become a regular in the prison Visits section. That permitted me to confirm the rumours about the 'conjugal rights' that were being regularly exercised by the prisoners and their partners during visits.

The staff in Visits had told me that prisoners regularly had sex with their visitors in the visit cubicles. They advised me that if this happened while I was in charge of a visit, I should move to the side and ignore it.

When a visitor on a normal visit entered the visit box, if the rules were applied rigidly the visitor would perhaps hug or kiss the prisoner and then they would sit down on opposite sides of the small table in the cubicle. The visit would last approximately forty minutes and at the end of that time they would hug or kiss again and then each would leave by the appropriate door. The visitor would be escorted back to the Visits area exit, where they would wait for a van to transport them back to the visitors' entrance; and the inmate would be returned to the compound where he was housed.

What actually happened, I was told, was a very different story. The visitor and the inmate would sit at the same side of the table in the cubicle, and talk would be the last thing on their minds. Any conversation would have been done through telephone calls and letters, leaving visiting time free for fulfilling the physical needs of both the prisoner and his visitor.

I refused to accept that this sort of thing went on, until one day when I was supervising a visit between a prisoner and his visitor it actually happened.

The female visitor, a beautiful girl dressed in a long cream coat with black boots, entered the cubicle, walked past the guy she was visiting and positioned herself in the blind side of the cubicle. As she brushed past the visiting table her coat fell open, revealing that she was wearing nothing more than the cream coat and black boots. I was shocked. It was like a scene from a blue movie, or so I imagined. I couldn't understand how the visitor had got into the prison dressed—or, more to the point, not dressed—as she was. The only conclusion I could come to was that on the way up to Visits in the back of the van she must have hidden behind the other visitors while she stripped down to the condition of which I had just had an eyeful. I froze, knowing full well that while the practice I was about to witness was not against the rules of nature it was definitely against the rules of the prison.

The girl was now standing in the blind corner of the cubicle. Her coat was fully open. Although it was the blind corner of the visiting box, from where I was positioned I could see everything. Hence the advice from the other staff telling me to move to the side so that the 'view' was blocked from my sight. But I couldn't move either my body or my eyes: I was frozen to the spot. I could clearly see the girl's heaving breasts. Her body was porcelain white, her nipples were erect and judging by the moans I could hear she was obviously very aroused. Still neither the visitor nor the prisoner spoke. The prisoner reacted at a frantic pace as he moved square on to the girl. He placed his right hand behind the girl's head and drew her lips towards his. He kissed her passionately and at the same time his left hand sought out and found the girl's right breast and nipple.

They were both oblivious to me. Suddenly my embarrassment brought me to my senses and I discreetly moved to one side so that the entwined couple were no longer in my direct view. Despite this, the rustle of clothes, the sounds of zips opening, the bodies thumping off the wooden walls of the cubicle and finally the sounds of male and female moans of ecstasy gave me a clear mental view of the remainder of the 'action'. I was embarrassed in the extreme. Remember, this was 1977 and as a twenty-two-year-old from the sticks I had never experienced the sexual freedom that is more than apparent among today's youth.

The visit ended with the prisoner mumbling his thanks. Was the visitor a prostitute? I wondered. Perhaps in name only. I had heard the other staff talking about girls being sent up to keep up the men's morale, among other things. Perhaps this was one of those girls. The visitor closed her coat and as she left the cubicle she smiled and winked at me. She knew that I had seen her! The colour that had just left my face returned with a vengeance. The prisoner pushed past me and I had to shake myself back to reality and quickly follow him to escort him back to his compound.

When I returned to Visits I was met by a chorus of catcalls, whistles and laughter. I had been set up! This was a weekly occurrence with this particular prisoner and the guys had deliberately got the detail fixed to ensure that I was the one who got the eyeful on this particular occasion. I had the last laugh, though, as the officers who had previously been in charge of the visit had, to a man, always moved to a respectful distance as soon as the girl entered the visit cubicle, so they had never been privy to the sights that I had been blessed with that day. I had strange dreams that night, to say the least!

There were many other incidents that happened during my tour of duty in Visits, some interesting from a learning perspective, others just plain shocking. One appalling example that springs to mind was a visit that took place between a prisoner and his female visitor.

It started like any other normal visit. The visitor, a good-looking girl, smartly dressed, was the first to arrive. She was shown into the visiting cubicle and sat down waiting for the arrival of the male prisoner. She appeared agitated, which drew her to the attention of the staff, as this usually indicated the visitor was smuggling some contraband into the prison. Although visitors were thoroughly searched by the search staff before they went to the Visits area, there were never any internal searches or anything remotely resembling an internal search. The amount of grief the search staff got for asking a visitor to remove their shoes was bad enough; I dread to think what a visitor's reaction would have been like if they were asked to strip!

Security was well aware that certain female visitors were visiting the prison with illegal items secreted inside their bodies, items that they would remove after they had passed through the search area. The usual method was to ask to use the toilet, where they would remove the smuggled items and pass the prohibited articles on to the prisoner they were visiting. Of course the prisoners were searched following their visit and the 'find' percentage by the staff was quite high.

The prisoner finally arrived and was searched before going into the visit cubicle where the girl was sitting. The principal officer in charge, who had been alerted by the state that the girl had arrived in, a state that had become progressively worse the longer she waited, had asked the staff supervising the visit to pay close attention to what went on.

As the prisoner entered the cubicle the staff noticed fear in her eyes. The prisoner remained standing with his arms open, inviting the girl to come to him. There was a brief moment when it seemed she would remain sitting, declining his offer of an embrace. The prisoner called her name in quite an aggressive tone and the girl jumped to her feet, in fact she nearly jumped out of her skin. She moved slowly round the small wooden table, tears running down her cheeks as if she knew what was about to happen. She was shaking.

Two staff had now moved into position and stood ready on the off-chance that the prisoner might turn violent. They had figured that the girl was the prisoner's wife, because they shared the same surname. Perhaps she had sent him a 'dear John' letter during the week and he had sent his mates round and forced her to come to see him so that he could try to talk her into staying with him. (A 'dear John' is prison slang for a letter sent from a girl to her prisoner boyfriend or husband finishing the relationship: this type of letter has triggered more than one suicide in prison.)

As the girl reluctantly let herself be drawn into the arms of the man, he grabbed her and threw her against the wall of the cubicle. It all happened so quickly. The buttons burst from her blouse as he attacked her like an animal. One hand was on the girl's breast as forced his hand inside her bra. He was using his body to pin the girl to the wall and his free hand was beneath the girl's skirt, making its way forcefully up the inside of her thighs. The girl was screaming. She forced her thighs to close on her assailant's hand, but he was too strong.

'Christ, he's trying to rape her!' shouted one of the officers, as he rushed into the cubicle. The second officer followed his colleague and it took both of them, supported by a third officer, to pull the prisoner off the girl and onto the floor of the corridor just outside the visiting cubicle. Other prisoners had to be restrained, as they believed that the scuffle was one of their comrades getting a kicking from the 'screws'.

The prisoner was dragged from the Visits and given a thorough search so that the staff could be sure that what they had witnessed was not a charade to cover the passing of illegal items from the visitor to the inmate.

The female visitor was sitting on the floor of the cubicle. She had been knocked to the floor during the scuffle and there she sat, her skirt up around her waist, her tights ripped to shreds, her blouse torn asunder, her breast exposed where it had been forced from her bra, just sobbing her heart out.

One of the staff reacted slightly quicker than the rest. He removed his jacket and tried to help the girl to her feet. He had a fight on his hands to help the girl, for as soon as he put his hands near her body she reacted like a wildcat. Her arms were flailing, she was screaming, as probably any girl would who had just suffered near-rape. The officer spoke softly to her, desperately trying to calm her, and slowly she fell sobbing into his arms. He placed his jacket around the girl's shoulders, pulling it across her half-naked body to shield her from the prying eyes of the other staff who had started to gather. 'Okay, lads, move on. The situation is now under control. Give the wee girl a bit of privacy.' The officer led the girl back through the rear of Visits and another female visitor who had travelled to the prison on the same bus took over and escorted the girl to a small holding room at the back of Visits.

The officer waited outside while the girl tided herself up. He needed to speak to the girl to try to ascertain what was behind the attempted rape. He knew he would be asked to prepare a report, which would also be needed should the girl make a formal complaint to the RUC.

The female visitor who had now taken responsibility for the assaulted girl came out of the room, closing the door tight behind her. The officer asked how the poor girl was recovering and added that someone was bringing a cup of tea for her. The visitor's eyes filled with tears.

'God, what's wrong?' asked the officer, concerned that the girl had been more seriously injured than he thought.

'That was her brother!' came the shocked reply. The girl was not only in shock following the attempted rape but also acutely embarrassed as her assailant was her own brother.

Interviewing her was a definite non-starter and the officer made his way back to the principal officer to inform him of the terrible details of this horrific assault.

Talk with regard to the incident in Visits had all but died down by the following Monday. This was the way of the Prison Service. There were so many different incidents happening all the time that an event from the previous week was quickly overtaken by something else. However, although this next visit was rather different from the previous week's assault of the young girl, the two were linked.

The girl's father came up to visit his son, and before his son arrived, the father asked for a few moments of the principal officer's time. The principal officer brought him into his office so that the father would have some privacy to discuss such a delicate subject.

'Thank you for seeing me,' he began. 'I believe that you were on duty last week when the incident involving my daughter and son took place in the Visits. First I would like you to convey my thanks initially to the three staff who pulled my son off my daughter and second and in particular to the officer who offered his jacket and comforting words to my daughter immediately after the incident.' The man was crying!

'I will pass on your thanks, but there is honestly no need for you to thank our staff. Contrary to speculation we do have some extremely conscientious staff and there are many of them who would have done exactly what the staff on duty did for your daughter. Now let me return my thanks to you. It is seldom that a prison visitor has a pleasant word for any of my staff, so your acknowledgement of my staff's actions is greatly appreciated,' the officer said as he shook the man's hand.

'Before I leave, Principal Officer, can I ask you one last favour?' the man asked.

'Depends what the favour is,' the principal officer replied. 'If it's possible and doesn't compromise either my staff or myself, then I'll certainly give consideration to your request. What is it?'

'It's just I don't know what got into my son and I need a few minutes to *talk* to him without any interference from your staff,' replied the man.

Something went unsaid between the two men in the office that morning. An understanding was reached without any further words being spoken. The two men shook hands for the last time and the father left, to be escorted back to the visiting cubicle to wait for his son.

The principal officer spoke to the member of staff who was responsible for supervising the visit, advising him of the conversation he had just had with the visitor and telling him that the man wanted and was to be given a few minutes to talk to his son. For the second time that day two men looked into each other's eyes and, as before, an understanding was conveyed and received without another word being said.

The prisoner arrived and was searched before being allowed to proceed onto his visit with his father. He was sweating profusely and shaking visibly. The supervising officer escorted him into the visiting cubicle and almost immediately turned and walked away.

He had moved only a few steps when the first blow landed. He kept walking. That first blow was followed by many, many more and was complemented by a series of kicks to the head and body of the man the visitor had once called son. The officer stopped and slowly turned, making his way back towards the visiting cubicle that he had left a few minutes before.

The assault had ended. The father was sitting calmly at the table, although the beads of sweat that ran down his forehead, the distinct red mark on his forehead and his bloodied knuckles were all an indication of the tools he had employed to leave his son a blubbing wreck lying curled up in a ball on the floor of the cubicle. The officer was sure that if he could have seen his feet the tips of the father's boots would have been scuffed as well.

The father stood up as the officer entered the cubicle to drag the son to his feet and remove him from the small room. For the third time that day two pairs of eyes met, one pair of eyes conveying the man's thanks, the other the acknowledgement of the supervising officer. But there was something else present in the father's eyes. At first the supervising officer thought it was anger. No, not anger, he realised: it was sadness. The realisation had just hit him: the realisation that he had lost his son.

The son had to be dragged out of the cubicle: such was the beating he had received that he was unable to walk. Another officer grabbed the prisoner's other arm and between them the two officers manhandled him out of the visiting area.

The principal officer had already organised a van to be on standby to transport the assaulted prisoner to the prison hospital so that his injures could be treated. As the prisoner passed the principal officer the two escorting officers stopped for a moment.

'How was your visit? Any complaints?' The principal officer directed his questions to the prisoner. Without lifting his head, the prisoner give a muttered response. 'No complaints, PO,' he moaned. From the laboured sound of the prisoner's breathing it was obvious he was suffering a great deal of pain. *Serves the bastard right*, thought the principal officer.

That was the way the service was then. Things happened. Heads were turned the other way. People were hurt.

Although I was now spending most of my time employed in the prison Visits my night guards ranged between Tango 7, one of the Towers, and patrolling in Compound Maze. The Towers were the best duty because there were little gas fires there, so covering this post meant that I was at least out of the rain and could keep warm as well. There was an added advantage in that there were blankets concealed in the Tower and sometimes (like the coat hanger man) you could manage to get a night's sleep.

During the course of the night the Control Room staff would interrupt you with radio test calls. These were to confirm that the staff member deployed to the Tower was alert and that his radio was working. 'Control to Tango Seven test call, Control over.' The response they waited for was 'Tango Seven to Control, message received, Tango Seven over.' Control would then respond 'Control to Tango Seven, your signals are good, Control over.' And again they waited for the reply, 'Tango Seven to Control, your signals are good also, Tango Seven out.'

However, a prison officer with time on his hands and annoyed at having his sleep interrupted on the one night he thought he could catch up on some much-needed rest very quickly came up with a solution. The officer simply turned off his radio and slept soundly, awakened in the morning either by the cold, if the fire had run out of gas during the night, or by the officer on day duty who was relieving him. But what of the radio test calls? Surely if he didn't respond someone would be sent to do a physical check on his post to find out why he was not responding? The answer was so easy. A colleague in the nearby H Block would simply answer the test call on his radio by responding with the Tango call sign. I never understood how management never picked up on this con, but then again in the Maze Prison management had many more higher priority problems to worry about.

I have to admit I never used the blankets or allowed anyone to answer my test calls. I was too frightened of being caught. There were many nights, however, when my eyelids fluttered with exhaustion that I was sorely tempted.

The new H Blocks were well under construction by late 1977 and after I had had a few extremely cold nights on night guard I submitted my name to the list of staff who wished to be considered for inclusion in the eighty staff necessary to man the soon-to-be-opened H Block 8. I was fortune enough to be selected and at the beginning of November 1977 took up my new post as a Prison Officer in H Block 8.

No one could have imagined then how these same H Blocks would gain worldwide notoriety for so many reasons: the dirty protest, the hunger strike, escapes, attempted escapes and, finally, murder would dominate the headlines for many years to come.

I would not have believed, standing there on my first day in November 1977, that one day I would be promoted to governor in charge of one of these same H Blocks and later in my career would be, on occasions, in charge of the whole prison. After all, I had just joined for a couple of years until I could get a proper job!

Another clear memory I retain from 1977 was the first week I received £100 as my weekly wage. The £80 offered in the advertisement was only the tip of the financial iceberg. Yes, £80 was the gross pay of a prison officer working a forty-hour week. I never worked a forty-hour week from the day I finished my training: it was normal to work a thirteen-day fortnight plus overtime covering association duties in the prison. (Association duty was the name given to evening shifts: it allowed the prisoners to associate with one another, perhaps in the block dining room playing pool or snooker, or just watching television.)

In addition to my salary I also received other allowances because I lived in at the Maze, in the Portakabin-type accommodation that was provided. At the time, for each night I lived in I received around £3.50, which was treated as tax free. I was also paid one return journey per week to my father's home, now in Crossgar, and received another £1 per night 'on call' allowance. The prison was still fairly unsettled at that time and paying this additional allowance meant that the prison management were able to order the live-in staff to report for duty in the event of a disturbance in the jail during the night.

So there I was; a twenty-two-year-old with more money than I could ever have imagined. Money that was burning a hole in my pocket, just itching to be spent. The solution arrived in the shape of a six-month-old bright red Toyota Celica. The car was stunning but that is not what I remember most about the purchase. It was more the way I bought the car. I walked into the showroom, checked out the car and told the salesman I would take it! Not 'What is the selling price?', not 'What discount can I negotiate?'; simply, 'I'll take it.' The salesman was dumbstruck. He obviously didn't know whether to believe this brash twenty-two-year-old flashing the cash.

I was not the only one of my colleagues who had plenty of money but no financial guidance. The prison staff spent their money as quickly as they earned it. I was one of the lucky ones: I didn't drink or gamble and was not about to get sucked into this money-draining, marriage-wrecking habit.

There was cheap drink to be had in both the sergeant's mess in the army camp and the Prison Officers' Club close by. Both of these 'drinking dens' were contained within the Long Kesh site, close to the outside wall of the actual prison, which was located on the same site.

Many men became embroiled in the many card schools at the prison. After work staff would go for a few drinks to relieve the stress of the day before heading home, and get involved in a card school; and some might lose their entire wage packet. There were times when the unfortunate player would throw his car keys into the middle of the table in a frantic last-gasp attempt to recoup his losses. At the end of a bad losing night an officer's hat would be passed around the players to collect some money for the loser to take home to his wife and children.

There were nights, as I made my way to bed, passing through the room where the card school was operating, when I subconsciously made a mental note of the identity of the players. On heading for breakfast the following morning I was never surprised to see the same officers, unshaven and red-eyed, still playing!

This was a failing of the service and although today the salaries are smaller in comparison to the pay in 1977, staff are still not given the necessary financial advice to help them avoid the same problems that still exist some thirty years later.

My time spent working in H Block 8 was short. The officers were a great bunch of lads and worked well with each other. The novelty of working in the new H Block after the compounds seemed to lift both staff and inmates, and there were few problems of any significance.

The one story that sticks out in my mind from my time in H Block 8 relates to an officer who suffered from a personal hygiene problem. Despite the strongest possible hints, he never attempted to address his colleagues' concerns. In an effort to provide proof of the officer's excessive body odour, staff placed a small, almost insignificant, dot of Snopake correction fluid on the back of the officer's shirt. Unbelievably, some two weeks later the Snopake was still there—the officer was still wearing the same shirt!

While I had been at the Prison Service College my tutor Dessie Stewart, who was full of good advice, suggested that if I wanted to give myself the best chance of promotion I should consider transferring into the administration grade. As I had been involved in administration-type work from the time I left school, and because at times I found the job of prison officer quite boring, I took Dessie's advice and applied for an advertised position, and on 9 January 1978 I started work in the Wages Office at the Maze Prison.

Chapter 4
Love and Death

It's strange how the whole of the rest of your life can seem to have become arranged for you within the space of two days. That was the thought that filled my mind when I awoke on Wednesday 11 January 1978.

I had started the latest phase of my career, this time in prison administration, two days earlier, and from day one I felt I had found my niche in the prison system.

I worked normal office hours, Monday to Friday, from eight in the morning till five in the evening, and there was always plenty of overtime available.

I felt that my future working life was now mapped out: despite my initial plan to join the service for just a couple of years, I had settled in completely. Not only did I enjoy the financial benefits of working for the Prison Service, but I was no longer working with terrorists, doing a night guard once a fortnight trying not to fall asleep in a bloody Tower. I had stopped wearing uniform and, best of all, still received the same remuneration as the discipline grade.

The second part of my future, I was sure, had been arranged the night after I started my new job, Tuesday 10 January 1978.

Tuesday night was Stormont night, the night I went to the Stormont Hotel in Belfast. I had been seeing a girl from Lisburn for the previous ten months and, although she was a great girl, I just felt that the relationship was not going anywhere so I had called it a day. Now I was back on the loose again, trying to convince myself that the single life was for me.

I arrived at the Stormont with my red Toyota not as beautiful as it had been a few weeks before. I had caused £1000-worth of damage to it in a recent accident and I was just waiting for a date to leave the car in to be repaired. The accident had happened in early December, during my first week's leave from the Prison.

I had been on my way to Downpatrick to leave my car in to be serviced and had pulled out to overtake a bus on my way in. As I pulled out, I thought 'Why am I rushing? I've got all day', and braked to move back in behind the bus. Just as I braked the car hit black ice and spun out of control, crossing over onto the other side of the road and swerving between oncoming traffic before coming to rest entangled in a concrete fence.

The glove compartment burst opened and the St Christopher I had received as one of my presents from the factory landed on the passenger seat beside me. The car, and of course the fence, were badly damaged but I was uninjured. Instead of being grateful and thinking that maybe St Christopher was responsible for my lucky escape, I jumped from my car and in my frustration flung the small statue as far as I could into the field to which my car now lay broadside. I often wondered whether my lack of injuries was anything to do with St Christopher or just plain good luck. When I did reflect on the day of my accident I must have had a subconscious positive feeling about St Christopher as the sterling silver medallion I had received as my second present from the factory staff was never far from me afterwards.

I parked up my car and headed into the foyer of the hotel. I knew that if my friends hadn't already arrived they would be there soon. This was the regular Tuesday night haunt and it would have taken at least a broken leg to keep any of us away.

I was walking towards the bar to buy a drink when I came across a lovely-looking girl I had never seen at the Stormont before. She was blonde, with a pageboy-style haircut, and had blue eyes. I still remember what she was wearing: a white blouse just off her shoulders and a navy skirt just below her knee.

There was a crowd of guys watching her waiting for someone to test the water. This was the norm for the guys when an attractive girl appeared available. No one wanted to be the first to approach her in case they were 'shot down', which would mean enduring their mates' banter for the rest of the evening and the days beyond.

The shyness I had suffered as a child and teenager had long since passed: money in the bank and a flash car can give your confidence a terrific boost. I had also lost a lot of weight by playing football and running around the wall of the Maze every day. This, perhaps more than anything else, gave me the self-confidence I had lacked.

As the girl was standing on her own I thought it more than likely that she was with a boyfriend, who was probably at the bar buying drinks. Did this deter me? Hell, no!

I caught the girl's eye, smiled and held eye contact as I walked up to her.

'Hello there,' I ventured.

'Hi,' came the reply.

Conversation down to me, I thought. 'I haven't noticed you here before—if I had I am sure that I would remember,' I said.

I thought she rolled her eyes and wondered if what I had just said sounded too corny. But no, what I had said was true. I definitely had not seen her at the Stormont before.

'Could I buy you a drink?' I asked.

'I don't drink, actually,' came the reply.

'Would you like to dance?' I was trying hard, maybe too hard.

'No, thank you, I am waiting for my friends.' Her accent was soft, but not Belfast. I couldn't place it.

The girl was obviously well brought up and had a definite air of sophistication. I was determined not to let her escape my clutches and, trying to show her I could be amusing as well as confident, explained that the crowd of guys further up the foyer were watching me talking to her, to gauge whether she was the dancing type or not. She looked over my shoulder at the crowd, blushed as she realised I was telling the truth and dropped her eyes in embarrassment.

At that moment her two friends appeared and as they approached us I realised that I had to go for broke or lose my opportunity with this lovely girl. They asked her if she wanted to come to the bar with them and before she answered I seized my opportunity. I had turned aside to the girl as her friends approached and taking her arm gently I said that we were going to dance and if they didn't mind we would be back shortly. Her friends laughed and walked towards the bar and I guided this attractive girl to the floor.

Just over two years later we were engaged and the following year, on 25 April 1981, the lovely-looking girl became my wife. It was her nineteenth birthday.

We had bought our first house, in Bangor, before we were married and were able to move straight in when we returned from our honeymoon in Florida.

The hunger strike was in full swing a couple of months before we were married and while we were on honeymoon the first of the hunger strikers, Bobby Sands, died. I could scarcely believe it: I never thought for a moment that Margaret Thatcher would let them die. Equally, I never imagined that the provisional movement would let their comrades die. This one deed, more than any other, brought home to me the dedication of many members of the Provisional IRA. As hunger striker after hunger striker died it seemed to me that the republican movement was on its knees. If Thatcher would not yield when there were men dying, what else could they as a movement do? Where could they go from there?

I was amazed, as were no doubt many other people, when the hunger strike was called off and within weeks the prisoners had been granted all the demands their comrades had died for. This, of course, gave the Provisionals a massive morale boost, and the movement went from strength to strength.

At this time, as with the 'dirty protest' and the 'great escape', I was safely ensconced in the prison's Administration section and to be honest was glad of it.

I had lost several colleagues by the time the hunger strike ended, the most notable being an Administration colleague from HMP Belfast who was murdered during 1979.

In December 1978 my then girlfriend and I had been away on holiday, our first holiday together. We had visited Palma Nova in Majorca and had returned, rested and relaxed, and looking forward to our first Christmas together.

The previous week there had been an IRA terrorist attack on three members of the Administration department staff as they approached Carlisle Circus shortly after leaving Belfast Prison. One of the officers had been killed and the other two were obviously badly shocked. Of course I was angry that a colleague had died and that two others had suffered physical injury as a result of the attack. However, as I reported for work on Monday morning, my annoyance at the attack on the staff had selfishly moved to myself.

The 'Stewart' (the management grade responsible for the Administration department) sent for me around nine thirty.

'Good morning, Billy,' Alec said as I knocked and entered his office. Before I could answer he went on, 'I know that you're only back from holidays and I am not sure if you've heard that there was a terrorist attack on three members of the Administration staff from Belfast Prison while you were away?'

The hairs started to rise on the back of my neck and a sickening feeling of dread, which would return many times throughout my career, came over me.

'I want you to report to Belfast Prison first thing tomorrow morning. You will be on detached duty to help out either until the two injured staff return or until other staffing arrangements can be made. While you are stationed at HMP Belfast you will be treated as on detached duty basis and paid travel expenses as per the regulations.'

'I'm sorry, Alec, but I can't go to Belfast Prison,' I explained. 'You see, my girlfriend lives in that district and my car is in and around the area all the time. Plus my wallet was stolen from my car when it was parked outside her house several weeks ago and it was found in Ardoyne with my warrant card missing, so no—I can't go.'

I was certainly not prepared for Alec's reply. The mistake I had made was in thinking that Alec had asked me to go, whereas in fact he was telling me I had to go!

'Let me remind you, Mr McKee,' he began, 'when you joined this job you signed a piece of paper that said that you agreed to serve in any prison that you were posted to, do you remember?'

'Yes, Alec, I do,' I replied.

'Well?' he said. I realised that this was a question he wanted answered not with words but with actions.

The following morning I drove to HMP Belfast, feeling worse that I had the last time I was there, and remembering how unpleasant my first experience had been. It didn't help my mood when I found out later that I was actually the second choice and that the officer chosen first had threatened to go sick if he was sent.

One complaint I had against the service was that there were people who refused to go somewhere or do something as instructed and some other mug was picked out instead. How many governors did four tours of duty in the Maze, for instance? Not many, but in the years to follow I was to get to know one such governor very well!

What was it Alec had said? 'You will be there for about three months and you will receive the appropriate expenses.' Three months my foot! It was not until ten months later that I was posted back to HMP Maze, and as Belfast Prison was still regarded as my home station I did not receive a penny in expenses. I refused to accept the non-payment of expenses and, as I had to do many times during my career, researched the regulations until I found a rule that I was sure I could turn to my advantage. Some ten years later I was finally reimbursed with the expenses. I suppose this is just one example of my determination and refusal to give up. If I felt I was right I was like a dog with a bone.

I enjoyed all aspects of my time in Belfast except for leaving the prison at night. Every night was the same: as the huge gates slowly swung open the dread would hit me as I drove out into the unknown. Would there be another shooting? Would it be my turn? Which way will I go? Turn down the Crumlin Road. Turn up the Crumlin Road. Go straight across and then down the Shankill Road. It was the same every night. My decision was always off the cuff, never planned.

I did not want to establish any kind of pattern: we all knew how the Provos worked. They watched. They recorded. They reported. They received their orders. They killed.

Fortunately it wasn't my turn to be targeted during that particular duty: that would come much later. Some twenty-six years later.

But this time it was the turn of a young man I worked with and with whom I became very friendly during my brief time at HMP Belfast. I had mentioned to my girlfriend that I had made friends with a couple of guys around my own age in the prison and who also worked in the Administration department. They were called Danny and David, and my girlfriend actually knew David—they had both attended Joanmount Church Youth Club. It's a small world. She, like everyone who knew him, felt that David was a really nice, genuine person with a great personality.

A few weeks before my transfer back to the Maze David had been telling me how he had settled into his new house and how secure he felt because most of his neighbours were members of the RUC. David travelled to work each day by bus, which was a concern to all of us. He felt that working in Administration, with minimal prisoner contact, coupled with the fact that he did not wear uniform, somehow reduced his risk of attack.

I was off duty on the day it happened. I had stayed the previous night at my girlfriend's parents' house and was looking forward to spending a relaxing day with her, probably shopping, coffee, more shopping, lunch, more shopping! Downtown Radio was playing in the kitchen while we were having breakfast. The pips came on just before the hour, and then the ten o'clock news.

I can't remember who the newscaster was, but I do remember the terrible news he read. 'This morning a young prison officer reporting for duty at the Crumlin Road Prison was shot dead by what is believed to be a lone gunman as the officer disembarked from a bus outside the prison just before nine o'clock this morning.' The rest of the newscaster's words tailed off as my mind tried to absorb the enormity of what he had said.

By this time I had returned to work in the Maze and coincidently young David had taken over the role that I had vacated when I left HMP Belfast.

I stood up and walked into the hall. The tears were running down my face. These were the first tears I had shed since the death of my mother some ten years earlier. I sat on the third step on the stairs and rested my face on my arms. My girlfriend came out of the kitchen and sat beside me. She put her arm around my shoulders to try to comfort me and quietly asked if I had any idea who the prison officer was. She hadn't made the connection.

There were two people whose names came into my mind. I knew from the time of the shooting that most of the staff would already have been on duty; and the only staff who would still be arriving at the prison at that time were the administration staff and governor grades.

The newscaster was clear: 'a young prison officer disembarking from a bus'. I was sure, but prayed that I was wrong—it was Danny or David. The description 'young prison officer', combined with the time of the shooting: it just had to be one of them.

The eleven o'clock news: 'The next of kin are being informed.' By midday I had received the call that I was dreading. 'It was David that was murdered this morning.' I couldn't even speak, I just handed the telephone to my girlfriend and returned to my spot on the stairs. I didn't cry any more. I just experienced the same old emotions: feelings that would become familiar, feelings that would come back so many times over the coming years, feelings of desolation, helplessness, sadness and, finally, anger.

Chapter 5
On the Move

My career in the service was going as well as could be expected. And it wasn't just my career that was going well. I had got married on 25 April 1981 and three years later our first son was born. We moved to a new build house in the picturesque village of Hillsborough. Life was good.

However, after six months in Hillsborough we decided to move closer to my wife's parents, and we moved back to an older house in Belfast.

I remember the day my wife and I went to view the house and walked around it for the first time. The ceilings were orange! The most amusing part of that first visit was when we were being shown into one of the bedrooms. The female owner of the house stopped and apologised before we entered and explained that she was unsure whether to allow us to view the room today. My suspicions were aroused immediately. More orange ceilings? A leak? A radiator hanging off the wall? No, of course that couldn't be it: the house didn't have central heating. Slowly the lady opened the door and there was her problem. No, her embarrassment. Her husband, at three o'clock in the afternoon, in bed blind drunk!

The amount of work that needed to be carried out on the house was extensive. As we were being shown around, each time I caught my wife's eye I shook my head and mouthed the word 'No'. Did that have any effect? Of course not. I don't know if it's something to do with her Taurus birth sign or whether determination (or stubbornness) is the main driver in her decision-making processes, but despite all my resistance we purchased the house.

It took about six months' work—no, six months' hard labour—by my wife and I, plus occasional involvement by qualified tradesmen, for the house to be transformed from the disaster it had been to a very comfortable home.

I always believed that my wife missed her calling. She should have been an interior designer: not only does she have great practical skills but she has an instinctive sense of style, which meant that the fabrics and colours she chose blended together seamlessly. I have not been the most skilful of handymen, but the basic contribution I was able to make to the refurbishment was enjoyable nonetheless. By the time our first Christmas in the house came round it had been finished to an exceptionally high standard.

After Christmas the rumour mill at work was in full swing, with mounting speculation that promotion boards were scheduled for some time in the spring. I felt I had the necessary experience and management skills to move on to the next level.

The rumours had been correct on this occasion, and I attended the board, after which I was promoted to clerk class 2, equivalent to the senior/principal officer discipline grade.

I was subsequently posted to HMP Magilligan in County Londonderry. This was good and bad news. Good news because I had been promoted, but bad news because the prison was seventy-eight miles from home.

My wife made it clear from the start that she would not consider relocating. She was happy now that we were living closer to her parents and that was that as far as she was concerned. I realised how content my wife had been since we moved to Belfast, and I felt her contentment was shared by her parents now that they had ready access to our son, their first grandchild.

I agreed initially that a move closer to Magilligan was not on the agenda. However, after four months the return journey of one hundred and fifty-six miles a day, seven days a week, was beginning to wear me down. There were evenings when I arrived home that I was unable to remember driving certain parts of the journey.

I knew then that I could not maintain this punishing schedule, but I also knew my wife's feelings. A compromise was needed.

I started to stay at Magilligan a couple of nights a week, but it just wasn't working. The crazy hours that I had been working in the Maze meant that I had effectively missed the first year of my son's life, and I just wasn't prepared to lose any more time with him. I didn't know then that the amount of time I would miss out on with all my children, when I could have been watching them growing up, would make that year pale into insignificance.

So another impasse in my life was reached. As I had only recently been promoted, and based on my knowledge of other such promotions, I could end up travelling to Magilligan for years. And it wasn't just the travelling, of course: I had a travelling allowance for the first three years only, which meant I would be landed with an enormous financial burden at the beginning of my fourth year.

My wife was still digging her heels in and refusing to consider a move. She had also secured a job suited to her skills: as a kitchen designer with a market leader in the industry.

I started to bring home brochures of 'new builds' in the Coleraine area and, whether I eventually wore down my wife's resistance or whether she realised that from a family perspective moving house was the right choice, within a few weeks the decision was made.

My wife designed a bungalow, in conjunction with a builder who passed our thoughts on to the architect, and about ten months later we moved into a beautiful purpose-built home in Coleraine.

Not long after we had reached our decision to move we had some good news: my wife discovered she was pregnant with our second child and on 23 December 1987 my daughter came into the world.

Being away from the Maze meant that I had committed the cardinal sin of allowing my security awareness to lapse a little and I had become complacent about my personal safety. I didn't have to wait long for a wake-up call.

Before the move I had made arrangements to car share with a couple of governor grades and that helped to alleviate the tiredness caused by excessive driving. The Security department had received high-level intelligence informing them that the PIRA were targeting a red car believed to be carrying governor grades to the prison each day. Of course it wasn't governor grades, it was me!

Those same governors, who I came to regard not just as colleagues but as friends, were with me on another night in the future when decisions would be made that affected me and added to the building bricks of my career, bricks that would eventually fall with appalling consequences.

After that warning I could not wait to move into our new home. I also changed my red car to a white one and got false, untraceable number plates.

As a family we were happy in Coleraine. My wife had continued travelling to Belfast three days a week to work in her new career as a kitchen designer but gave up the job after the birth of our daughter.

Within a couple of years I moved to the role of cashier in Magilligan, which was really a sub-accountant role. As I was required to go the bank each day it allowed me to go home for lunch and to see my wife, daughter and son. Yes, life was good, we were settled, and we were happy. But once again my career interfered with my family life.

A promotion board was called to fill four senior Administration posts equivalent to the discipline rank of chief officer 2. As there were staff of my current rank with many more years' experience than me I felt, even though I had decided to prepare and attend the board, that my chances of success were slim. In the event the board went extremely well and although I felt that I had given a strong account of myself, I didn't realistically hold out much hope of success.

The results of the board were published. The four positions were filled, and I was shocked to discover my name was on the list. Other colleagues in the service were obviously shocked as well. Of the thirty participants in that promotion board the only congratulatory calls I received were from the three other successful candidates. I did of course also receive a call from my good friend Alfie, the call that I really valued.

When I arrived home the day I received the letter confirming my success I tried to be coy with my wife, telling her that the results of the board were out. She obviously had a lot more confidence in my ability than I had and simply replied, 'You got the board, didn't you?'

She shared my disappointment when my promotion and posting were held up, but with her practical good sense accepted that there was nothing we could do but get on with our lives. There was one post available in Magilligan, which was filled by a colleague from the board who lived in Bangor, County Down; and another post at Maghaberry was filled by another successful candidate who lived in Ballymoney. The two would pass each other each day, on their way to their respective places of employment, each being paid ridiculous amounts of unnecessary travel allowance. Finally, common sense prevailed and each staff member swapped to the prison that was closer to home. Not only did the service gain two happier employees, employees who were arriving at work fresh and ready for the day, not tired after too much travel, but it also saved an immense amount of money.

So what about my promotion? Such was the level of resentment towards me that the Prison Service Personnel department would not post me, but instead allowed another colleague to act up to the new rank, an individual who had not even participated in the promotion board at which I had been successful.

I was annoyed for several reasons. First, it was not my fault that I had been successful on the board. Although I had enough confidence in my ability to be a success at my proposed new level of management I felt my colleagues' resentment should have been directed at the members of the board, not at me! Second, the fact that they would not post me to fill one of the vacancies cost me both credibility and financial reward.

I felt that the Sword of Damocles was continually hanging over us as at every major decision we had to make the same question would come up again and again. *But what if your promotion and posting came through?*

The people responsible for these postings clearly didn't understand the impact that failure to arrive at a prompt decision had on staff and their families. And from experience I knew that we were not the only family to suffer like this.

When the posting did arrive, three years later, there was a combination of happiness tinged with sadness and excitement. I suppose in a way my wife and I felt that we were moving back home again. My son was seven years old and my daughter was almost four, but we painted the picture of our impending move in such a way that the children also got excited.

My brother-in-law, also in the service, had recently been promoted and he and my sister had moved to Coleraine following his transfer to Magilligan. Unfortunately they were arriving just as we were leaving.

Before leaving Magilligan I was presented with the customary leaving gift and card signed by all my colleagues. However, the card that meant more to me than any of the others was from Victor, a very sincere individual who was employed in Administration and had worked with me when I was in charge of the Wages Office. Victor's comment in his card to me read, 'It is good to see that even in the Prison Service the good guys can still win.' Following the negative reaction I had received from my colleagues the comment on Victor's card was very welcome. While moving house earlier this year I came across that card again and when I read it I felt the same warmth as when I first received it all those years ago. Victor was a true gentleman, very much in the mould of my friend Alfie.

Something else of particular significance and great joy also happened at this time. Just as she had during our previous house move, my wife fell pregnant and on 16 December 1991 our second daughter was born. This arrival was to complete the McKee family.

We made a decision to move down country as soon as possible as we wanted to ensure that our son would be starting the new school year on the first day of the new term. We had also decided that the children's education was paramount and selected a prep school with a sound record of academic achievement.

Prior to my promotion coming through a massive change took place throughout the service, when governor and chief officer grades were amalgamated, which meant that there would be a surplus of grades. I had started to believe that I would never get to serve in my new rank. I often wonder where my family would have been now if that promotion had never materialised. I suppose I would have continued to work in Magilligan, the children would have gone to school in Coleraine and the upheaval that I had suffered as a child would have been alien to my own children. Many times I wished that the promotion had never arrived: but it did come, and history cannot be rewritten.

I couldn't imagine the repercussions that lay ahead when a letter landed on my desk at Magilligan one morning shortly after I had arrived at work. The letter was a posting, but not as a chief officer. It couldn't be—the chief officer rank no longer existed. The letter informed me that I was to report to the Prison Service College at the beginning of September to commence my training to become the first of the new governor grade in the Northern Ireland Prison Service.

This was something I had always aspired to but as the majority of the new governor grades were direct entrants with a university degree I felt that it would be a step too far for me.

Chapter 6
Parkhurst Experiences

After a short period of living in rented accommodation we moved into our new home outside Templepatrick on 17 November 1991 and our second daughter arrived a month later. I had started my governor training in October and had met the five colleagues who were to join me for the duration of the training, colleagues who would become firm friends by the end of the course. One of the five, a woman, had been in the service before and was returning after a career break; the remaining four had been selected by open competition from the principal officer grade. I counted myself fortunate that I did not have to participate in the open competition as I would not have been confident of success. Two of my new colleagues had university degrees, another was a former hospital officer, and the other two had been involved in the physical education side of the service.

I was now surrounded by five of the best new governor grades the service had to offer and as I had been selected through a different competition I wasn't sure how I would be accepted, or the level of credibility I would be afforded. I suppose what was of the most concern to me was whether I had the ability to be on a par with them.

My old friend insecurity had again raised its ugly head. For a short time my stammer even returned, but thankfully not with the same severity that I had suffered as a child. Up until the time I had commenced working at the shipyard I had always been known by my full first name 'William', but because there were no Williams employed in the yard I was renamed 'Billy' by the workers on the shop floor and the name just stuck: now, when I introduced myself to people it was as Billy and not William. While I could control my stammer most of the time, sometimes when I introduced myself to someone new I would say Billy, Billy McKee. From then on I was affectionately known as BillyBilly by my five colleagues.

My time at the college was fantastic. Not only was I being taught everything I needed to know for my new role but I enjoyed great comradeship, not just with my new friends but also with the tutors, especially the governor in charge of our training, Mr Pat Maguire. I could not have imagined then how our paths would cross over and over again through the remainder of my service, whatever prison I was working in.

Christmas that year couldn't have been any better. I was enjoying my latest career direction, we had a comfortable new home and, best of all, we had a beautiful new daughter. Although we had moved in only a month before our second daughter was born the majority of the house was decorated. In fact the night before our daughter was born my wife was hanging curtains, such was her determination to have our latest home ready for the new baby.

I still had no inkling of the terrifying circumstances that lay ahead for me and my family. Circumstances that were directly connected with my becoming a member of the governor grade of the Northern Ireland Prison Service. Yet another brick in the wall, the wall that was my life, the wall that would come tumbling down—not yet, and not by my own doing, but by events that I found myself drawn into, events that would ambush me in the future and all but destroy my life.

The training continued to go well. Pat set us a great example of man management. He had a relaxed style that gave us confidence in our individual abilities combined with a knowledge of the role which led us to believe that we would succeed in our new careers as prison governors.

Part of our training was a period of detached duty to another prison in a different jurisdiction from our own, and I was fortunate to have the opportunity to be posted to HMP Parkhurst on the Isle of Wight.

The film *Trains, Planes and Automobiles* came to mind as I completed the final part of my journey to the Isle of Wight. I had flown from Belfast International to the United Kingdom, caught a train to Portsmouth and then a boat to the island.

During the duration of my detachment I was able to do something that I could never have considered when employed in the Prison Service in Northern Ireland: I went to and from work each day on a bus.

That first morning as I made my way to Parkhurst on the bus, and especially as I disembarked, my mind drifted back to a friend who had done the same one morning thirteen years earlier but was greeted not by a friendly face but the covered face of an IRA assassin, an assassin who murdered him in cold blood. I felt shivers run up my spine at the thought and quickly pushed it to the back of my mind.

The governor of Parkhurst was a certain John Marriott, a gentleman in every sense of the word. I could not have been made more welcome by John, but apart from him and his deputy Kevin Rodgers, I detected a coldness from the rest of the governor grades. I wasn't sure if it was just an 'English thing', but John and Kevin were English themselves and still offered me what I can only describe as Northern Ireland-type hospitality. The coolness never thawed during the few weeks I was at Parkhurst and to this day I still cannot put my finger on the reason. Did they feel threatened by me? Maybe. I just didn't know.

John Marriott was a 'one off' in No 1 governor terms. To start with he insisted that everyone address him as John, while in our home service some of the No 1s wanted to be saluted! John had ideas that I believed were more suited to an open prison or to a young offender centre. On one occasion he brought an ice cream van into the prison and paid for ice cream cones for the prisoners; on another he organised a gigantic barbecue. He would later suffer ill health and serious stress, which in my view contributed to his death, after his dismissal from the service following an escape—but I shall come to that soon.

Kevin Rodgers was another 'one off' but in an entirely different way from John. My initial impression of him was that he bordered on the eccentric. He had an incredible likeness to Postman Pat, including the mass of curly hair, Roman nose and glasses. He appeared to revel in his similarity to 'Pat' and took delight in mentioning it at every opportunity. My suspicion of Kevin's eccentricities was totally confirmed, however, by John Marriott. In fact when I heard the tale I initially did not believe him, convinced that it was a joke. Well, it was a joke, but not in the way that I had imagined.

John explained that he had been having his office refurbished while Kevin was on annual leave and had moved temporarily into Kevin's office. Unfortunately the work on John's office had taken longer than anticipated and when Kevin returned from leave he was unable to use his office because John was still there. Kevin had apparently moaned about it so much that John had promised him that as soon as his office was finished he could arrange to have it refurbished any way he chose. Kevin took him at his word and several weeks later had his office wallpapered with Postman Pat wallpaper! This was the office of the deputy governor of one of the most important prisons in the English penal system and it was decorated with Postman Pat wallpaper. I only accepted John's story after I had visited Kevin's office. Eccentric? Most definitely!

Kevin's career moved on as well, and the last I heard of him was an article in the *Prison Service News*. He had become governor in charge of a prison in Doncaster, a private prison owned by an American company. The article referred to a quote from Kevin in a local Doncaster newspaper assuring the public that the prison was secure and that prisoners would not be permitted to escape into the local community. However, someone had added, it should have been more of a concern that the governor in charge was at large in the community at night! Obviously Kevin's eccentricity had followed him from the Isle of Wight to Doncaster.

John had asked Kevin to prepare a schedule for the duration of my posting and it presented me with a comprehensive introduction to one of the most infamous prisons in the English penal system. Parkhurst was one of eight 'dispersal prisons' in the system. These were prisons to which prisoners unable to settle to prison life, and who were usually serving long sentences, would be dispersed. Fortunately or unfortunately prisoners allocated to Parkhurst seemed to settle. Was it the sea air? The way they were treated? The ice cream vans and the barbecues? More knowledgeable professionals than I have considered this question and none to my knowledge has ever reached a persuasive conclusion. Many infamous prisoners had passed through the gates of Parkhurst, including the Yorkshire Ripper, who ended up in Broadmoor Mental Institution; the Black Panther, a serial rapist; and many other career criminals.

At the beginning of my detachment John explained to me that he had his problems at the prison and welcomed my appointment and also that he wished to use my 'fresh eyes'. He asked me to prepare a comprehensive report on my stay at Parkhurst. He encouraged me to be forthright in my observations and recommendations. As part of my undertaking to Pat Maguire back at the college I had to prepare a report on my stay, so John's request was not going to cause me much additional work.

Parkhurst was a prison that probably hadn't changed much in its outward appearance from its origins in the Victorian era. As I passed through the jail I believed that was probably true of the interior as well. Just like HMP Belfast, our own example of a Victorian prison, the prison was divided into wings with three or four landings where the prisoners were secured in cells. Space was at a premium and many cells housed two and sometimes three inmates. One of the largest wings I found quite frightening. There was a landing full of Rastafarians, another of Africans who all appeared to be six foot six and weigh over three hundred pounds, one for terrorists and finally a landing for gangsters.

In the Northern Ireland Service the annual cost of keeping a prisoner in custody at that time was £78,000 per year per prisoner, with eighty-five per cent of that cost being taken up by staff salaries. The equivalent cost in the English service was £23,000 per year per prisoner and I could see why there was such a difference. In Northern Ireland there were three prison officers for each prisoner—this was because the majority of Northern Ireland prisoners were terrorists—while in Britain there were three prisoners for each member of staff.

The English service also saved staff—and therefore money—by using a 'pass key system'. This system didn't require an officer on the outside gate of any of the wings as the staff inside had the key needed to leave and enter the wing at will. This was a practice that I found difficult to comprehend. It would have been acceptable in a low-category security rated prison, but a category one dispersal prison? An accident waiting to happen!

I asked one of the few officers who were employed in the wing why he locked the entrance grille. He looked at me, puzzled, before answering that it was to keep the prisoners in. I shook my head and walked away. There were approximately one hundred and eighty prisoners unlocked in the wing for the majority of the day, and twenty-seven staff. The staff inside, with the prisoners, had a key to the grille on their belts. Do I need to point out the possible consequences?

I heard many interesting stories during my time at Parkhurst, but most interesting was the day I was given access to the old prison journals dating back to the late 1880s.

As I flicked through the pages, studying the names and ages of the offenders, noting the actual crimes they committed, crimes of which they were subsequently found guilty, my attention was drawn to one in particular. Offender: Thomas Brown; Age: Nine years old; Crime: Charged with stealing a hand bag; Punishment: Prison ship to

Australia. I couldn't believe that a nine-year-old boy would be taken from his family and put on a ship to spend months at sea; and if he was fortunate to survive the crossing he would receive a pardon on his arrival. The pardon was actually an abdication of responsibility by the authorities at that time. When I told my own children of the story, they laughed and I was unable to convince them of the truth. It reminded me of a story from the last time the English cricketers were playing in Australia. One of the sports reporters was stopped by customs at the airport and asked did he have any criminal convictions. The reporter, being a somewhat sharp individual, replied that he didn't realise that having a criminal record was still a prerequisite for admission to the country.

Other tales from Parkhurst made me laugh at times at the sheer stupidity that led to some of the disasters that befell the prison. For example, thousands upon thousands of pounds was spent on building a new front gate to the prison. Apparently it was magnificent, and any governor would have been proud of it. The only downside was discovered when there was a fire in the prison and the fire engine could not get in because the concrete head above the gate was too low.

Another crazy example was the construction of the new laundry. The floor had to be several feet thick to withstand the constant vibration of the huge commercial washing machines. Unfortunately the builder misread the plans, which resulted in the huge commercial washing machines vibrating their way into the shallow floors and the three-foot thick roof causing the walls to buckle with the unnecessary weight. The plans had obviously been read upside down.

There was an unsuccessful escape attempt during my time in Parkhurst. The prisoners had large pinboards on the walls of their cells and at night, when staff levels were at their minimum, they were using plastic forks, knives and spoons which they had stolen from the dining room to work their way through the cell walls. Each night after they had finished they replaced the pinboards to conceal their labours. I suppose that highlights the disadvantages of permitting inmates to view films detailing escapes from prisons as in *The Shawshank Redemption*, which obviously provided both the inspiration and method to implement just one of a number of escapes and attempted escapes from this category one prison that was Parkhurst.

The area immediately outside the prisoner accommodation at Parkhurst was like a building site, and the prisoners were able to dispose of the rubble from their labours by simply throwing it out of their cell windows.

Eventually their concerted efforts resulted in a 'window' in each cell wall being created from one end of the landing to the other. In all other wings in the prison the end cell had additional strengthening, but in this particular wing the end room was not a cell but a medical room where the additional strengthening had not taken place. When the night of the planned escape arrived the prisoners removed the pinboards and passed through from one cell to the other until they reached the last cell. They only had to cut through the final cell wall into the medical room and then dig through the exterior wall. This was achieved with a minimum of effort.

The escape might well have been a success if it had not been a warm night in early summer: as a night guard officer opened a window to get some fresh air he witnessed the prisoners dropping one at a time down knotted sheets. The officer froze for a few seconds as he checked to confirm he wasn't dreaming—after all, prisoners escaping from a prison using knotted sheets was more like a scene from *Escape from Alcatraz* than the mundane reality of prison life.

After this attempted escape I made a telephone call to our research and development department asking for advice on how to prevent the fabric of the cells being interfered with. It was a fairly simple matter of painting the cells with ultraviolet-based paint. During cell searches the prison officers would scan the walls with a lamp sensitive to ultra-violet light, which would determine whether any part of the wall had been damaged or interfered with. I also recommended that any wall coverings such as the pinboards should be secured in such a way that it was possible to check behind them during a cell search.

The attempted escape took its toll on John Marriott and a few months later a successful escape finished his career and led to the ill health that ultimately ended his life. John had settled into life on the Isle of Wight and when he left the service he sought and gained employment with a hospital trust on the island. I was sad to learn of his death some years later.

The area of greatest interest to me in Parkhurst was their special supervisory unit (ssu). This unit was used to hold extremely danger-ous inmates who had the financial means to fund an escape attempt. While I was there I spoke to one of the prisoners held in the unit who was a member of the gang responsible for the gold bullion robbery at

Heathrow and another prisoner, Valerio Vicci, responsible for the Knightsbridge safe robbery. There were also IRA terrorists held in the unit.

I could understand and accept the top security set-up but not the regime set in place for the inmates. For example, the prisoners were able to spend huge amounts of cash on themselves. It is normal to set a limit on the amount of money that a prisoner is allowed to spend in prison. If there is no such limit the prisoner will become a prison 'baron', selling for an inflated price items purchased on the 'outside'.

The situation in the SSU was such that an officer's only role seemed to be running back and forth to a store in the nearest town to buy expensive Italian food for the Italian who was responsible for the Knightsbridge robbery.

Most of the prisoners in the SSU were reluctant to get into conversation with me, except for the Italian. He told me that a deal had been done with the Italian authorities and he would be returned to Italy within a year and released from custody soon after. I recall reading in the *Mail* later that year about the prisoner's subsequent transfer home, as per our conversation, which was correct except for one crucial detail: a short time after being released from Italian custody he was killed.

On my last day at Parkhurst I recall jovially thanking John for arranging to make my detachment more exciting by arranging the attempted escape. At the time we laughed together, but the next escape from Parkhurst was successful and I can guarantee there were neither jokes cracked nor laughter heard in the corridors of power in London when John was called to account.

I completed my report on my visit to Parkhurst some weeks later and, as John had requested, was forthright and indeed critical where I believed it was appropriate. I sent John a copy of the report and it was some four weeks before I heard from him. At one point I started to fear that perhaps I had been too critical and was concerned that our friendship had been damaged. My fears proved fruitless. I received a lengthy letter from him thanking me for my report and detailing which recommendations he could take on board and the constraints that prevented him following the others. Two of my recommendations might have gone a long way to preventing the escape that was eventually to cost John his career but unfortunately they were never implemented.

Before leaving Parkhurst I had raised my concerns with John about the operation of the pass key system in a high-risk dispersal prison. I pointed out to him that the prisoners could easily empty B Wing by securing the key to the outside grille from one of the officers working inside the wing. One hundred and eighty inmates could then make a bid for freedom. John explained that they would be contained in the area immediately outside B Wing, which was surrounded by the high fence that separated the prisoner accommodation from both the Administration building and the main entrance and exit of the prison. He also pointed out to me that if an inmate had got hold of a pass key it would be of no further use to them as the gates through the fence to the Administration building were electric and operated from the Control Room in the prison.

I diplomatically demonstrated to John that although the pass key would not allow the inmates to exit through the gate operated from the Control Room, the key could be used to bypass this gate by entering the football field by one gate and exiting it through another, which would leave the inmates outside the Administration building and, more crucially, at the main exit from the prison. John was stunned! 'Couldn't see the wood for the trees,' was the phrase that came to mind.

I reminded John of this particular security issue in my report, but whether he addressed the problem or not I don't know. At the time of the inquiry into the escape it was suggested that I should forward a copy of the report to the inquiry team. John didn't need that. If I had been asked for it of course I would have been obliged to release it. But I wasn't asked, and the complete report lies gathering dust in a filing cabinet in some corner of an office somewhere within the prison estate. Its contents could no longer pose any threat to John.

The man heading the inquiry was a certain Martin Neary. Ten years later this same man would be at the head of another more serious inquiry a little closer to home, this time involving escape/murder, possible collusion, alleged security forces involvement, and . . . me!

Chapter 7
Back to the Maze

All good things come to an end, no more so than when the governor training finished. Our respective postings arrived and, thankfully in one respect, I was posted to HMP Maze, along with the governor to whom I had been closest on the course, a governor who has since reached the heights in his career to which I once aspired. Despite the intervening years this relationship has developed and I still regard this individual as one of my closest friends. We have shared laughter and tears over the years and have formed a slightly macabre pact: whichever of us dies first, the other will speak at the funeral!

There were easier places than the Maze to be posted, but I felt at the time that it was better to get the difficult postings over first. How wrong could I be? This was my second posting to Maze and over the following years I would discover that it would, unfairly, be just one of many. While several governors went through their entire service without once working in the Maze Prison, it seemed the staff who did all that was asked of them, and never argued about their postings, were the first to be detailed to the more challenging posts in the service. The phrase 'the willing horse for the hard road' comes to mind.

Upon arriving at the Maze most governors would start work at the sharp end: the H Blocks where the prisoners were secured. This, after all, was the bread and butter of the service.

We were introduced to our line manager, Governor 'Del' Smith, and after minimal instruction were each allocated responsibility for an H Block. There was one governor in charge of each block and I was given responsibility for a mixed block, H Block 6. Looking back now I feel it was ironic that out of a possible eight H Blocks I was allocated H Block 6, as this was to prove central to a drama that would enter my life in the years ahead; a drama that would almost lead to my suicide, my murder, and, combined with other factors, all but destroyed my career, my health, my mind, and ultimately my life.

H Block 6 was one of the Provisional IRA blocks in the prison, but only two 'legs' of the 'H' held PIRA: the other side was the accommodation for the orderlies in the prison. The orderlies were made up of what were known as ODCS, or 'ordinary decent criminals'.

The PIRA OC in H6 was a prisoner called 'Tim' and during the time I was in charge of the block we developed a reasonable working relationship. That's how it was in the Maze. The heavy hand approach rarely worked when dealing with paramilitaries in the prison. By a strange coincidence, the one ex-prisoner I meet more than most in my life after the Prison Service is Tim. After his release under the Good Friday Agreement he settled in an area of Belfast that was close to where I lived. When we meet, as with most ex-paramilitary prisoners, we stop, say a few words and pass on.

I remember one occasion when I met the OC of PIRA while walking through Castlecourt in Belfast. He said hello and extended his hand and when that happens it is instinctive to respond in kind. He asked how I was and inquired if I was now working in that other 'big house', which he and I both knew was Maghaberry Prison. I responded with some similar small talk and we moved on. Of course, as Castlecourt is full of cameras there was more than a chance that the meeting had been recorded. I had to submit a short report to the Security department detailing why I was in Castlecourt shaking the hand of the OC of PIRA in the Maze Prison.

My time in H6 passed quickly. I had a great working relationship with the principal and senior officers who were my second and third in command, and the quality of our officers meant that the block, I am proud to say, was one of the better H Blocks in the Maze.

My day normally began with dealing with prisoner requests. Each morning at unlock the prison officer on the wing would take prisoner requests at each cell door. These ranged from requests to see the governor, doctor or dentist, to asking for an extra visit or occasionally to be permitted to have something left into the prison that was outside the normal rules.

The PIRA continually tried to bend the rules that the prison authorities had set for them, and on many occasions they were successful. I believe they used these attempts to build and maintain morale amongst their volunteers.

For example, there was one prisoner who put his name down to see me at least once a week about conjugal rights in visits. I would of course listen to the prisoner's arguments, which would have been rehearsed with his colleagues before he came out of the wing to see me. His co-prisoners would try to predict my responses to his questions so that when our meeting took place he was able to defend himself against all my arguments with confidence. There were occasions when I came up with an argument that they had not anticipated, and when this occurred the prisoner, rather than counter-argue, would simply bring the conversation to an end and return to the wing. I knew, however, that he would be back next week with an answer that would contradict the challenge I had raised.

Although I was happy to talk about whatever topic was up for discussion, I had no authority to agree anything as controversial as conjugal rights in the prison. The prisoners would be issued with petitions, which were really letters addressed to the offices of the Secretary of State, and his policymakers would reply to the prisoners outlining all the various reasons why the subject of their petitions could or could not be agreed to.

It was a game. We knew it, they knew it, and they knew we knew.

The PIRA also continually subjected all prison staff to a process of 'conditioning'. The best example of this was revealed in a conversation between 'Tim' and myself. He was thanking me for my co-operation in the way I managed the block and worked with him to resolve difficulties and by doing so helped both to keep the tension in the block down and to maintain a workable relationship between prisoners and staff. I thanked him in turn for his co-operation in the way he managed his men and in particular for helping to reduce the amount of swearing at my officers. Tim suddenly interrupted me. He realised that I had been playing him at his own conditioning game and as he turned to leave my office he simply said, 'We are the ones who do the conditioning, not you.' He tried to hide it but I saw a faint smile spread across his face as he closed the door behind him.

I remember another incident with a member of the PIRA. He was a hardliner and couldn't be bothered with this pleasant conditioning approach. Sadly his father was either dead or dying and he wanted to be let out of the prison on a visit.

I should explain at this point that there was an instruction from the PIRA to their volunteers that any prisoner out of the prison on compassionate parole must report back to the prison. They realised that as soon as one individual didn't return the whole compassionate parole privilege would be at the very least reviewed or at worst stopped immediately. On one occasion a volunteer chose to ignore the order and the PIRA on the outside collected him and escorted him back to the jail.

This prisoner came to see me about his request for compassionate parole. There was no eye contact to start with, which was unusual for a member of PIRA. I spoke. He listened. I struggled to get more than 'yes' and 'no' answers from him. Security was not happy to support the request but with a little pushing from me I managed to secure the man his visit. He went on the visit and, whether it was down to pressure from his OC or his conscience I don't know, but some two weeks later he asked to see me to thank me for sorting his visit. As we talked we went around in circles as he struggled to get the words formed and out of his mouth. Eventually they did. 'Thanks,' he mumbled as he got up quickly and left the office.

This was part of my conditioning of the prisoners. I regularly went out of my way to solve problems, real and perceived, painting a picture of 'the helpful governor'. The working relationships that I established in my first years in the Maze, with PIRA in particular, would be of great use to me in solving future problems that presented themselves as I moved up the career ladder.

I don't want to paint the picture that these prisoners were really a pleasant bunch of men and we were all happy together in H Block 6— far from it. Not only were we detaining some of the most dangerous and knowledgeable terrorists in Western Europe but they were, to a man, committed to their cause, and any change of policy from the leadership could lead to mayhem.

But this was the Maze Prison and the way I ran my block was a small-scale example of how the whole prison was managed.

The other crucial aspect of my new job was completing the life sentence reports on each prisoner serving a life sentence in my area of responsibility, in this case H Block 6. The reports were requested by Prison Service Headquarters at various stages during the prisoner's sentence and I would review the prisoner's main file, which, of course, revealed the crime for which he was serving the time. The file gave all the gruesome details of the crime in addition to the background of the convicted individual. Reading these files was a reminder, if it was needed, that the prisoners were far from a pleasant bunch.

In a normal prison environment the preparation of a life sentence report involved reports from the wing officer and other staff who had a working knowledge of the prisoner. The prisoner would also have sight of the contents of the report so that he was fully aware of what was being written about him. But this was not possible with the terrorists, mainly because of the risk of intimidation. I could imagine the reaction of a prisoner reading a report recommending that I did not believe he had shown remorse for the crime he had committed and that I also believed that if released he would still be a danger to the public. This type of report, more than anything else, ensured that a prisoner's release would be delayed at least until the next year's report.

There were many events in my time in H6 that stand out in my mind, some serious and some amusing. One of the more light-hearted occasions just before Christmas. I had bought individual Christmas cards for every member of staff on the H6 detail. I handwrote the cards and on some mentioned my thanks for some little service that had occurred at some stage throughout the previous twelve months. The senior officer was a well-known joker, and as the cards were being handed out to the staff he decided to set up a member of the group. The senior officer opened and resealed his card after placing a ten pound note inside. He ripped the card open in front of the 'set up' officer and of course the ten pounds drifted to the floor. The 'set up' officer who had just received his card quickly ripped his open to get his tenner, at which point he was engulfed by the shouts and laughter of his colleagues. These moments of humour were very important: there were times ahead for all of us when laughter was the farthest thing from our minds.

As time went on in the Maze staff gradually withdrew from the wings. The legs of the blocks became a no-go area for staff. The OC had appointed the orderlies of his choice and the prison paid them the appropriate wage for their services.

The search team still carried out regular searches of the blocks, and that was the only time when staff went down on the wings, except for a regular appearance every Friday morning by two officers who refused to give up any area of the prison to the paramilitaries: 'Big' Norman Henderson, the principal officer of H6; and me, the governor.

I would have my coffee with Norman every morning, and at the same time each Friday Norman would stand up, put his cap on his head, a cap with the peak slashed and turned down so as to make him hold his head high, and say, 'It's time, Governor.'

We would then leave his office and make our way into the circle, standing aside as the officer on the circle grille let us through as we made our way to the two legs of the wing where the PIRA prisoners awaited us. Of course they knew when to expect our visit. (The circle was not really a circle, but the rectangle that formed the 'bar' of the H: the word circle had been used to describe the same area in the old Victorian prisons like Crumlin Road, and the name had stuck.)

It happened the same way every time we entered the wings. As we walked through the final grille we always paused while the key turned in the lock, securing us in the wing with approximately twenty-five PIRA prisoners.

The prisoners always gave us the impression both by their body language and non-verbal contact that they were no more interested in us than the man in the moon. We then slowly and deliberately walked towards the bottom of the wing, Big Norman in full uniform, boots shining, shoulders back, his hands behind his back as he walked, myself strolling almost casually beside him. Neither of us ever spoke until we had reached the end of the wing. As we neared the end of the wing, Norman would always lean close to my ear and whisper 'squeaky bum time'. We would turn and steel ourselves for the onslaught that would ambush us as we headed up the wing towards the exit. The prisoners, who had shown us zero interest on the way down the wing had been 'switched on', batteries recharged, and the verbal assault and finger-pointing began.

No matter how many times it happened the effects, on me at least, were the same. Raised body temperature, profuse sweating, dry mouth. Why do we put ourselves through this week after week? This was a question that neither of us put into words, but every time we entered the wing, whether we went down the right side or left, the look that we exchanged asked the question. The answer was not given in words but rather by the determined expression that appeared on our faces. We were two stubborn bastards.

Norman left it to me to repel the assault. I would just pick out one individual prisoner who had asked a question that I felt I could deal with. I would make eye contact with him and waffle away, dragging out my answer until we made it to the top of the wing where the officer was always ready, key in the lock, to open the grille as soon as we arrived to allow us to escape. But then we had to repeat the complete exercise all over again in the other leg of the wing.

We both knew that this was the conditioning process at its worst. The prisoners resented Norman and me invading their space and hoped to wear us down with the constant threatening behaviour. They never did. Norman had been in HMP Belfast for the majority of his service, and in that prison the staff were in control. He had a strong personality and I leaned on it many times during the period we worked together.

That Christmas I took Norman and the senior officer out for Christmas dinner to thank them for their tremendous help and support throughout the year. We had booked a table at the Saints and Scholars restaurant in Belfast and had spent a great night enjoying each other's company on one of the few occasions away from the stress of the PIRA, H Block 6 and the Maze Prison. Throughout the evening Norman kept encouraging the senior officer to drink up: 'after all, the governor's buying'. I laughed, not minding how much the bill was, as the guys thoroughly deserved it. With every course the same thing happened: 'Order plenty, the governor's buying.'

As the evening came to a close the waiter returned and Norman ordered us all cigars. I still didn't care because when I reflected over the year thinking about our Friday mornings and the visits to the wings and all the other support these two had afforded me they were welcome to their cigars and more.

The meal was eaten, all three courses, the drinks were drunk, the cigars were smoked. The only thing left to do was pay the bill. I made my way to the cashier to settle the bill but I was too late. All the non-sense about 'eat up, drink up, smoke up, the governor's buying' was another of Norman's wind-ups: the two of them had split the bill. As I stood, gobsmacked, muttering, 'Thanks, but you shouldn't have', Norman turned and said, 'You didn't have to do this to demonstrate how much you value us because we know that, but we felt we needed to show you how much we value you!' Another precious memory, one that showed me the strength of character of colleagues who became friends. It was they who gave me the purpose and determination to survive as a governor in HMP Maze in the dark days that lay ahead.

The years rolled on. I was well established as a 'block governor' and felt comfortable with all aspects of my role.

For as long as I could remember, the administrative side in the Prison Service had always been staffed by prison officers. Everyone (with the exception of the direct entrant governor grade) joined the service as prison officers; some then became hospital officers, trades officers and clerical officers. As I've mentioned, I had taken Dessie Stewart's advice from college back in 1977 to join Administration because it would bring more opportunities for promotion. Of course he was right and he had pointed me in a direction that had led to me becoming a governor in the service.

The fact that prison officers filled all grades within Administration, and received the same pay as the discipline grade, meant that simply running Administration placed an immense financial burden on the service. A decision was taken and a package agreed with the Prison Officers' Association to replace the prison officer clerical grades with more cost-effective civil servants. Two of my colleagues, who had been part of the same batch of recruits as me, had followed me into the clerical function: one was my good friend Alfie and the other an officer who is no longer in the service. Under the new arrangements, any clerical officer who wished to leave the grade and the service was able to take advantage of a financial exit package: others were assimilated into the discipline grade and retained their status so that, for example, clerk 2s became principal officers, and so on. A decision was taken that HMP Maze was the first prison to be 'civilianised', in the term used to describe the change.

The No 1 governor at Maze, requested that I attend a meeting in his office one morning. When the No 1 sent for a governor it was usually for one of two reasons: the governor had committed some indiscretion, work-related or otherwise; or he was being transferred. As I made my way to the No 1 governor's office on the top floor of the main Administration building my mind was full of thoughts concerning my impending conversation with the boss. The governor and I had enjoyed a strong working relationship when he was the No 1 at HMP Magilligan and I was employed there. While I was there I had been part of his command team that brought to an end an unsuccessful hostage attempt that had involved the prisoners and a prison officer. He had come up through the ranks and to reach the rank of No 1 in the Maze was a great testimony to his management ability and leadership skills. There were few people who rose through the ranks nowadays to reach the dizzy heights of No 1 governor in charge of a prison.

So was I to be transferred? No, I didn't think that was the reason. I knew from my annual reports that my career was going well and that

I was a valued member of the management team in the Maze Prison. So as I climbed the stairs and approached the office of the Governor I was starting to worry. What had I done recently that would have brought me to the governor's attention? I knew that I bent the rules when necessary to ensure the smooth running of the prison, but I wasn't alone: we all did that. Too late now, anyway, I thought as I knocked on the heavy door to his tastefully decorated office.

'Come in,' boomed the voice from behind the door. The governor was a big man in every way: size, height, personality and character.

I entered the office and waited for the reprimand that was to follow, by now convinced that I had been overdoing the rule stretching.

'Good morning, young William,' came from behind the desk.

That expression took me back to many years before when I had worked in the factory in Downpatrick, as that was the term of endearment used by the two directors when they spoke to me. I felt better: the memory of the factory give me a good feeling. The governor asked me to sit down while he explained what he needed me to do for him, something that would benefit the service as a whole.

Even though, after just fourteen years in the service, I had already reached a rank one rung higher than I had previously aspired to I was still very ambitious. Anything I could do that would benefit the service would obviously also benefit my career. I listened intently and became a little excited as I wondered what role he had in store for me.

I had left the administration role way behind as I progressed into the governor grade, so I was shocked by the role that The governor had envisaged for me. He explained that civilianisation was necessary to make the administration of the service more cost effective and that individuals were being selected from the various Civil Service departments in the Northern Ireland Office and beyond to fill the new roles in the Prison Service. I was still lost as to why we were having this conversation and could not see what my involvement would be.

'So, William,' he continued, 'as you have vast experience of the main functions, important functions within Administration, I want you to be the facilitator for the complete transfer of the Administration departments from the current incumbents of the clerical functions to the new Civil Service grades.'

I just sat there. What? I thought. Where would I even begin to set about organising that?

The governor was waiting for my answer.

'Governor,' I began, 'I'm sorry, but with the greatest respect you have no idea the enormity of the task you're asking me to undertake. Are you aware that we have people in the general office with twenty years' experience who are still learning, discovering the odd piece of legislation or reading the outcome of a legal challenge that changes the way they carry out their job? These are changes that, if missed, can mean a prisoner being released early or, worse, retaining him in the prison too long. Also there are areas of the administration that I have limited knowledge of and others that I have no knowledge of at all. My time in Administration was spent on the financial side and therefore my strengths lie there, but even with that, my last experience there was quite a few years ago.'

The governor had a very simple answer. 'Look, as far as I am concerned I know you, and the efficient no-nonsense approach you adopt as you address the prison side of our business. The people at Headquarters obviously know more about your previous roles and talents in the administration side, so you are the man we collectively believe is the right individual to undertake this extremely important role.'

He continued, 'I can't stress enough the importance of the task as there are certain people who want it to fail and ultimately leave us with the embarrassment of having to retain the current extremely expensive prison officer grades in their current roles. The Maze is the test bed and biggest prison, so it is essential that the transfer to the civil servants is both seamless and an unmitigated success.'

The way the governor had finished the conversation was classic. Before I could even speak again, he was on his feet with his hand outstretched, a bit like a used car salesman who has just closed a deal.

'I have told the department that I would release you from your current role as H Block governor and you can start your new role room from next Monday. I have let Del Smith [my line manager] know he is losing you and when you have this job done you are being transferred to HMP Belfast. I am sorry to lose you and you will know that, but someone with a bit of clout has asked for you to go to Belfast.'

I was now on my feet, knowing that the conversation was over. Talk about a double whammy!

First, despite my protestations with regard to the Administration challenge I had no choice in the matter. I was allocated the task and that was that, and to stop me thinking too much about it the governor drops into the conversation the fact that I am being transferred to Belfast!

I shook the governor's hand and left the office. I can't remember if I spoke or, if I did speak, what I said. The next thing I remember was heading back to my office with a dozen different thoughts whirling through my mind. I hadn't a clue where to start with the Administration task. I would think about the implications of the transfer to Belfast at a later date. But that was me: even under pressure I was still prioritising.

The task facing me was immense and the number of my former colleagues still involved in Administration who gave me the old 'rather you than me' comment did little to encourage me.

The staff had been chosen from the clerical grades of the Civil Service and the quality of the staff selected was the first positive feeling I had about the whole project. They had all the qualities that were necessary to adapt quickly and efficiently to their new roles, provided they were instructed correctly. And that was my responsibility.

The outgoing prison staff were obviously not in a charitable mood with regard to the hand-over process, so another important part of my role was to build relationships in an attempt to make the transition as smooth and problem-free as possible.

The staff coming in from the Civil Service were not all known to each other, so a team-bonding exercise took up the first week of the new phase of their careers.

Using my background knowledge and with the help of other current administrative grades we achieved what I had initially thought was nigh-on impossible. There were headaches along the way, but a lot fewer than anyone could have anticipated.

I argued strongly for retaining prison officer clerical grades within the general office, the office that dealt, among other things, with calculating prisoners' sentences, court productions, working out prisoners' fines and collating the life sentence reports. I explained that a simple course would not come close to giving even the most intelligent person the necessary knowledge to manage the office effectively. I was subsequently proved right: all these years later there is still a uniformed senior officer grade employed there. The fact that it is my good friend Alfie pleases me immensely.

The system of job allocation, tried and tested in the service over many years, went out of the window when the Civil Service grades moved in. For example, my administration experience had been gained in the financial side of the business, while Alfie's experience was, for the majority of his service in the general office, prisoner-based. This meant that experience was built up in a particular field and this experience kept mistakes to a minimum.

After the Civil Service took over this function, staff were almost routinely moved in and out of the general office, which did not give them adequate time to learn and grow into their new posts.

Alfie became the continuity of the office and there was no better man to fill that particular role. His years of experience, combined with his courteous, calm manner, ensured that the governor could focus on more contentious areas of the prison in the knowledge that he had the best of the best managing one of the most important departments in the prison.

As I write yet another of Alfie's little phrases comes to mind, a phrase that says a lot about the man who coined it: 'A little courtesy goes a long way.'

I was pleased with my success and felt the letter the governor had placed in my file would be a help when the next promotion board came around.

Everything appeared to be going in the right direction in my life. Even the transfer to Belfast Prison worked to the advantage of the McKee family. I was able to nip out for ten minutes in the afternoon, collect the children from school and drop them at my wife's parents, and then collect them after work each day.

I received my transfer date and the Saturday before I was due to start at Belfast one of my governor friends with whom I had travelled to Magilligan a few years before invited my wife and me, along with our other travelling colleague and his wife, to dinner. I enjoyed a great relationship with these two particular governors, one of whom left the service, only for our paths to cross in a different environment some years later. The other enjoyed a meteoric rise to the top of the governor grade and is currently No 1 governor of HMP Maghaberry. That night we sat laughing over dinner, recalling amusing incidents from both our work and personal lives. The telephone rang and our host excused himself from the table to take the call. The rest of us chatted on for a few moments before he returned to the dining room.

As he entered the room we saw that the smile had left his face and had been replaced by a look of great concern. 'It's Maghaberry Prison looking for permission to have the names of the control and restraint-trained staff released. They need to be contacted at once. There is a massive riot taking place in Belfast Prison. The loyalist prisoners are going through the walls, floors and ceilings in an effort to get to the PIRA inmates. They think they might lose the jail.'

Everyone at the table froze. The details of what we had just heard filtered through our minds. I started to laugh. 'Very good, Alan! You really had me going there. I almost believed you.' I thought, since he knew I was starting work at Belfast in two days' time, that he was trying to wind me up a little before Monday.

'I'm not joking! Honest to God, I am not joking!'

My God, I thought, great timing, this.

The Maze had now settled and was no longer regarded as the difficult prison it once was; and now I was transferring to the most problematic jail in the system! I looked across at my wife and saw the despair in her eyes. Her expression said it all: 'Why you? Why is it always you?'

The problem behind the disturbance at HMP Belfast was a segregation issue. In the Maze the paramilitaries were all sentenced prisoners and were segregated in their own blocks, while in Belfast the prisoners were on remand waiting either trial or sentencing. At the Maze, after the prisoners received their sentence their status changed from remand to sentenced and they were then transferred to the segregated blocks. The remands in Belfast were mixed, with prisoners from different factions being secured in alternate cells. This meant that when prisoners were entering and leaving the wings the staff had to try to minimise the contact between opposing groups as much as possible. If a republican was out of his cell the staff shouted 'Taig out', and if it was someone from the opposite faction they shouted 'Prod out'. Whenever the opposing factions met they attempted to assault each other, so it was imperative that the chances of this happening were as few and far between as possible.

On one particular occasion three PIRA tried to ambush one of the leaders of the UVF, David McCullough, as they returned from the Visits. Now David McCullough was an extremely fit guy, a big man who hadn't reached his position in the UVF leadership without being able to handle himself. The three PIRA must have regretted their actions—after they regained consciousness. According to staff McCullough exploded into action when he saw who stood before him. He moved so quickly that there was not a visible mark on him after the attempted assault by the PIRA. From a staff perspective it also let them know what to expect if they ever found themselves on the wrong side of David McCullough. I was to recall this event later in my career when McCullough and I crossed swords in the confined space of the governor's office in an H Block during yet another posting back to the Maze Prison. On that occasion only the actions of a brave female principal officer saved me from serious assault and injury.

I believe that there was a concerted effort by both sets of inmates to use threats to each other's safety to support their case for transfer and segregation to HMP Maze.

Well, they had played their ace card this time.

The dinner finished and no one present was in any mood to continue with the conversation. At that stage we had no idea whether any staff had been hurt or what the repercussions would be for the service.

I telephoned the governor at HMP Belfast the following morning and volunteered my services a day earlier if he felt I could help.

Chapter 8

Wing Governor, Office Politics and the End of the 'Crum'

The jail was in such a mess that any help offered by experienced personnel was gladly accepted. Within the hour I was making the familiar journey to HMP Belfast.

The damage to the cells was horrendous. The loyalists had come up through floors and gone through walls and ceilings in any way they could in order to get at the PIRA prisoners. It was just as Alan had told us on Saturday night at dinner. The bed frames had been destroyed and the bed ends had been used as tools to break through the fabric of the cells; no doubt they were also intended as weapons to attack, maim and probably kill the occupant of the cell they were attempting to enter. Thankfully the PIRA inmates had been moved from their cells in time and murder was averted.

The loyalist prisoners were secured in their cells by three-man control and restraint teams who had handcuffed each prisoner to prevent further damage and injury.

As I made my way around the wing I noticed that there was none of the air of euphoria that normally followed intervention and success in a battle with the paramilitaries. I believe that even though Belfast Prison was not to close immediately the staff could now see the writing on the wall. I did not yet know the important role that I would have to play in its closure.

A political decision was taken to relocate all paramilitaries to the Maze Prison and hurried arrangements were made to have the necessary accommodation prepared to permit this to happen. This had to be done immediately because the A Wing accommodation in Belfast was totally wrecked and the loyalist cells in particular were in such a state of disrepair that it was uninhabitable. It was not just a simple matter of putting the prisoners in a van and throwing them into the Maze—far from it. The staff who were employed in A Wing with the remands had to be posted to the Maze, some on the Sunday, to help prepare the two H Blocks for the prisoners' arrival; the rest were deployed in searching the prisoners and accompanying them in vans, with police escorts, to their new 'home' at the Maze Prison.

Remand prisoners have few restrictions on the number of personal items they are allowed and a separate van was required to transport their property. It wasn't just a matter of bunging their stuff in bags. Each cell had to be emptied and its contents recorded and checked against the records held in the prison. Failure to do this would result in massive compensation claims from the prisoners.

I was called to the governor's office. As I entered the office the first thing that struck me was how pale and stressed the governor looked. Not that I was surprised—far from it.

'Sorry, Billy, that I'm only getting a chance to speak to you now. Obviously you will understand that other rather more urgent matters have had to take priority over that.' He smiled as he finished speaking to me. I admired him for that. The prison was coming down around him and he still managed a smile.

'Glad to be here, Governor. Sorry about your current difficulties. What have you planned for me?' I asked.

'Well, young man, what I had originally planned for you will have to wait. I have had you posted back to Maze on detached duty again from today. I need to use your experience managing an H Block to get these bastards sorted out and settled,' he explained.

I couldn't believe it; this was the third time I had been posted back to Maze and the task I was being given was a throwback to the bad old days. I was expected to try to manage staff and prisoners, none of whom were familiar with the procedures or the layout of an H Block. The prisoners would be on a high because their objective had been achieved, and they were difficult enough to handle on a normal day in an environment that they were familiar with. Thankfully I wasn't the only one who was aware of the potential problems, and the staffing difficulties were partly solved by mixing experienced staff from Maze along with the inexperienced officers from Belfast.

The main problem that lay ahead for the staff from Belfast was their non-existent relationships with the former Belfast prisoners. As a result of the harsh regime that was in place in Belfast I had no doubt there were many prisoners who felt that they had scores to settle with some of the staff.

I headed off to the Maze, spoke to the governor and went down to the blocks that were been hastily prepared for the transfer of the inmates. It was as if I had never been away.

The staff had responded to this latest situation the way that they had reacted to countless others over the years. They were used to dealing with this kind of problem and worked quickly and efficiently with a minimum of direction to have the necessary preparation finished in time to accept the warring factions from Belfast. The number of times they had to deal with a wreck in the Maze—too many to recall—meant that staff were skilled in preparing alternative accommodation quickly and relocating the offending inmates efficiently.

The actual decant from Belfast to the Maze went as well as could have been expected. The prisoners were hardly going to cause us any problems, as being transferred to the Maze was what they wanted. The inmates were searched, then re-handcuffed and placed in their little individual cells in the large transportation vehicle that was to ferry them to Maze. A large police presence was necessary: the Northern Ireland Office could not take a chance on further embarrassment caused by a vanload of terrorists being hijacked by their supporters on the way to the Maze.

As each prisoner arrived in the H Block where they were to be housed I took a few moments to speak to each one and make myself known to them. They were grinning from ear to ear.

The loyalists came from various paramilitary factions. It was the governor's intention to split each faction into their respective groups—he was wise enough to know that if he didn't do this now, within days he would be forced into doing it anyway. That was the way things were in the Maze. We collectively tried to envisage what demands prisoners were going to push for next. If we knew that in the end they would achieve their goal, causing perhaps thousands of pounds of damage—and staff assaults—along the way, a pre-emptive strike could be carried out to give the prisoners what we knew they would get eventually.

By the end of the first day the loyalists were safely ensconced in their H Block in the Maze. They were not separated at that stage but in my opening address to them I told them that once the Security department had confirmed which faction they were affiliated to they would be allocated a wing along with their comrades from that faction.

Joe Helm was the governor given the task of sorting out the PIRA when they arrived the following day. Joe was an ex-chief and operated as if he was still a chief. He could not tolerate any of the paramilitary prisoners and made sure they knew it. The PIRA move was not running quite as smoothly as the loyalist move the previous day and I was sure Joe's attitude to the inmates was not helping. He was a Belfast prison governor and was used to treating the prisoners the 'Belfast way'.

For example, in the Maze the prisoners tended to wear shorts all the time, so that was how they were dressed when they presented themselves for governor's requests. In Belfast that was never allowed, so if a PIRA prisoner in the Maze on that first day asked to see the governor, Joe would not see him unless he had trousers on.

The governor asked me to go to the H Block for which Joe was responsible to try to move the whole process forward—he didn't want the staff still working at midnight. I spoke to Joe and introduced myself, as I had never met him formally before.

'Hi, Joe,' I said, 'I'm Billy McKee. I saw you in Belfast the day of the wreck-up but never got a chance to speak to you. The boss has asked me to come over and see if there's anything that I can do to help.'

It was about six o'clock by this time and I was tired. That last two days had been so busy I honestly hoped Joe would say he was fine and sure as I was clearly knackered I should just head on. He was aware that I had spent the previous days sorting out the loyalists. Joe looked at his watch. 'That's great, Billy, I have an appointment I need to get to.' He then turned on his heel and walked out of the H Block. I was stunned and just stood there and watched him go. I called the governor and told him that Joe was gone. Fat lot of good that was. 'Good! That will give you a chance to get the PIRA sorted. You did a good job yesterday,' came the reply.

I reported to the loyalist remand block the following day and by close of play had the UVF and the UDA separated.

Then the claims started. One of the former administration grades came to the H Block in an effort to resolve the problems caused by items that were allegedly missing. It was during one of these interviews that I overheard the comment from a prisoner to him: 'Fuck away off, you're not in Belfast any more, this is the Maze. Just get this fucking sorted for me!' This was to set the tone for the relationship between ex-Belfast staff and their former prisoners for the foreseeable future.

For some reason the remands never settled the way the sentenced paramilitary inmates did at the Maze. I believe that was more because of their prison status than anything else. A remand prisoner, regardless of his crime, has far more variables in his life than a sentenced inmate does. A sentenced prisoner knows he is convicted; knows the length of his sentence; whether his appeal has been successful or not; and in most cases whether his partner is going to stand by him and support him through his sentence by sending him parcels and clothes and coming to visit him. A remand only knows that he is remanded on a charge. He doesn't know, for example, whether the police will get sufficient evidence to bring him to court. Might he get bail? If he gets sentenced how long will he serve? Will he appeal? If so will his appeal be successful? Will his girlfriend/wife/partner support him and wait for him? These were the variables that made the remand prisoners feel unsettled.

I stayed on at HMP Maze for three weeks until the dust had settled and the new regime for the remands was up and running. The OCS had made themselves known to me and, as was the way of the Maze, it was the OCS we talked to if we had a prisoner-related problem. Everyone— staff and prisoners alike—felt it was just like a big prisoner of war camp.

I reported back to Belfast Prison on Monday morning and felt relieved. I realised then that I needed a break from working with the paramilitaries. It was starting to wear me down. Every time I left I thought, 'well, that's my turn over', but a nagging doubt always remained.

I was introduced to what remained of the management team at HMP Belfast at the governor's meeting on Monday. Several had already left, posted to HMP Maze, and the gaps in the structure now had to be filled.

My desk was in an office at the top of the spiral staircase that I shared with the other wing governors. I was to be responsible for C Wing, a three-landing wing that housed ODCS—'ordinary decent criminals'.

That first day Barry Lorimer, a long-serving governor five, had taken me with him to deal with the governor requests, fifty in all, in C Wing. Barry was a kind-hearted individual but gave the distinct impression that morning that he was trying to impress me by demonstrating that he was in charge and that the prisoners knew it. His style was not my style. But so as not to appear ungrateful for his 'guidance' I just bit my tongue, knowing that I would be on my own within a few days. The second day with Barry was worse, as a consequence of the offhand way he had dealt with the requests the previous day. Not only had he the requests for the current day to deal with, he also had the spillover from those of the inmates' requests from the previous day that he had failed to deal with in an appropriate manner. There were seventy-two requests that morning.

I had a quiet word with Gary Hall, the governor three, and mentioned that I felt capable of dealing with c Wing myself from now on. Gary raised his eyebrows and asked who I was currently shadowing in c Wing. I explained that Barry was showing me the ropes. His eyebrows rose again for a second time that morning. Now, although Gary was renowned for his dicky bows and red braces, he also had a sarcastic wit and I am sure behind his smile there were words forming to suit this particular occasion. However, he resisted. 'I will speak to the No 1.' That was that.

I took charge of c Wing the following morning. The first thing that struck me about c Wing was how dirty it was. There were orderlies employed to clean it but in my opinion they were not doing a satisfactory job. Of course I didn't want to jump in blowing trumpets and beating drums. I knew very few of the staff or management grades and anyway that type of reaction would have been foreign to my style of management.

I started slowly. First I made a reasonable show of cleaning my own wing-based office with the help of one of the wing orderlies. Obviously people trying to be friendly with the new wing governor would pass comments, and I would draw them into conversation, highlighting the fact that I preferred working in a clean environment. That was my approach: lead by example. Don't ask someone to do what you would not be prepared to do yourself.

The orderly who was helping me became my conduit for letting his fellow orderlies know the standards that I expected. I can't, however, claim a great success. It was just barely enough to satisfy me. There were restrictions caused by the fact that Belfast was an old Victorian prison, far from the shiny new H Block that I had left behind at Maze. The additional problem was, of course, the remand prisoners. They couldn't be forced to work so they were on the wings more than the sentenced prisoners on D Wing and as a result of this it was a Forth Bridge scenario: as soon as the orderlies had finished cleaning, the state of the wing was such that they needed to start cleaning it all over again.

I had started to believe that being in charge of a wing of ODCs was a gift compared to dealing with the paramilitary prisoners. I was soon to learn that each type of prisoner brings different problems. For example, the suicide rate among paramilitary prisoners is virtually nil, mainly because they are a cohesive group and each member feels they have the support of an extended family all around them in the wing. Not so, however, with ODCs. ODC remands can arrive in the prison knowing no one, and at risk of being bullied, on top of all the other worries that I have already highlighted. These prisoners, some of whom have low self-esteem and minimal coping strategies, can find it extremely difficult to deal with prison life. There are too many inmates for the staff to give each the attention they need. In order to compensate for this, staff try to identify the vulnerable ones and raise a form (an IRM21) to raise their concerns so that everyone who needs to know is fully aware of the inmates who are regarded as at risk.

Unfortunately, this did not stop me losing two prisoners to suicide during my first two weeks as the governor in charge of C Wing. We lost one young man at the beginning of the week and the other followed five days later. The first was not expected. Some prisoners are good at hiding their fears and if we miss them at that stage the second stage is harder to detect.

The second stage is when the prisoner has made a conscience decision to commit suicide. When he arrives at the decision, the sense of relief he experiences is often such that being in prison with all its associated problems no longer matters because he now has an exit strategy to escape them all. He becomes detached, no longer worries about his problems because he knows they will soon be over, and he may even demonstrate a contentment that can be interpreted by staff as having accepted and adjusted to prison life. Next thing we know he is dead.

The other real concern is 'copycatting'. Sometimes when a prisoner commits suicide you will hear comments in the wing where he died such as: 'That's his worries over'; 'At least he is happy now'; 'He will fear no one now.' All it takes on occasions like this is for a vulnerable prisoner struggling to cope to pick up on one or more of these comments. He can then convince himself that this is his 'way out' as well and next thing you know you have lost another prisoner.

I was annoyed about the first suicide, but was helped to come to terms with it when my staff convinced me that there were no visible signs. This was not so with the second.

I would like to think that the more capable members of staff are aware of the consequences of 'copycatting' and therefore would be extra vigilant following a suicide in the prison. Imagine the dismay I felt when I checked through the wing file of the second prisoner. There, in large letters, just inside the front leaf of the file, were the words that could have saved him. 'MUST NOT BE SINGLE CELLED.' Someone knew he was at risk but the clear warning in his file was missed: the prisoner had been moved from the cell he was sharing with another prisoner to a cell on his own. He was now 'single celled'.

The experts tell us that when a prisoner decides to commit suicide the intended action moves from 'if' to 'when', meaning that once he reaches the point of no return the individual will wait until the opportunity is available, then he's gone. Thinking back to my father's saying, 'Good care cuts the head of bad luck', I wondered if we had taken 'good care'. If we had read the prisoner's file would we at least on this occasion have averted a suicide? Probably.

There have been occasions when a prisoner has confided in their cellmate that they intend to commit suicide and the cellmate has respected his decision and sat quietly, not raising the alarm until his fellow prisoner was dead.

Needless to say, I did not miss any staff in the debrief that followed the two suicides. I set in place a new rule that any doubled-up prisoner being moved to single-cell occupancy had to have the move approved by me first. The staff were left in no doubt of my feelings on the suicides, and something must have got through: I went through the remaining years as a governor five without losing another prisoner to suicide.

My stay in c Wing was short-lived and as soon as the extensive damage to a Wing had been repaired the governor told me to make the necessary arrangements to relocate the c Wing prisoners.

While the paramilitary prisoners were secured at HMP Belfast the ODCs were just small fish in a big pond, but once the paramilitaries had been transferred to the Maze the little fish tried to become big fish. One particular remand prisoner, 'Berto', was a particular handful, always involved in fights and generally making a nuisance of himself. I often felt that part of Berto's problems and that of other likeminded individuals was boredom, and their troublemaking was partly caused by simply having too much time on their hands.

The refurbished A Wing was getting new furniture, and equipping out the three landings was a labour-intensive job. Remand prisoners cannot be forced to work so we had to rely almost on 'good will' to finish the wing off so that the decant from C Wing could proceed.

Berto was a body builder and was incredibly strong. I was a great believer in utilising the resources available whenever possible, and I believed Berto was one of these resources. Berto ran up and down the stairs carrying wardrobe after wardrobe, bed after bed and never complained once. Banter, yes; but complaints, no. Obviously he was doing the work all on his own but I would estimate that he equalled the workload of at least four other inmates in his overall output in preparing A Wing for the transfer.

Our paths were to cross later, and that next meeting resulted in a photograph of Berto and myself appearing on his mother's mantelpiece somewhere on the Falls Road in West Belfast. There are not too many prison governors who could claim that privilege, but then again not many would want it. Berto had been successful in some gym-related test and I had been asked to present him with his certificate of accomplishment. A photograph was produced to commemorate the presentation.

The move to A Wing went well and it gave staff and prisoners a psychological lift: the wing had been refurbished, repainted, supplied with new furniture; and of course the actual move broke the monotony of remand prisoner life.

But another problem soon became apparent. A clique of prisoners had formed in the wing: nationalist prisoners who were all remanded on allegations involving the illegal drug trade in Northern Ireland. At that time there were a few female prison officers among the A Wing staff. One of these officers was an extremely attractive young woman who became the subject of abuse from this particular group of inmates. They accused the officer of spying on them when they were naked in the showers and made other derogatory remarks when she passed by, such as 'What's that pissy smell?' and other similar comments. The officer was obviously greatly distressed but did not want them to win. I was keeping the situation under observation and was prepared to remove the officer from the wing if necessary. However, the problem was taken out of my hands and resolved within a few days.

An ODC with loyalist connections was chatting to me one morning and mentioned that he felt the 'druggies' had dropped to a new level with regard to the way they were treating the 'wee girl'. I started to say that I could not discuss this or any other prison matter with him or any other prisoner, when he interrupted me, saying, 'I could sort them out for you, Governor, if you wanted.' I was shocked by what he was saying and in an effort to dissuade him from any such action replied that I could not sanction or support any such action. He smiled, winked and sauntered off down the wing towards the dining room.

The first of the offenders he met went down at the first blow. Teeth, blood and tears was what I was greeted with as I ran to the scene. The prisoner who had offered his help was still moving. I still don't understand why the officer opened the grille to allow him into the dining room, though I have my own private thoughts on the matter. Two further assaults were perpetrated in the dining room. Two more prisoners hit the floor. More blood—a lot more. By the time of the last assault the alarm had sounded and staff were responding, rushing to the area of the incident. Why did it take until the third assault before staff hit the alarm?

I walked on down the wing, heading towards the dining room. Halfway there I met the big prisoner who had carried out the three assaults. He greeted me with a smile and a wink. The staff escorting him stopped while I spoke to him. 'I know why you did that. I told you that I could neither support nor condone an attack by one prisoner on another, or in this case an attack on three others. You will most likely have been seen by both cameras and witnesses, which draws me to the conclusion that you will probably be found guilty at adjudication and suffer a loss of remission as a result.'

He was still smiling. 'Look, Governor, those bastards got what they deserved and anyway once sentenced I will be going to Maze and whatever I lose at adjudication I will get it back there, so no problem.'

I just shook my head as the staff escorted him to the cell block to await his adjudication. But he was right. When he went to the Maze he would apply for and get his lost remission reinstated. That was what happened in the Maze.

The three assaulted prisoners got the message. The other prisoners decided their behaviour was unacceptable and dealt with the matter themselves. Needless to say, the abuse of the female officer stopped, but it was too late for the service to save her career. She subsequently left the service and joined the RUC. The Prison Service's loss was definitely the RUC's gain.

A few weeks later a new prisoner arrived in the wing, awaiting trial for alleged drug charges. I knew from the initial wing interview that he spelled trouble. His whole attitude told me that being in prison was just an inconvenience for him, just a break between jobs, and nobody would be telling him anything. The other prisoners seemed to hold this inmate in awe. Another bad sign. The temperature in the wing changed almost overnight. Staff reported that more and more prisoners were asking to be locked up in their cells and were not taking advantage of either their association or exercise periods. It was all down to one man, the latest addition to A Wing. He was cute, always using his henchmen to carry out his dirty deeds.

My chance, however, arrived sooner than I thought. One morning, while doing my rounds of the landings, I walked down the left-hand side of the second landing, known as the 'twos'. The problematic inmate was on the other side of the landing. He was full of himself.

'This is my landing,' he shouted over at me. 'The prisoners do what I say.'

I thought, Keep talking, you clown!

He behaved as if he were one of the Kray twins. But he had said enough.

'Take him off my wing,' I shouted to the staff.

Before he could move, control and restraint arm locks were applied and he was dragged off the wing, screaming obscenity after obscenity, all directed at me. The final outcome of the matter was that the prisoner was charged, adjudicated on, found guilty and placed on Prison Rule 32 for the remainder of his remand time. The Board of Visitors, who are really the overseers of the prison, had little difficulty in signing the Rule 32 order. Their discreet conversations with other prisoners in A Wing had supported my allegation of the problems the offending prisoner was causing on the wing.

Rule 32 meant that he was on twenty-three-hour lockup, allowed out for one hour's exercise per day. He was isolated from all other inmates. This lasted for approximately ten months. A Wing returned to normal.

Such was his hatred for me that almost three years later, when he bumped into one of the A Wing officers at the local shopping centre, his first words to the officer were, 'Where is that bastard McKee working now?' This was something that went with the territory but it was nothing compared to the threats that would be directed at me in the years to come.

Another problem followed, a problem that threatened the health and safety of staff and prisoners alike on the wing.

Fires were continually being lit on the wing. These were the responsibility of one young prisoner who had made his way through Borstal and the Young Offenders Centre and had ended up in A Wing. No doubt a career criminal in the making.

In an effort to eliminate the threat I took the decision to remove all lighter fuel from the wing. The fires stopped, but the tension in the wing was a little higher than normal. The No 1 governor sent for me.

'Good morning, William,' he began. 'What's this I hear, that you have taken a decision to remove all the lighter fuel from A Wing?'

'Yes sir, that would be correct,' I replied.

'Did you not think to run your thoughts past me before you took your decision? After all, I am the governor of the prison.' Oops! Judging by his tone, he wasn't pleased with me.

'So how do the prisoners get a light for their roll-ups?' he went on.

I composed myself. This was the first argument I had got into with this No 1.

'Staff on the wings give them a light, Governor,' I replied, in a tone that had a hint of aggression or perhaps assertiveness about it.

'And if staff don't smoke, what then?' the No 1 asked.

'Then they do without, Governor!'

I had overdone the tone and the expression. The governor exploded.

'You will get the bloody wing wrecked!' he shouted.

The telephone rang and broke the hostile atmosphere. It was obviously something more important than A Wing getting burned down, as he waved me out of his office.

I returned to the wing feeling annoyed. I knew that I had made the right decision in removing the lighter fuel—the fires had stopped. I was also annoyed by the aggression I had allowed to creep into my conversation with the governor.

Just before lunch a knock on my office door was followed by the No 1's head appearing round it. 'Let's walk,' he said. I came around my desk and joined the Governor to walk down the wing. He lit his pipe before he spoke. 'You okay?'

I looked at him. 'I am, Sir, are you okay?' I asked.

'I am okay too,' he replied.

The matter was forgotten. He never mentioned it again and neither did I. He had made a point and I had made a point.

The prisoners who were frustrated at having to wait for a light for their cigarettes sorted the problem for us. They 'spoke' to the inmate who had been starting the fires and advised him of the frustrations that the other prisoners were enduring because of his nonsense, his life-threatening nonsense. They then approached me and asked whether, if they guaranteed me that there would be no more fires, I would consider returning the privilege of the lighter fuel and lighters.

I asked them to let me consider their request and had a word with the man who not only turned out to be one of the best principal officers I ever worked with, but also made the jump to the governor grade and went on to be one of the most effective managers in the service. He agreed that the time was right to return the lighter privilege, but I did so only after consulting the No 1 about my intentions. Lesson learned there!

David was my third principal officer since I had arrived in Belfast. The first was an ex-Maze man who, despite being told the direction I wanted to take the wing, tended to want to do things his way. The third time this happened I went to see Pat Maguire, my former tutor from the Prison Service governor training, who had recently been posted to work in Belfast, and told him I wanted the principal officer replaced.

Pat responded to my request and I was given a different principal officer from the following Monday morning. The new man was also the local chairman of the POA (Prison Officers' Association) and was not always present in the wing. To make matters worse, one of my new senior officers was also the POA secretary, which meant that at times I had to operate with two managers down.

I was extremely fortunate with the quality of my managers in A Wing: four of them went on to governor grade and a couple of the senior officers moved up to principal officer rank. Looking back to my early days in the service, back in 1977, when I had noticed that there appeared to be two managers in charge of the wing; now I understood how that situation worked. The principal officer was really responsible for the discipline of his staff managing the prisoners. The wing governor's role was to ensure that the policies of the governor were being implemented on the wing and that the prisoners were being dealt with accordingly. Of course there was some overlap between the two roles, and a good working relationship between the two managers was essential to promote the smooth running of the wing. That was not the case with this particular principal officer and me. Now, I liked the guy. He had a tremendous sense of humour and was a good manager of his staff. He did a great impression of Reg Holdsworth from *Coronation Street*. I tried to talk to him to explain that we needed to pull together, and although he always agreed I always left the meeting feeling that we were no further on.

A Wing, like most of the prison, was always short of staff. This affected the smooth running of the wing as I was unable to deliver all that I wanted to in respect of the regime—I simply didn't have the manpower to resource it. I had started to look at all the posts in the wing to assess which, if any, I could do without entirely, or how I could reduce the number of officer hours worked on the wing. I started with the posts that required the most cover and hadn't got far when I discovered that the parcels officer post was seven days a week, twelve hours a day. A total of eighty-four hours a week, equating to two officers' full weekly hours. That was unbelievable. The more I considered those figures the more convinced I became that if I could eradicate this post, or deliver the same service in a different but equally efficient way, I could gain the equivalent of two additional staff per week.

I was excited. I spoke to my staff and managers to ascertain their thoughts but received no encouragement. They couldn't see the wood for the trees: they were looking at the problem from the wrong perspective. They all kept saying the same thing: 'But you need the post manned seven days a week and twelve hours a day.' I wasn't even sure whether we did need the post manned twelve hours a day, seven days a week, but whatever hours were required, did it need to be manned by the equivalent of two expensive prison officer grades? Of course it didn't.

The parcels office was located in a converted cell on the left side of the wing, sandwiched between the principal officer's office and that of the governor. On the right side of the wing another cell was converted into an office where the member of staff kept a check on the wing's prisoner numbers and as prisoners left and returned to the wing he would adjust the numbers accordingly. This was one of the most important functions on the wing—it was imperative that the numbers were one hundred per cent correct at all times. It was particularly important that prisoners' destinations were recorded whenever they left the wing.

Another important function of this office was censoring letters. All letters entering and leaving the prison were checked in case they contained illegal items and the letters were read to ensure there wasn't anything controversial in written form either leaving or entering the prison.

My solution to our 'parcels' problem was fairly straightforward; but two things had to be agreed upon first.

First, I had to convince the union that my solution was not going to reduce the staffing level on the wing, but I did not have the authority to give an assurance on that. I briefed the No 1 and left him to come up with a form of words that would satisfy the POA.

The second issue required the active participation of the Works department. It was my intention to relocate the parcels office next door to the censor's office. I then wanted the tradesmen from the Works department to knock a door through the wall to connect the two offices. The shelving from the previous parcels office also had to be dismantled and rebuilt in the new one.

When the physical alterations had been finalised, all that remained was to staff the office or in fact to 'prisoner' the office, because that is exactly what I did. I appointed a prisoner to the post with a deputy, also a prisoner, so that when the original inmate was on a visit he had a trained substitute to step right in.

The purpose of having the door between the parcels office and the censor's office was to enable supervision of the prisoner.

'I love it when a plan comes together,' to quote an old television star from the era of my childhood.

Of course there were detractors who refused to accept the workability of the plan and continually tried to undermine the new arrangements and detect flaws in the system. There were no flaws and, in addition, under the new system there were fewer claims about missing parcel items than there had been under the previous system.

I also submitted a claim under the Civil Service financial savings scheme for the percentage of the staff savings that my new scheme had achieved. Because of the colossal amount of annual savings I qualified for the maximum payment of £15,000. In order to substantiate my claim the adjudicators of the scheme wrote to the No 1 governor asking him for verification.

I never received the payment. The governor confirmed that the savings had been achieved, but added the killer line that he would expect his wing governor to identify and implement savings in the course of fulfilling his designated role.

I was disappointed. Not just because it felt like I had the £15,000 snatched from my open hand but more because I felt I deserved it. I knew that the entrepreneurial approach I had used to solve the problem was not common in the modern-day Prison Service and believed that by not awarding me the payment the service in effect dampened others' enthusiasm and discouraged them from trying to make savings too. Imagine the motivation that could have been gained by recognising my achievement, publicising it and using it as a tool to inspire other managers to look really hard at their own area of responsibility with a view to matching my success and collecting their financial reward. The Prison Service was renowned for its short-sightedness and the handling of this particular issue just confirmed that thinking.

My only consolation was that my new arrangements were a success. Imagine, then, how I felt when I reported to the wing on Monday morning only to find the new parcels office closed and the previous office resurrected with a prison officer back behind the hatch. I entered the principal officer's office. Luckily the door was open: if it hadn't been I probably would have kicked it in. I exploded.

'What the hell is going on? Why and on whose authority has the parcels office been relocated to the previous location?'

The principal officer's face was white. He had just seen a side of me that he did not know existed. Even *I* had just seen a side of me that I didn't know existed!

'I decided to move it because . . .'

I don't care what you thought,' I interrupted him. 'I would have preferred that we ran this wing together but it would appear that is no longer possible. Get the parcels office back to its new location now, get the officer redeployed to more essential duties and bring the nominated prisoner back to the parcels duties.'

I was shaking with rage and was just managing to bring it back under control as I turned to leave the office. 'And don't ever change anything in this wing again without consulting with me first. Is that clear?' I never even waited for his reply. I just had to get out of the wing.

By lunchtime that day the parcels office was back to the area I had designated but the damage to the relationship between me and the principal officer was beyond repair. Over the next few weeks we just kept out of each other's way, but there was a definite change in the atmosphere in the wing. It took me a while to ascertain what the problem was, and a couple of times I caught staff whispering in one of their offices with the door closed. Whenever I entered the office the conversation would stop abruptly and although I didn't really believe that the conversations were about me they were definitely something to do with the way the atmosphere had changed.

I decided to call a meeting of all the wing staff who were on duty in an effort to clear the air and resolve, or at least attempt to resolve, whatever the difficulties were.

I had assumed that the regime in the wing was the same on all three landings. It wasn't. It turned out that the bottom landing was running a tighter regime than the other two landings and this was causing friction between staff and prisoners on all the landings. The staff had thought that I was responsible for the change.

I addressed all the staff, explaining that the regime on the wing was to be the same on all three landings and that I as a 'servant' of the governor had the responsibility to ensure that his wishes with regard to the regime were implemented in their entirety. I then pointed out to the staff that we had discovered that 'happiness is not door-shaped' (an old prison slang meaning that if the prisoners are locked in they can cause no problems). I believed that spending less time (within reason) behind the door actually had a positive effect on prisoners' behaviour. I explained to the staff that if they were honest with me and themselves they would have to accept that the way I was managing the regime was making their jobs easier.

Finally, I asked if there were any staff currently employed in A Wing who didn't agree with the way I ran the wing and felt that they didn't want to be part of it. I suggested that they let me know and I would arrange for them to be moved to another group first thing the following morning.

One officer stepped forward. He was the No 1 officer employed on the bottom landing, the one that was out of sync with the other landings. As he stepped forward he looked directly at the principal officer, who turned away and folded his arms. That sent a clear message to me about who was really behind the change in atmosphere in the wing.

I had nothing but admiration for the officer who stepped forward.

'Look, Governor, I'm just an old long-in-the-tooth warder and can't change and don't want to change. I'm not into this modern thinking and I would prefer if you would get me a transfer.'

Now was a dangerous moment. Would the floodgates open? Would more staff step forward to ask for a transfer?

Thankfully, not one other officer moved. I took that as a vote of confidence in my management style and closed the meeting, thanking the staff for staying behind to help sort the problem. I also reminded them that hiding in office corners whispering was not the best way to let me know what was wrong in the wing and took the opportunity to tell them that in future the prisoners would be locked half an hour early once a fortnight and we would have a meeting to discuss any problems and observations in an attempt to nip concerns in the bud.

Now the time had arrived for me to deal with the remaining source of conflict on A Wing. The relationship between me and my principal officer was at an all-time low and this in itself was placing a strain on the other managers in the wing. I had to tread carefully because the senior officers and other principal officers in the A Wing group, since they were all members of the discipline uniform grade, might easily fall in behind my opponent, which could lead to my position as the governor in charge of A Wing becoming untenable. As it happened, circumstances were to present themselves during the next few weeks that allowed me to solve the problem.

One morning I entered the wing to deal with that day's requests and stumbled on a meeting taking place behind the closed door of the principal officer's office. I don't know why, but I knocked on the door and walked in. It was obvious that I was the subject of discussion as the conversation died mid-sentence when I entered the room.

The principal officer liked to play to the crowd and perhaps over-estimated the support that he believed he could solicit from his colleagues. After some small talk he took his opportunity. He thumped the Prison Standing Orders on the desk and almost shouted, 'From now on, Governor, I will be running this wing my way and if you don't like it you can remove me from the wing!'

I smiled inwardly. 'Your request to be removed from the wing is granted as of now. I will speak to my line manager this morning and arrange for a replacement to fill your now vacant post.'

The office went deadly quiet. You could have heard a hair drop, never mind the proverbial pin.

First to react was the senior officer who was also the secretary of the local POA committee. He jumped to his feet and with voice raised offered his opinion. 'If the principal is leaving the wing then I am as well!'

'No, John,' I began. 'Sit down. You are too angry to discuss this issue today. I will talk to you in my office first thing tomorrow morning and if you still feel the same then that will not be a problem either.'

I turned on my heel and left the office and the wing. I had nothing more to say. The principal had said it all for me.

I walked through the circle and climbed the spiral staircase that took me to the wing governors' other office. The other wing governors had already left to deal with the prisoners' requests in their own wings, which left my line manager David Morrison.

David was a strange kettle of fish. Both his appearance and accent might have led you to believe he was an army officer. He had spent a period in the UDR as an officer and whether this had any influence on his persona I don't know. But I liked him because he let me do my job and respected my decisions: well, he had done so up to now. I wondered how my latest decision would go down. I think David's time in the officer rank of the UDR had made him aware of the importance of rank and the absolute importance of staff having respect for their superior.

I related not just the events that had taken place in the principal's office that morning but also the brief history of our deteriorating relationship and finished by saying that I now required a new principal officer for A Wing. I took a breath and waited. David, who was obviously taking in and dissecting what I had said, paused before replying.

'The remaining senior and principal officers in the group, how do you believe they will react?' (A reasonable question to ask.) 'Might your problems be exacerbated if they decide to lend their support to the principal?'

'That will not happen,' I said.

'Okay. Well done. Well handled. I'll let the No 1 know and we'll get you a replacement sorted.' With that he left the office.

The call from the No 1 came just after lunch. Before it came, David Morrison, the principal officer who was leaving A Wing and myself had a meeting in which the principal officer, to give him his due, substantiated the events that had occurred earlier that morning. There was something false about it all, though. The principal was too amenable to everything. He was also a sharp individual. Who had really won today? Him or me?

I had the feeling that he might have played me, that he had his eye on some other post, and my moving him from the wing had somehow played into his hands.

Sometimes in the Prison Service two equally good managers can come together only to discover that their two distinct management styles conflict and as a result a parting of the ways has to come sooner or later. I was sure that this was what had happened here. Personally I had no problem with the individual and have to admit that on an informal basis I enjoyed his company, but our professional relationship was quite another matter.

'What are you trying to do to me?' were the first words to hit me as I entered the No 1's office. He was at his desk with his head in his hands as if emphasising the seriousness of the latest predicament that the governor of A Wing was bringing to his door.

'Your principal that you have removed from A Wing is the chairman of the local bloody POA—what were you thinking? And can I remind you that the decision you made this morning was not your decision to make. You are not the governor of this prison yet and until that time will you please leave No 1 governor decisions to the No 1!'

A small smile appeared on his face. (A little sooner would have been appreciated!)

'I am going to give you a new principal officer. He is now your third in your time working in Belfast, so try to hold on to him for at least a year,' he said sarcastically.

With David, the new principal officer, joining our ranks in A Wing we went from strength to strength in every respect.

The following morning I reported to A Wing and met with John, the senior officer who had asked to leave the wing the previous day. John was an outstanding senior officer and I didn't want to lose him. I told him as much and asked him to give it one month under the new principal officer's stewardship; if he still wanted a move at the end of the month I assured him that I would support his request. I was not then aware of the existing friendship between David and John—they had worked together in the immediate reaction force in the prison.

A few weeks later another character was remanded to A Wing— Frankie 'Boogaloo' Mulholland. Frankie was sometimes described as a Catholic drug dealer and sometimes as a body-building drug pusher. He was about six foot six inches tall but never caused me a single problem the whole time he was in A Wing. Unlike the alleged drug dealer we met earlier in the chapter, by whom the majority of prisoners were clearly intimidated, 'Boogaloo' was quite different. The inmates showed him respect and staff regarded him as a 'gentle giant'. I believe Frankie quickly understood the way A Wing worked and accepted that playing ball with the staff and conforming to the rules made it easier to put in your time on the wing. He may well have shared his thinking with the other prisoners, because while he was on A Wing there were seldom any serious disturbances.

Although Frankie was a Catholic he had no problem crossing the sectarian divide if it meant he could do business with the 'other side', and he allegedly traded with both republican and loyalist paramilitaries. He felt he was untouchable. Perhaps because he was supplying both sides he believed that gave him the security necessary to take risks and at times pull a fast one on the people he was dealing with. He told me that on one occasion he had, for a considerable amount of money, sold Johnny Adair a bale of peat briquettes that Johnny had believed to be a bale of cannabis. This was a classic example of Frankie's sense of invulnerability.

After Frankie had been discharged from the prison he slipped from my mind until one day I heard his name on the news. Frankie had allegedly been involved in setting up a drug deal with a gang of Protestant paramilitaries when he was shot dead at close range as he sat in the driver's seat of his four-by-four. The murder was claimed by the Red Hand Defenders, a cover name used by both the LVF and UFF. Frankie had also been on a hit list of Direct Action Against Drugs, a name used by the IRA in their attempts to clamp down on drug dealers. I think it had become a matter not so much of whether but when he would be killed. I could and would never condone the supply of drugs to anyone—I know only too well the misery that they bring. However, like a lot of prisoners I have encountered over the years, it was hard not to like Frankie.

Christmas went well and as usual I was at home on Christmas morning where the usual McKee ritual was followed and enjoyed by all. I didn't know then that these moments of happiness were to be all too brief.

Just after Christmas there was a lot of speculation that HMP Belfast was to close and the reaction of the staff reminded me of my time in

Harland & Wolff. 'The Crum will never close'; 'They couldn't afford to close the Crum.' That last statement was the opposite of the truth. 'They', the Prison Service, couldn't afford *not* to close the 'Crum', and to demonstrate how serious they were, when the decision was finally taken 'they' had not asked for a budget for the following financial year, so it had to close.

Chapter 9
The Willing Horse and Another Hard Road

Pat Maguire, a governor three by this stage, was asked by Headquarters to make the necessary arrangements to ensure that Belfast Prison was closed by the end of March. It was then 9 February. Pat, whether it was confidence in me or if he was just passing on a problem that he didn't want to deal with, recommended me to Headquarters as the man to carry out the task. I was getting thoroughly annoyed at this stage by the Prison Service's attitude of 'just make it happen'.

Certainly there were occasions, many occasions, when staff would give a manager a dozen reasons why a particular piece of work couldn't be done. Usually that came down to resistance to change. No one wanted it, no one liked it—I knew, because I felt the same. Resistance to change is a natural human trait. We all have our comfort zones and pushing the boundaries can create all sorts of concerns and worries. However, if change is carried out in a measured, controlled way, with a sensible approach and realistic expectations, a degree of success can be expected.

Closing Belfast Prison in the space of a few weeks was not realistic, it was bloody mad! I told Pat as much and he admitted that it was a 'big ask', but as there was no budget to run the prison for the next financial year it had to close, end of story.

I arranged a meeting with the then governor No 1 of Maghaberry Prison, Barry Wallace. Of all the No 1 governors I had worked for, Barry was the only one with whom I had never enjoyed a warm relationship. He had been my No 1 governor in Magilligan and the fact that an oversight of mine had resulted in the number one account in the prison going £130,000 into the red for a week did absolutely nothing to help the relationship. At that time the temperature of our relationship went from lukewarm to extremely cold.

So here we were again: Barry on the other side of the desk facing a governor who had let him down in the past, a governor who was here to organise and set in place procedures that within the next seven weeks would almost double the population of his prison, change the way he managed some of his prisoners and generally turn the jail on its head. If I was in his position I wouldn't have been happy either.

If nothing else, Barry was one of the coolest-thinking individuals I had ever worked with. That was clearly evident that morning as we spoke and I saw him grasp the enormity of the task that I was facing in getting Maghaberry just to the preparation stage for handling the decant of the majority of prisoners from Belfast Prison to Maghaberry. His thoughts seemed to be a few steps ahead of mine, focusing particularly on the days following the arrival of a type of prisoner that Maghaberry's facilities were neither physically nor organisationally ready for.

He asked me to prepare a list of objectives that had to be achieved regarding accommodation and regime to enable the transfer to be completed within the designated timeframe.

He added that I should talk to Jimmy Kidd, a senior civil servant in the prison, to ascertain where he was in relation to the ordering and supply of the necessary cell furniture, etc. I agreed to deliver a list within a couple of days. That in itself was quite a challenge. Where would I start?

I was pleased that there had at least been some forethought regarding the move and welcomed the fact that the cell furniture and suchlike was at least a starting point. Yet another incorrect assumption. I met with Jimmy and after the formalities were dealt with I asked for an update on delivery dates for the prisoners' cell items.

'What cell items?' was Jimmy's response. I explained that Barry had mentioned that he was handling that part of the operation and I just wanted to confirm, first, that there were enough cells to house the prisoners; and second, that the cells were or would be equipped to the necessary standard by the end of March.

'Nobody tells me anything. There is nothing ordered and nothing will be ordered until I have an understanding of what is happening, the proposed date that it is happening and the number of bodies involved.'

I had just received the first item for my list.

I quickly brought Jimmy up to speed with all the information that he required and stressed the absolute necessity that the transfer happened on 31 March.

Jimmy, being Jimmy, gave me all the reasons why the task he had just been set was totally impossible and why the time constraints were completely unrealistic. I explained that I was meeting with Barry in two days' time and if he could not deliver I needed to know before that meeting. That final comment to Jimmy was probably all the motivation he needed to meet my requirements.

I set up a meeting with the local POA to attempt to bring them on board in the hope that they would support the move and not place obstacles in my way. Second item for my list.

The POA were not remotely interested in putting their considerable clout behind the closure of HMP Belfast and assured me that Belfast Prison would still be up and running come this time next year.

Thankfully the 'experts' from the reception area and general office in Belfast Prison were quickly able to identify the necessary structural changes that were necessary to facilitate the dozens of additional daily movements of inmates to and from court. This part of the transfer was outside my remit and therefore did not need to be added to my list.

By the time Barry and I met again my list had grown to thirty-one items. The list had made its way to Prison Service Headquarters and that brought home to them the full scale of the unrealistic task that they had set. Now I had another meeting to attend each week because they also wanted a continuous update. I could have done without this additional meeting in my diary.

I worked literally day and night for the following seven weeks. David, my principal officer, and one of my senior officers from A Wing proved invaluable to me in providing expert input to the new regime that I was planning for the remands. We worked efficiently and over the following weeks things came together at an unbelievable speed.

Jimmy had managed to secure the cell furniture and after the 'house' to which the prisoners were to be transferred was thoroughly cleaned, he set about getting it kitted out.

I had worked hard to establish a strong working relationship with the POA, using the phrase 'them and us' to give the impression that we were on the same side, both trying to ensure that our staff were not going to be done over by 'them'. I also told the POA that the move was going to happen, with or without their support, and that it was in their members' interests for the POA to be involved. First of all, they would be able to find out what the new arrangements were and what implications these had for the staff; and second, their presence at those meetings would ensure that the views of the staff and their representatives would also be heard.

The day of the move came and went. The only teething problem on the day was that the plugs on all the televisions had to be changed because they were not compatible with the sockets in the prisoners' cells. Yes, that's right: each prisoner had a television in their cell courtesy of the taxpayer.

The only sad event that disrupted the smooth running of the move was the death of a prisoner, who suffered a heart attack during the move. The medical staff fought long and hard to save the prisoner's life, and the sheer physical force used in their desperate attempts caused fractures to the prisoner's ribs and severe bruising to the his chest. Unfortunately the other prisoners did not accept this explanation for the injuries and were convinced that the prisoner's heart attack had been brought on by a serious beating by the Maghaberry search staff who were assisting with the move. This caused resentment towards the staff employed in the prison search team, a resentment that remains even today.

I put on my jacket at three o'clock that afternoon and headed for home immensely satisfied by the success of the 'impossible' move.

As the majority of the prisoners were 'my' remands from A Wing I fully expected to be taking responsibility for Foyle House, where they were now secured.

I did get a letter from Dick Mullan, one of the senior governors at Maghaberry, who wrote on behalf of Barry Wallace thanking me for my contribution to the success of the move. Even though it was only two lines long I still felt it was better than nothing.

Another disappointment came in the next few days. A formula was devised to determine where the surplus staff from HMP Belfast should go. Although I had left HMP Maze only eighteen months earlier, and had already served three tours of duty there, I was now, unbelievably, being sent back for my fourth. When the governor informed me I laughed—I honestly thought he was joking—but when he didn't crack a smile I realised it was true. And again, other governors who had never once served in the Maze were overlooked. Yet again it was a case of 'the willing horse for the hard road'. Well, this particular horse was getting tired of it!

I reported to the Maze the following Monday and, whether it was out of guilt or embarrassment, instead of returning to work in the H Blocks I was detailed to the role of governor five in Inmate Services.

Pat Maguire was also posted to the Maze, and I often wondered if that had that any bearing on the way the formula was used to post me back there as well.

Chapter 10
Streamlining Visits

So here I was again! How many more times? This 'same old same old' Maze bloody Prison was starting to annoy me. There had been other management changes and an English governor, Martin Mogg, had now been appointed the No 1 governor at HMP Maze Prison. Ken Crompton was the deputy governor and of course Pat Maguire was third in charge as governor three. My new boss in Inmate Services was a woman, Miss Orr, and the other governor five, who shared the responsibility of that department, was Joe Helm.

My actual responsibilities covered, among other things, two of the most contentious areas from an inmate's perspective: letters and visits. (I don't think *that* allocation of duties came about by chance!) Inmates Catering was Joe's responsibility, and that area also proved problematic.

These areas were contentious because if any of them were not functioning as the prisoners expected their dissatisfaction was very soon made known to management: and that annoyance would not be relayed by a politely written letter. Far from it.

The prisoners in the H Blocks had largely settled, with only the UDA/UVF mixed block a subject of annoyance for both governors and staff.

Visits was at that time easily the most difficult area to manage, and the managers employed in this area were by far the most stressed people in the entire prison.

I had only been back in the Maze a week when I was approached by two of the senior officers from Visits. These were two exceptional managers who were not content to accept the old Maze cliché, 'It's the Maze and you will never change it.'

It was so refreshing to hear their views as I, like them, would never accept that bad practice could not be made better.

They told me that they were disillusioned by their previous governors and had rarely seen them: the closest these governors got to

Visits, they said, was when they walked past on their way in and out of work each day. I would have been horrified if any of my staff had regarded me in this way.

But the senior officers were not there to complain about anyone, they were there to paint a picture of the difficulties they faced and the reasons for these problems.

I listened to the Visits managers for at least an hour, and that in itself seemed to be a positive start from both our perspectives. The longer the meeting went on the more enthused the senior officers became about trying to improve Visits by resolving their difficulties, and their enthusiasm was infectious.

It was impossible to take on board the sheer volume of the problems that the senior officers brought up at that meeting. It wasn't just in the Visits complex where the problems lay: other areas in the prison were making a significant contribution, including the H Blocks, the transport department and the visitors' car park.

Next stop Miss Orr, my line manager. She listened and was surprisingly sympathetic. (I don't know why I was surprised: I didn't really know her either personally or professionally. My opinion probably came from first impressions, which were perhaps incorrect.) I didn't really expect her to do anything but give me her approval to look into the senior officers' concerns. That *was* a problem.

Visits were so contentious that there was a genuine fear that interfering might exacerbate the problem. The paramilitaries had succeeded in conditioning sections of the management to such a degree that any ideas they might have had about trying to alter prisoners' perception of things was simply a non-starter. I believe this type of thinking had prevented the previous incumbent of my job even attempting to resolve the difficulties in Visits. This realisation, however, did nothing to dampen my growing enthusiasm for what I was starting to see as a 'project'.

Second stop Pat Maguire. Pat was probably the most forward-thinking governor I had ever worked with, and the more I got to know him, the more aware I became of his talents and personality. He gave his managers freedom to act on their own initiative, but he was always on hand to offer advice and constructive criticism. I laugh when I mention 'constructive criticism': he was particularly good at dispensing that when necessary. I both liked and admired Pat. Pat had been a direct entrant and eventually overtook the other governors he had trained with. I knew from those early days that a No 1 governor's office door someday in the near future would have Governor Maguire's name upon it.

Pat accepted that I had not come to give him solutions to the Visits problems, but rather to seek both his permission and support to research the problems and perhaps, just perhaps, find solutions that could make a difference. After our experiences together in the likes of A Wing in Belfast and the Belfast decant to Maghaberry we had a confidence and a trust in each other that, despite the difference in rank between us, allowed us great freedom of discussion.

'All I really need, Pat, is your permission to have a look at the Visits,' I explained. 'I'm happy to prepare a paper for you identifying the problems, and also to offer solutions. I can guarantee that any proposed changes would only be implemented with your or Martin's approval.'

Pat trusted me, so I imagine it was relatively easy for him to give me the answer I sought.

The lack of trust between staff and management, combined with the POA's understandable concerns, turned out to be the biggest obstacles, not the anger or the challenges that everyone told me I should expect from the prisoners. I couldn't understand that point of view anyway: why would the prisoners be interested in restricting or even preventing me implementing improvements in the conditions in Visits that would allow everyone to benefit?

There were ninety-four officers employed in the Visits group, six senior and two principal officers. That of course did not include the van drivers or the staff employed at the car park where the visitors entered the prison, which was also where the prisoners' parcels were delivered. This was a staff-intensive, expensive part of the service to run.

The staff soon got wind of my interest in Visits and my intention to introduce positive change. Staff believed management never or rarely did anything to improve their working conditions and that any change that ever occurred was to benefit prisoners. I was determined to change that perspective.

The rumour mill had gone into overdrive before I had even had a chance to discover what the problems were. I therefore decided to address the staff and put to bed all the nonsense and speculation. Because of the shift system it took two meetings to speak to the majority of the staff in the Visits. Addressing two fairly hostile groups, each of about fifty, was pretty intimidating.

I explained that Visits was regarded as currently the most contentious area in the prison and that it wasn't just prisoners who were affected by the system's failings. I went on to say that no decisions had yet been made, and that I could not think about solutions until I knew what the problems were. The staff, of course, didn't trust what I'd said, and when I had finished they started rattling off all the rumours they had heard.

I was fast losing control of the meeting and realised that I had to say or do something to bring it to order. The solution came to me in a flash. I raised both hands and slowly lowered them as if to speak and the staff gradually became quieter.

'I can see that a lot of you here today are very concerned about the changes that may or may not take place in Visits. I am also aware from some of your comments that you are currently not happy belonging to the Visits group and may therefore not be happy to buy into the necessary changes that may be required, so what I am prepared to do is to offer any officer who no longer wants to be part of the Visits group or to buy into the probable changes a move to another group as soon as possible.'

The room went totally quiet. I continued: 'So anyone here today who wants to take me up on my offer please submit your request in writing to me through your line manager.' Silence.

I knew and they knew that a transfer from Visits meant a return to work in the H Blocks, and I knew exactly how attractive that was.

There wasn't much eye contact any more. What I had actually said—and no doubt the staff listening had been reading between the lines—was simple: anyone who was not prepared to make the small effort to work with me wouldn't be here much longer.

It was only after I had left the service that I heard that some staff called me 'Governor My Way or No Way'. I don't believe that was how I operated: yes, I was decisive, but wherever possible I always took into account other people's views before making a decision. Whenever a manager informs his subordinates of probable change, some will embrace it, while others will resist it.

I knew after that particular meeting that what I needed in Visits was a principal officer with strong man-management skills. Bertie was that man. Like me, Bertie had worked in the administration side of the service, so I knew his abilities well. He was naturally reluctant to take on the post, based on what he knew about the Visits and what he had heard from the current incumbent of the post. Although most of the staff on Visits had an easier job than those in the H Blocks, this could not be said of the principal officer: he would be summoned by prisoners to deal with even the most insignificant problems.

I arranged for Bertie to meet me and the two senior officers who had first approached me, and half an hour later we had our man. The current principal officer, who had been in charge for about three years, needed a break. He had been subjected to verbal abuse and threats for the entire time he had had the job and he was not only glad of the move from Visits: he deserved it.

I started focusing on the actual Visits area but soon discovered that most of the problems were in the two areas that fed Visits with visitors and prisoners.

I first looked at the car park, the area where the visitors were processed before being transported to the Visits complex.

I then went through the various procedures followed by the visitors to ascertain what was causing the delays from this area. It was strange: as I passed through the turnstiles the visitors were all chatting away to each other oblivious to the fact that a prison governor was among them. The chatting continued until we got on the bus that was used to transfer the visitors from the car park to the Visits complex. I felt this was a good time to introduce myself to the visitors.

'Good morning,' I began. 'My name is Governor McKee and I have just taken over responsibility for prison visits. I have been made well aware of the problems that you and the people you visit are experiencing.' (It's always best to avoid using the term 'prisoners' or 'inmates', especially to their loved ones.) The other conversations on the bus ended as soon as I started to speak and there was not another word spoken until the visitors had got off the bus and were safely ensconced in Visits. Well, that felt like a wasted exercise, but at least I felt—wrongly, as it turned out—that I could safely discount the car park as a problem area.

I followed the visitors through Visits, watching while they were processed and directed through to the table they had been allocated. Now where was the prisoner? Why was he not here waiting?

I thought it was time to meet with the ocs in the H Blocks. My first meeting was with Harry, a member of the PIRA army council in the prison, and it was the first of many. (My final meeting with him left me an emotional wreck, but that lay a few years in the future.) As I had expected, Harry welcomed my intervention in Visits. He didn't need me to tell him that management in particular was reluctant to open dialogue with the PIRA, since on occasions in the past this had been akin to opening Pandora's Box. Dealings with PIRA always began in a professional way. No threats, no one getting angry. It was only later, if things didn't work out to their satisfaction, that they could, and did, turn nasty.

I hadn't a lot to tell Harry other than I was as aware as he was that the systems in Visits were not working efficiently and that a review and reorganisation were long overdue. He agreed and said that his side would set up their own working group and prepare a document for my attention outlining their perspective of the faults, possible solutions to rectify those faults and another 'list of additional changes' that they wanted to be implemented. Well, that was Pandora's Box well and truly opened!

I wasn't surprised by Harry's proposed list of extra changes. The PIRA never offered something for consideration: they went straight to the point. This would be a list for implementation. But unlike certain other governors, I didn't have a problem saying no to prisoners, regardless of factions in the Maze Prison.

My meetings with the other sections were similar to my meeting with Harry, but I had to suggest to the loyalist factions that they should set up working groups and prepare a list of any complaints for my attention. Giving people ownership or at least partial ownership of a problem that affected them, I believed, was guaranteed to get them involved and communicating. On many occasions throughout my career I discovered that the people with the solutions were often the people who were most affected by the difficulties.

At that time the atmosphere in Visits was poor. The prisoners collectively had the incorrect impression that the prison staff were deliberately delaying visits, and the prison officers were in turn reacting to the verbal abuse that was being thrown at them. During my talks with the inmates I sought and got agreement from them to knock the abuse on the head to allow me the opportunity to identify the problems and try to resolve the difficulties that were responsible for the current conflict. They gave me two weeks.

The biggest complaint was the delays, which meant that either the visitor was waiting fifteen minutes for the prisoner to arrive, or vice versa. I had already established, or so I thought, that the car park was not part of the problem. Now I decided to focus on getting the prisoner to the Visits on time, and I was dismayed when I discovered what was causing the delays. The visitor would arrive at the car park. Once they had been processed a call would be made to the Visits complex confirming that a visitor had arrived to visit a certain prisoner. A prison officer would then request a van to deliver him to the H Block where the inmate was housed. The van would drop the officer off and then leave to collect another officer or wait for a request to go elsewhere in the prison, and the officer and prisoner would wait to be taken back to Visits. This whole process could take half an hour on a good day.

The delay was caused by the existing system, so I devised an alternative system and did a test run. I simply allocated two officers and a van to the H Block. Instead of the escort officer having to wait for a van to take him from Visits to the H Block an officer was already there; and instead of the officer waiting for a van to come and collect him and the prisoner from the H Block, the van was already there.

I had to listen to all the doubters giving me a dozen reasons why my proposals wouldn't work and that they would cause more disruption. The proof of the pudding is in the eating, though, and within a few weeks I had two escort staff and a van detailed to each of the H Blocks.

The system seemed to be working too well. Now the prisoners were arriving at their visiting table well before the visitors. I had already checked out the car park, had travelled with the visitors, tested the system and could find no faults. But there must be. I must have missed something. So back to the car park.

I went first thing in the morning on a busy day and watched every aspect of the process, trying to spot the elusive gremlin. When there were a lot of visitors passing through there were no problems because as soon as one of the four vans and buses returned from dropping off the previous batch of visitors it was filled again; but when the initial rush had eased and the visitors were coming through in dribs and drabs the staff were holding the van or bus until they had a full load.

A simple written order instructed the staff to ensure the van moved off every time there was a gap in the queue of visitors leaving the car park, even if this meant taking just a single visitor in the van. That was the biggest problem solved and there was a significant reduction both in the tension and the verbal abuse directed at staff.

Two positive things came from this earlier-than-expected success: my credibility with both staff and with prisoners had grown considerably. However, I felt that acknowledgement of this success was grudgingly given by some of the prison officers. Some staff believed that, because the conflict and the causes of it had been resolved, 'that governor' would soon be out of their hair and no longer dementing them with his endless questions, always why this and why that: But *why* do you do it that way? Well, they were in for a shock. I had the bit between my teeth and as far as I was concerned meeting the biggest challenge in Visits was only the beginning.

The paramilitary factions were delighted with the changes in Visits but of course took the credit for them themselves. I didn't mind in the least. The people who, in my eyes, really mattered knew where the plaudits should really be directed. The real success for me, however, was having built and established stronger relationships with the leaders of the various paramilitary factions in the prison.

My next step was to address the cleanliness—or lack of cleanliness—in the Visits complex. Cleaning was the responsibility of civilian cleaners and their efforts left a lot to be desired. For example, on one occasion when I inspected their work I discovered that their interpretation of washing the floor was to push the mop up the middle of the floor as they passed through!

Throughout my career I always tried to adapt and use whatever resources were at my disposal, and on this occasion I figured that the people who used the Visits were the most appropriate people to be allocated the task of cleaning. I needed Security's approval for this and I knew they would find it easier to say no than yes. I discussed my thoughts with Pat and, though he initially sided with Security, after a few days he gave me the go-ahead to discuss the matter with the prisoners.

I met with each of the factions to discuss the Visits area and deliberately let them bring up its lack of cleanliness.

'Another thing, Governor, the state of the Visits is ridiculous. How can we be expected to sit with our families in that filth?' was one comment.

'You could probably make a better job of it yourselves,' I suggested.

'Of course we could,' came the reply.

'Good idea, that,' I ventured; 'but I would never get Security to agree to it!' (I already had approval.) 'But if I can get approval, would you be willing to supply a prisoner each Monday [a visit-free day] to deep clean the Visits in your designated area and also each evening for, say, an hour to keep on top of it?'

'We would do that all right,' came the reply. 'Do your best for us, Governor.'

Mission achieved! That's the relationship direction I was aiming for: '*The Governor is on our side. He is trying to help us.*'

The conversation went along similar lines with the other factions: except for PIRA. They were too cute to fall for the approach that I had used with the loyalists and INLA. I had to make my proposals in a different way. I explained that I had got approval for the loyalists to have one of their prisoners appointed as a cleaner for their own visits but wasn't convinced that I could get approval for PIRA to be offered the same facility by Security. (Another white lie.) What this approach did was to move the PIRA's focus from being asked to supply one of their men to clean to the fact that the loyalists were getting something they were not. Of course they demanded that they were afforded the same conditions as the loyalists and naturally after a couple of days I confirmed that I had managed to secure them that right. There's more than one way of skinning a cat.

That was the cleanliness issue dealt with, and of course another benefit was that the prisoners could no longer complain to me if the Visits area was dirty. It was no longer my problem: it had now become their problem and theirs alone.

There were two remaining issues that still had to be dealt with: the non-existent crèche facilities; and the expensive tea and coffee machines. These machines were constantly breaking down and needing the attentions of an engineer, and despite the terms of the contract repairing the machines was proving extremely difficult. There was nothing to be gained by pointing out that it was the inmates' own children who were most often responsible for the damage to the machines: they were bored and tended to run amok around the Visits while their parents made up for lost time together. But getting a crèche for the children was proving an impossible challenge. The cost of employing eight crèche supervisors and their reliefs could not be approved. Fortunately the Quakers came to my aid and agreed to supply the necessary staff if the prison kitted out the crèches. Back to Pat. The money rabbit appeared out of the financial hat and within a short time I had eight crèches up and running and staffed.

All the time my hidden agenda was to build and develop my working relationships with the different factions in the prison. I knew that I would have bigger fish to fry in the future and might just need to call in a few favours.

The troublesome tea and coffee machines were now on my radar.

The machines were costing the prison £30,000 per year and the contract had many years still to run. Despite my suggestion that we could cancel the contract because the terms relating to repairs weren't being honoured, the service still paid up the contract to avoid legal challenge. I needed to find another way of providing tea and coffee for the prisoners and visitors before removing the machines could even be considered.

My solution was to fit eight hot water boilers in the Visits. Since the service was saving £30,000 a year, and as another sop to the prisoners (who were unaware of the massive savings my latest scheme would yield), I made a big issue of supplying them with free tea, coffee, milk and sugar. All was going as planned until the POA got wind of the hot water boilers. They were up in arms, and went straight to see the No 1. I ended up having to prove that the temperature of the water in the hot water boilers was the same temperature as the water in the tea and coffee machines that I intended to remove.

There was still resistance, and only after securing a guarantee from the paramilitaries that their men would not attempt to scald staff did I finally succeed with the final piece of my jigsaw in making Visits better than could ever have been expected.

I eventually lost Bertie from Visits when he was assaulted by a loyalist prisoner who threw a can of Coca-Cola at him. The principal officer who took over Bertie's mantle was Jim Murphy. I really liked Jim, despite his short temper. I had more rows with him than with anyone else during my twenty-seven years in the Northern Ireland Prison Service, especially when I was implementing changes. The arguments always ended the same way. 'If you aren't happy with the job I'm doing in Visits just move me!' Jim would say. 'I just might!' would come my reply. But the next day we were on speaking terms again. He certainly had a short fuse: but on occasions perhaps I did too!

Chapter 11

Buckingham Palace— and Promotion

Following my success with Visits I was ready for my next challenge. I arrived in for the morning meeting on Tuesday still slightly euphoric after bringing the last eight weeks of successful work in Visits to an end. The previous day was the first time I had stayed in my office, on the top floor of the Administration building, for a full day since I had begun my efforts on the Visits.

I hoped that the governor wouldn't labour too much on the success of the Visits project: that would only further alienate me from those in the governor grade who had already shown more than a little resentment towards me. Thankfully he mentioned it only briefly as he went round the table in the boardroom asking each of us for an update on our various areas of responsibility.

'Visits all sorted then, William?' he asked.

'Yes, Sir, that's the best can be done at the moment,' I replied. 'I just want to keep an eye on it to ensure there is no slipping back to old habits and would be grateful if the Duty Governor on Saturdays could include it on their 'walk about'.' (Duty governors were detailed to visit all areas that were open on a Saturday and Sunday and this was known as the 'walk about'.)

'You all heard what William has asked; please ensure that his request is carried out. It is the least we can do to support the good work he and his staff in Visits have put in over the past two months.' That was it and he moved on to the next person at the table.

I didn't mention my next intended 'project'. Time enough for that once I had done a little research into the matter and ensured that I could actually do something positive about it.

The Inmates Catering section had endured losses of £½ million per year for the past five years and was desperately in need of a thorough examination.

We all knew the stories of how full meals were rejected by the prisoners and how the catering staff would have to prepare a further meal in an effort to keep the prisoners happy. There was yet another cliché that I heard so often following my return to work in the Maze: 'I'm not getting the jail wrecked over the price of a few fish suppers.' When the prisoners refused their designated meal the catering staff would contact a governor. It was usually the evening duty governor and he would *always* approve the preparation of a new meal. I had done it myself.

Before I could mention my intention of taking on the Inmates' Catering problem I had to have another chat with Pat. Inmates Catering fell under Joe Helm's remit so I could not just ride roughshod over him. As always, Pat made the conditions right for me to make my move. What he told Joe I wasn't sure but all that mattered was that I was clear to go!

The first item on my agenda was to attempt to understand how the catering budget was arrived at and to find the cause of the massive deficit. I discovered was that the weekly menu for the inmates was overpriced by approximately £5 per prisoner per week: this, multiplied by fifty-two, amounted to a tidy annual sum.

A short chat with the staff told me all I needed to know. They were embarrassed by the situation and believed that with the right support from the governor they could haul back at least some of the overspend. At the next morning meeting I laid before the governor my latest aspirations regarding the Inmates Catering budget.

'Just to let you know, Governor, I am starting to look at the Inmates Catering budget, examining the practices and procedures to see if there is any way we can at least make some inroads into the massive and totally unacceptable overspend.'

The next comment was the most motivating thing ever said to me by one of my fellow governors.

'The only way you will ever make a hole in the catering budget is if you get the cooks to make a big pot of stew and give the prisoners that twice a day.' Alan McMullan was the governor who made the statement and he accompanied it with a huge belly laugh, which prompted smiles from the other governors who were too polite to laugh.

The governor gave a look that silenced the room. 'Do you really believe that you can reduce the overspend?'

'I can only try, Governor. I have had a chat with the cooks and they are willing to support my efforts. I also believe that we should strike while the iron is hot. I've developed a reasonable working relationship with the various factions because of the positive changes in Visits and at least that credibility should allow me the opportunity to discuss the catering problems with them.'

The governor sat quietly for a moment, obviously turning over my proposal in his mind.

'Okay, William, go for it! I trust you to tread carefully and keep Pat updated with what you are doing. And, as always, don't get my jail wrecked!'

'One last thing, Governor,' I asked. 'From now on, if any of the factions refuse their meal can I be permitted to make the decision to agree to replace the meal or not?'

The Governor did not have to think about his answer. 'No, not at this moment. Maybe in a few weeks. That is a responsibility that is better spread among us all at the moment. But I will review that decision in a couple of weeks.'

The milk was my starting point. Every day the cartons of milk would be counted to ensure that the correct allocation was delivered to each of the wings. It was then delivered to each block, and checked again before the orderly was called to carry it into the wing. Ten minutes later, however, the same orderlies would come back with the claim that some unrealistic amount of milk was missing, and the milk was replaced without question. The overspend on milk was horrendous.

I set up meetings with the paramilitary representatives to discuss the catering budget in general and the milk issue in particular. I met with PIRA first.

I explained to the representatives that there was an overspend position which could no longer be tolerated. (The prisoners had no idea of the amount of the overspend, and I did not enlighten them.) However, I said, the governor did not want the prisoners to be disadvantaged by decisions that could disrupt the good working relationship that had been achieved in the prison. Therefore I had been given the job of negotiating savings. Because of the relationship I had developed with the prisoners I felt able to throw in a joke now and then, which cooled tempers when the going got tough.

I told the prisoners that I fully understood and accepted that the current allocation of milk had been calculated at a time when the prisoners were locked in at half past eight each night. Since the prison had now moved to a twenty-four-hour unlock this allocation was now insufficient to meet their needs. Give a little, get a little. This was my philosophy at the beginning.

I then made my first bold statement of the discussions: I said I was prepared to give them an additional four pints per wing per day. They obviously knew that was more than enough: and as with any negotiation the negotiating works two ways. They were approaching the discussions in the same manner as I was: give a little, get a little. I had no problem with that. That approach would keep them receptive to my ideas.

The loyalists were the next to the negotiating table. For once they drove a harder bargain than PIRA and received six pints of milk per wing per day.

The result was that the milk bill was reduced by £13,000 per year! That was easy, but there was still a long hard road ahead to achieve even greater success.

At the next morning meeting I told the governor about our quick win. This let him know that the negotiating door was open, and that in itself was more encouraging than the £13,000 in milk savings. It is hard to believe, but this was the way the Maze was. Rarely was anything imposed on the inmates. The way it was in the compounds had just carried on to the new H Blocks and as every year passed the prisoners' position became more entrenched.

At the next meeting with the prisoners I suggested that any food they didn't like be removed from the menu and replaced with something different. However, they accepted that the prison was still legally obliged to provide balanced meals as per the dietary scale.

The next step was to have the cooks recalculate the 'prisoner cost' of the menu, which was £5 per prisoner per week over budget. This was done and I simply sold it to the prisoners as a menu change.

Two wins in the first few weeks. As I had in the Visits project, I spent the majority of my time either talking to the prisoners or in the kitchen, challenging everything that was done. The catering staff were motivated now. They were seeing progress.

Unfortunately, the prisoners continued to refuse meals, and the governors who were asked to allow the meals to be replaced still said yes.

A few more weeks passed and the two quick wins seemed a distant memory. Heads in the kitchen were started to drop as the cooks tried to convince themselves that the two wins were more than could have been expected and that perhaps that was the best we could collectively hope for. I would not give up. I knew and the cooks knew that the meal replacement scenario was a big part of the problem. I needed this to stop.

I spoke to Pat. He would still not let me stop or even make the decisions regarding the meal replacements. I had a further meeting with the cooks. I believed that if I could secure one or two more victories, we could probably convince the boss to pass to me the decision of whether to supply replacement meals.

Back to the drawing board. With the help of a female catering officer I started to look at the storage, ordering and wastage procedures of the department. I discovered there was an unacceptable waste of fresh vegetables and found that the new vegetables were being stored on top of the previous day's, so by the time the cooks worked their way down to the ones at the bottom they were spoiled and had to be dumped. I instructed the principal catering officer to immediately review all the other practices in the kitchen and to adopt a more hands-on supervisory approach to ensure no expensive short-cuts were taking place in his kitchen.

Back to the prisoners. I asked the orderlies who served the food in the wings to let me know what food was being thrown out. I was shocked at the amount of food that was ending up in the bin. The prisoners received for their supper each night a 'Paris bun' and it appeared that the majority of these went straight in the bin. Baked beans, peas, carrots . . . you name it, it was being thrown away. One look in the inmates' wing bins would have confirmed the terrible wastage.

I thought the supper situation could be turned to our advantage. After telling the inmates the actual cost of suppers per wing I invited them to choose their own suppers.

The loyalists were straightforward in their choices. A catering size tin of corned beef, the same size tin of tuna and a large block of cheese and they were happy.

PIRA, as always, were more difficult. They requested a Mr Kipling price list and each week submitted an order up to the value of their allowance. The only difficulty with this was that some of the staff also shared a taste for Mr Kipling and of course the PIRA order started to arrive a few buns down.

I had to instruct the cooks to seal the Mr Kipling delivery to the blocks and informed the prisoners to refuse to accept the order if it was interfered with. No more buns went missing.

Another win: not really in monetary terms but in relationship building.

The next thing I turned my attention to was the wastage of vegetables on the wing. Again the inmates were consulted. They explained that when food came down cooked, if they didn't want it, it could not be stored, so of course it ended up in the bin. My solution to this was to send the allocated vegetables down to the prisoners uncooked and unopened. I had initially believed that we would not achieve a financial gain from this: but I was wrong.

The prisoners started to stockpile the tins, which were the large catering size. As their stock built they wanted to barter. Seeing the financial advantage to be gained from this I advised the cooks to calculate the cost price of the tins the prisoners were offering, ensure that they were not out of date and allow the prisoners an exchange of goods equal to half the cost. This meant each time an exchange occurred we pulled back fifty per cent of the original cost.

That was all my ideas exhausted. The projected budget usage for the year had dropped significantly and I am sure the savings achieved would have been enough to satisfy the governor. But not me. I needed to be in control of the meal replacement decisions. Whether I wore the No 1 down with my 'Jack Russell with a bone' attitude or whether he actually started to believe that I wouldn't get his jail wrecked by refusing to replace a meal some evening, I really didn't know. What's more, I didn't care. All I knew was that I and I alone would from now on make the decision of whether meals that were refused were to be replaced.

I didn't have to wait long to test how far my relationship with the prisoners had developed. I received a telephone call from the catering principal officer confirming that the UDA in one of the H Blocks were refusing to accept their tea. I could hear the tension in his voice: he knew this was the litmus test. If I refused to replace the meal would we get away with it without confirming the governor's expectation that he'd get his jail wrecked?

I could easily have telephoned the H Block Principal Officer and passed my decision to him to tell the prisoners. The fact that he was a former colleague of mine from Administration had nothing to do with my decision to meet with the prisoners and tell them face to face my decision regarding replacing the food. I walked to the H Block for my meeting and that gave me the opportunity to marshal my thoughts prior to the confrontation. I had already formulated a strategy.

I entered the block and the principal officer greeted me in quite an agitated fashion. 'Listen,' he said, in an almost threatening tone, 'Don't you even think about refusing the meal exchange.' He had already reckoned that if I was going to replace the meal I wouldn't have taken the trouble to walk all the way from the Administration building to visit the H Block. 'My staff and I have to work with these bastards and it is difficult enough without you winding them up by refusing to exchange their meal.' This block was, incidentally, the most contentious H Block in the Maze.

Two UDA prisoners came into the governor's office to discuss the issue. They were not members of the UDA inner council, which was disappointing because I already had an established working relationship with the prisoners who sat on the council. The principal officer showed the two men into the room and withdrew. He expected a bad reaction and didn't want to be any part of it. Their reaction to me was exactly as I expected: threatening and abusive. They wouldn't sit down and started swearing and making demands even as they were walking into the room.

I interrupted their abuse. 'You sent word to me that you have a problem with your meal. I am here to discuss and hopefully resolve the problem. But let me assure you that unless the swearing and abuse stops I will leave the room and with my exit you will lose your opportunity of sorting out the meal issue.'

They stopped talking and just stared at me open-mouthed. If you treat people differently from how they are used to being treated you can stun and confuse them.

'Now!' I went on. 'What exactly is your problem with your meal?'

Usual response. 'The meal is shite—we want fish and chips!'

'I need to know exactly what the problem is with the meal. In fact, bring a sample of the meal out to me and explain what the problem is,' I said.

The pair of them left the office and returned a few moments later with an individual portion of their tea. I sampled the meal and was happy with both quality and content.

'Look, lads,' I began. 'I have explained to your inner council the budget difficulties and you are all aware that I have introduced lots of positive changes to the inmates' catering. I have also agreed that in the event of a meal being served at less than the acceptable standard I will replace it with heart and hand. The meal that I've just sampled, however, is in my opinion palatable. Therefore I will not be replacing this meal.'

The prisoners looked first at me and then at each other. They had been conditioned to expect getting this type of request granted, so they were lost as to what their response should be. The atmosphere was tense. We were all just sitting looking at each other. I knew what their next step would be and I braced myself for it. I wasn't disappointed.

'We'll fucking wreck this place! The men will fucking wreck this place when we tell them!' they shouted as they jumped to their feet.

Did I detect a tiny hint that my decision might be accepted? 'When we tell them'—I was encouraged by that. 'Look, lads, I'm genuinely sorry, but this is the way things are now. Your inner council know all about it. Now I'd hate it if you were to wreck this block, but I also have to make it clear that the cost of the repairs will not come out of my kitchen budget!'

I knew that what I was saying could be interpreted as provocative and that the No 1 governor would be pulling his hair out if he knew anything about this conversation. I felt it better that he did not know about it until after the event, and perhaps then in a slightly watered-down version.

We had now reached a defining moment. I had turned down the prisoners' request and knew that this could go one of two ways. If it went the wrong way the No 1 would wash his hands of me because my actions would have contributed to an H Block being wrecked. If it went the right way a new line in the sand would have been drawn.

I knew that the argument would have been over if the two prisoners were sitting here discussing their own two meals, but they were not. They had ninety-eight other mouths waiting for fish and chips and if they backed down with me they would then have to try to explain it to the others. I had no illusions about the pressure they were under.

'Fuck you!' signalled the end of our meeting. I had got away with it! The prisoners kicked back their chairs and stormed out of the office.

I have no idea what they told the other prisoners but I suspect it wasn't that the governor had said no.

The principal officer burst into the office. 'Well?'

'Well what?' I replied.

'Are you replacing the meal?' he asked.

'No. The meal will not be replaced,' I assured him.

He muttered something under his breath and stormed out of the office. I understood where the principal officer was coming from. This Block was probably the most contentious in the Maze and what I had done was in effect to leave him and his staff with a hundred annoyed prisoners. But it had to be done. There were new lines being drawn in the Maze now and for a change they were being drawn by management and not by the paramilitaries.

Of course I knew that the following day I would be summoned before the UDA inner council to deal with the fallout of today's decision. But that was tomorrow. Today I would take pleasure in having slotted in another important part of the jigsaw, a jigsaw that when completed would end the horrendous financial deficit that the service had now faced for five years too long.

I rang the catering principal officer and told him the good news. He burst out laughing. 'You have some balls, Governor! I've held all the cooks back as I thought for sure we'd be cooking fish and chips before we went home tonight. Sorry for the lack of confidence, Governor. See you in the morning.'

As I returned the phone to its cradle I smiled, realising that it wasn't just a catering principal officer I had just spoken to: he was also my friend. Just as with Visits, the difficulties and our attempts to resolve them had galvanised and strengthened working relationships that eventually grew and turned into friendships, friendships that were to last for many years to come.

By the time I had returned to the Administration building all the governors, apart from the duty governor, had gone home. I let the duty governor know that I had refused a meal exchange for the UDA and that the prisoners were a little annoyed to say the least.

The next day two things happened as a result of my actions the previous night.

First, the UDA asked for the principal officer in charge of their block to be removed. Apparently they believed that he had not put up a strong enough argument regarding their meal replacement. The principal officer contacted me later in the day with an extraordinary remark: 'You could have given them a tin of corned beef or something.' He still didn't get it.

The second issue I had to deal with was, as expected, a call from the UDA inner council. It went better than I thought it would. There was a reluctant acceptance from the prisoners, just maybe because I had warned them I would be starting to refuse meal exchanges before I actually did it: I had structured their expectations.

I had to let the boss know about the events of the previous night. 'And then what did they say?' he asked.

'Ah, Governor, they just said "dead on, Billy",' I said, tongue in cheek.

The governor looked at me, shaking his head. 'Get out! You'll get this jail wrecked yet!'

By the time the authority to sanction meal replacements was delegated to me I had already been working on the various factions, convincing them that the budget could no longer sustain the number of replacement meals that were being asked for. They, on the whole, had agreed and the issue had started to recede.

I had explained that the open chequebook days of the Maze were now over and that, because providing meals for the prisoners was a legal requirement, when the kitchen budget was exhausted funds would have to be transferred from other budgets in the prison. I said, for example, knowing how important the gym was to inmates, that this would probably be the first budget to be hit and we all knew how that would impact on the prisoners. (Another white lie.)

On one occasion, when the duty governor had agreed to exchange a meal of steak pieces, I told the cooks to make a beef curry for the following night, using the steak that the prisoners had returned.

By this stage of the project we were seven months in. The results that we had achieved in such a short space of time were nothing short of miraculous. The cooks were satisfied. The governor was impressed. But I wasn't. We still needed to identify some savings to put the catering budget back in the black every week, and I had run out of ideas.

I spoke to Alison, the civil servant who managed the ordering of goods. She explained that because of the system she followed she knew exactly when her budget was exhausted each week. I instructed her not to order any more goods when her budget limit was reached. I then told the cooks of the change to their ordering procedures. There was a sharp intake of breath, but their terrific accomplishment to date was enough to steel them for the final push.

We made it, and I took great delight at the morning meeting, some eight months from when I had begun the project, of informing the

Billy Wright, the charismatic leader of the Loyalist Volunteer Force. (*PA Photos*)

Crip McWilliams (*foreground, right*), the INLA gunman who murdered the LVF leader. (*Reuters*)

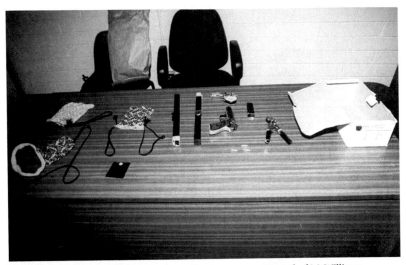

Items recovered from the three-man assassination team composed of McWilliams, Kennaway and Glennon. (*Pacemaker*)

One job too many! Martin Mogg, Governor of HMP Maze in addition to Director of Prison Operations. (PA *Photos*)

COPS SAVE JAIL BOSS FROM MURDER GANG

UDA-LVF in joint bid to kill prison governor

BY ALAN MURRAY

A PRISON governor was dramatically evacuated from his home, last week, amid fears that a UDA gang was on its way to kill him.

The governor was the man loyalist claim ordered the removal of a sentry from a tower overlooking the Maze prison courtyard, where LVF leader, Billy Wright, was shot dead.

The 45-year-old senior officer was hurriedly placed in a police car, outside his house, on the outskirts of south Belfast, 10 days ago, after information was received that loyalists planned to assassinate him.

It is believed the attack was intended to be the UDA's 'big hit' against the Prison Service, following a

statement read by masked men before TV cameras days earlier.

"He literally didn't have time to pack a bag of clothes," a colleague said.

"It was virtually a case of, 'we're the police, you need to get into that car

now, we've to get you out of here pronto'."

A spokesman for the Prison Service confirmed that a governor was moved from his home in recent days, because of a loyalist threat to kill him.

It is believed police had

received vital intelligence information, that the UDA and the LVF had agreed to mount a joint operation to kill the governor that evening, at his home, where it's understood he lived alone.

"They were insistent that he left that night, not the next morning or in an hours time even, so they must have received a late tip-off that the gunmen were literally on their way to his house," a Prison Service source said.

Loyalists have previously claimed that the senior

officer was the duty governor, in charge on the day Billy Wright was gunned down inside the Maze Prison by INLA inmates, in December, 1997.

Wright was shot dead in the exercise yard of H-Block 6 as he sat in a prison van, waiting to be driven to a rare Saturday morning visit.

No explanation was given, at the inquest into Wright's death, why the tower was left unmanned that particular morning.

H6 was the only H-Block shared by deadly enemies

in the LVF and the INLA, and the tower was normally manned around the clock.

A governor who gave the order for the sentry to be stood down did not give evidence at Wright's inquest, and it is not known if he was made available to speak to retired Canadian Judge Peter Cory, who has recommended an inquiry into Wright's murder.

The name of a governor, who allegedly gave the order, has appeared on websites linked to the illegal LVF

Courtesy of *Belfast Telegraph/Sunday Life.*

Memorial to all the staff that lost their lives. A memorial that my name was almost added to on at least two occasions.

Billy Wright Inquiry in sitting. The truth will be told! (*Press Eye Ltd*)

governor that Inmate Catering was now being operated within budget. A few days later I found myself in the governor's office speaking to Ken Crompton, the deputy governor. He brought up the subject of Inmate Catering and congratulated me on our achievement. Before I could speak, even to say that I couldn't have managed it without the help of the catering staff, he went on to say that he felt it better if senior management remained in the dark about how I had achieved my success: perhaps they could not and probably they would not have given approval to the methods I had used to turn around the catering budget deficit. I wondered if he had heard about the recycling of the steaks!

Because of the positive support and contribution of all of the catering staff, including Alison, I put a letter in each of their files highlighting their particular involvement in the success of the project. I also ensured that a copy of the letter, which I had had signed by the No 1 governor, was sent to each staff member's file at Headquarters, which would be consulted in the event of a promotion board. The next round of catering promotion boards saw two senior officers promoted to principal officer, two officers promoted to senior officer and Alison promoted up a level. I hoped that the letter the No 1 had prepared, signed and placed in my file would do my future promotion chances no harm either and, sure enough, at the next governor four board I was found competent to proceed to that level.

In annual reporting terms the Prison Service operated the same 'box marking' procedures as the Civil Service. Box 3 meant the member of staff had performed at an acceptable level over the course of the year. Box 2 meant he or she had performed at a slightly higher level than the norm. In the Prison Service I believed that a Box 2 was normal: during my career to date I had always received that particular marking. I was pleasantly surprised when I received two consecutive Box 1 markings from Pat for my first two years in Inmate Services and no doubt that painted a strong picture of my abilities for my next promotion. My two Box 1 reports were countersigned by Ken Crompton, the deputy governor, and I was pleasantly surprised to read one of Ken's comments: 'Governor McKee has the ability to identify problems and have them solved prior to senior management even knowing that the problem existed.'

I was obviously thanked by the governor, but the real vote of appreciation came from a member of staff who nominated me for an award under the Butler Trust for my efforts in both Visits and Inmate Catering, an award which I received and was presented with by Princess Anne at Buckingham Palace the following year. My son, who was fourteen years old at the time, accompanied me to Buckingham Palace for the presentation. This was an occasion I was glad we had shared.

Although I was absolutely delighted to have been nominated for the award I always felt it was 'our' award: it belonged as much to the people who had supported me in both projects as it did to me. The citation for the award read as follows:

In less than two years, Mr McKee has taken the lead in transforming two areas that are vital to all prisons—visits and catering. By a combination of imagination, practicality and extreme commitment, he has reconciled conflicting interests and brought innovative solutions to long-term problems. Both staff and prisoners have been fully involved in these solutions. The morale of staff has been raised, sick leave has been reduced, wastage has been diminished and prisoners now enjoy good food and high quality arrangements for visits which reinforce their home ties. Mr McKee's contribution to a particular difficult prison has certainly been exceptional.

Chapter 12

Threats, Fear and Exhaustion

'What a year. What a bloody year. I can't believe that it's Christmas already. I can't believe that we as a family have made it to Christmas after the unbelievable events of this past twelve months.' As I sat there in the front room, third glass of red wine of the day in my hand, my mind wandered back to the beginning of 1997.

My achievements in Visits and Inmates Catering and my subsequent award were a great start to the year, but as the year progressed my life had gone into freefall.

The LVF were not flavour of the month in the prison. None of the other paramilitary organisations would allow the LVF to have their family visits in the main Visits complex. A case of the tail wagging the dog: but this was the infamous Maze Prison, and very little of importance happened without the prisoners' agreement.

I was the governor in charge of Inmate Services, so Visits fell under my jurisdiction. The area where the legal visits were held was attached to the main Visits complex and for a short time I had managed to facilitate the LVF visits there. However, once the other factions discovered this, the No 1 governor was told in no uncertain terms by the other paramilitary leaders to put a stop to it.

The LVF were then allocated spare accommodation in the prison hospital for their visits. The LVF leadership believed this was unacceptable. I had spoken to the then governor of the prison, Martin Mogg, stressing that the tension coming from Billy Wright and company in relation to this issue was unbelievable and that staff were constantly on the receiving end of their annoyance. Martin had assured me that Prison Service Headquarters were well aware of the situation and that he had also requested funds to set up alternative accommodation for the LVF prisoners' visits.

Unfortunately, accommodation was only part of the solution. The additional staff who would be required for the new area were not available and the high level of staff sickness meant that this part of the equation was more difficult to resolve.

I believe, on reflection, that when I was sent to meet with Billy Wright and explain to him that we understood his concerns about the inadequate visiting facilities for his men and their families, and that Mr Mogg was doing all in his power to bring a speedy resolution to the problem, I was in fact being used as the conduit for a stalling process. The fact was that there was no chance of a resolution to the problem, due to the lack of staffing resources. If there were insufficient staffing levels, why not recruit and bring the numbers up to the necessary level? It is so easy to say, but the reality was that the process of getting new staff—placing the initial advertisement, setting the entrance exam, security vetting, interviews, references and training—took months.

There are three main issues in the prison that are sacrosanct to prisoners—visits, letters and food. If the prison managed to keep on top of all of these areas, things were generally quiet, but if one or more of them was not up to the standard expected by the prisoners the prison quickly became much more difficult to manage. The longer the issue went unresolved the more the atmosphere of the prison deteriorated.

So what of the LVF and the continuing problem of their lack of acceptable visiting arrangements? The situation came to a head when the LVF realised that they were being stalled, and Billy Wright was coming under continuing pressure from his men for answers. One particular day when Wright was both threatening and verbally abusive towards them the staff phoned across to my office in the main administration building and asked me if I would come and speak to him in an effort to calm him down. I immediately left what I was doing and made my way to the area in the prison hospital where the LVF visits were taking place. As I walked I tried to work out what I could tell Billy Wright that he hadn't heard half a dozen times before.

I entered the hospital and was met by one of the LVF Visits officers. He was visibly distressed, sweating and nervous, as he spoke to me. I was not alarmed by the state of the officer—I had witnessed this type of reaction from staff many times—but I was concerned. The officer briefed me, stressing that this was as bad as Wright had ever been. I touched the officer's arm to reassure him and went into the small annexe outside the room where I knew I was to be confronted by Billy Wright.

I had of course heard of Billy Wright when he was being held in HMP Maghaberry and also through various reports in the media. He had first become prominent in the Drumcree protest in July 1996 when he was seen on television meeting the Ulster Unionist leader David Trimble. This obviously raised concerns as to whether Wright's activities were capable of inflicting significant damage on the peace process.

Billy Wright had allegedly been a member of the Ulster Volunteer Force, a Protestant paramilitary organisation, from which he had been dismissed during 1996. He had then allegedly set up his own organisation, the Loyalist Volunteer Force, whose first victim is believed to have been a young Catholic man named Niall Donovan who was found knifed to death in June 1996 following a visit to relations in Dungannon. This assumption was based on the evidence presented to the coroner at the inquest into Mr Donovan's death by Inspector Ian McDonald, a detective involved in the investigation. This particular case is one of many currently being revisited by the Historical Enquiries Team, a unit set up by the government to investigate unsolved murders that occurred during the Troubles.

The activities of the LVF had continued to worry the government and there were real fears that the murder of a Catholic taxi driver, Michael McGoldrick, a murder that was attributed to Billy Wright and his LVF associates, could further disrupt the peace process.

Billy Wright had been arrested in January 1997 and sentenced to serve a term of eight years' imprisonment at HMP Maghaberry for making threats to a Portadown woman. At the time Wright was obviously extremely annoyed by his conviction and subsequently denied the charges, saying that although he had done many things that he should not have, this was not one of them. He speculated that this was a trumped-up charge to get him off the streets of Ulster.

While he was serving his sentence at Maghaberry, Christopher McWilliams and John Kennaway, two members of the Irish Nationalist Liberation Army (INLA), a nationalist paramilitary organisation directly opposed to the LVF and its activities, had managed to smuggle two weapons into the prison, with which they had gained entry to the residential house where they took a prison officer hostage. Although at the time it was thought that their intended victim was a former INLA terrorist, Kevin McAlorum (believed to have been responsible for the murder for a former leader of the INLA, Gino Gallagher), who was also located in that prisoner accommodation, there was also speculation that their real intention was to murder Billy Wright.

Billy Wright had requested a transfer to HMP Maze, insisting that he and his LVF colleagues should have their own segregated accommodation as they now were recognised as a separate paramilitary organisation. He further threatened to go on hunger strike until his wish was granted. On 22 April 1997 Sir John Wheeler, the Security Minister, decided not to proceed with the transfer of Billy Wright to the Maze, but two days later, following a meeting with senior prison officials, he reversed his decision and the transfer went ahead on 25 April 1997.

Billy Wright, along with other members of his organisation, was moved to H Block 6 at the Maze. He was housed in the only H Block at the Maze that also housed a different and directly opposing faction, the INLA.

Around the same time as Wright's transfer two other prisoners were transferred to H Block 6 from Maghaberry: they were two INLA members, Christopher McWilliams and John Kennaway.

My first encounter with Billy Wright was in H Block 6. H6 was a block that I had worked in as an officer and later in my career as governor in charge, and I had first met the head of the LVF in the prison when dealing with the catering reforms.

I reported to the principal officer in charge of the H Block and asked him to arrange for Billy Wright to come out to see me. I really didn't know what to expect.

Dealing with PIRA was normally quite friendly and businesslike: they tried to make you believe that you were a great governor and that they really appreciated the way you were trying to resolve their problems. This was part of their conditioning process—they would encourage you to drop your guard in their company in the hope that you would approach later, more controversial, requests in a more favourable manner.

The UDA and UVF were more hostile groups to deal with, resorting to threatening and abusive behaviour the moment something was said that they didn't want to hear. On one occasion Skelly McCrory, one of the UDA inner council, had me by the throat and up against the wall over some minor issue. Another time, when I said something that annoyed the head of the UVF, David McCullough, it was only Principal Officer Johnston's refusal to leave the office that saved me from 'having the head kicked off my shoulders', to quote the prisoner. So I had mixed feelings as I sat waiting for Billy Wright to enter the block governor's office.

The principal officer opened the door and in walked Billy Wright. First impressions? He looked just the same as the photographs I had seen in the media. He was calm and surprisingly courteous. He was dressed in a football shirt, shorts, socks and trainers. This was the standard dress in the wings of HMP Maze. The only time the inmates dressed any differently was if they had to attend court either on appeal or to answer further charges.

'Good morning, Governor,' he said.

I think it important to say at this stage that in a normal prison I would be accompanied by a senior officer when attending to a prisoner's request. The prisoner would be escorted into the office by a prison officer and he would then stand to attention and state his name and prisoner number. But then the Maze was far from being a normal prison, or anything close to it.

Billy Wright stood with his arms folded and waited for me to answer. The principal officer retreated from the room and closed the door. I was nervous and was annoyed at myself for being so. That nervous cough again: I hated myself for that.

I introduced myself and asked the prisoner how he was settling in to life at HMP Maze. It was no more than small talk, but I was surprised by how courteous he was towards me. It was not the same as the conditioning that I had experienced from the PIRA and I was slightly taken back. I invited him to take a seat, which he did, and offered his thanks.

I moved quickly on to the subject of inmate catering and explained in fairly simple terms the system that had been recently introduced to enable the prison to deliver a selection of meals within budget. To my surprise Billy Wright appeared to take on board all that I had said and thanked me for taking the trouble to come down to see him and explain it. He asked for clarification on a few minor points, but nothing of any real substance.

Over the following months I developed a reasonable working relationship with Billy Wright and the LVF. Staff were aware of this and when they were getting it 'tight' with any of the factions they would ask me to intervene and, as Governor Maguire used to say, 'pour your silky oil on troubled waters', a reference to the calm approach I adopted when communicating with the paramilitaries, sometimes on quite contentious issues.

So here I was, heading for a difficult confrontation with Billy Wright, and he in a foul mood, to say the least. As usual I hoped that the working relationship we had developed over the previous months would be enough at least to permit me to talk to him and try to calm him.

I had arrived at the locked gate that separated me from the raging LVF leader. I was greeted by another nervous, sweating officer, fear etched clearly on his face. 'Thank God it's you, Governor McKee, Billy says if it was that bastard Smith he would have pulled the head clean off him.' (David Smith was a colleague and friend of mine, who had joined the service with me in 1977. He was the type of man who said it how it was, no matter who he was addressing.)

I asked the officer to unlock the grille and entered the room to face Billy Wright. He was in a right state, pacing up and down the small annexe. His face was like thunder. I waited for him to speak.

'It's just as well it's not that fucker Smith!' he growled.

I explained that staff were concerned at his demeanour and had asked me to come across and meet with him to attempt to get an understanding of what the problem was and to try to offer a solution if possible. But the silky oil was not working for once.

He raged on. 'It's this bloody excuse for Visits that you and bloody Mogg have stuck us with, and you're doing fuck all to fix it.'

I began to speak, again trying to explain, as I had done so often, about trying to get additional funds and staff to address the problem. By now he was right in my face. This was a tactic employed by all factions when they had their angry heads on. I didn't dare speak. I thought, 'I'll let him sound off to me and perhaps eventually he'll calm down.' It was all right for me—I could take the abuse for ten minutes and retreat to my office for the rest of the day—but the poor officers were not so lucky.

Billy Wright's onslaught continued. 'That bastard Mogg sends you down to fill our head with shite, but no more—we want to see changes now! I mean, Governor McKee would you bring your children to visit in this excuse of a visiting room?'

I replied that not only would I not bring my children to this visiting room, I would not have them near the prison at all. Billy seemed to regain his composure.

'Okay, then, so are you prepared to come into the visit room with me and address the LVF prisoners and their families?' he asked.

I assured him that I had no problem with that and he opened the door and I followed him into the visiting room. The room was abysmal. At the very least it needed a fresh coat of paint. The next thing that I noticed was the hard plastic chairs and rectangular tables. In the main prison Visits area there were more comfortable and private seating arrangements.

The main Visits had a crèche where the wives and girlfriends could deposit their children into the care of the Quakers. That was another privilege not afforded the LVF. My thoughts were interrupted by the voice of Billy Wright bringing the room to order.

'This is Governor McKee,' he said. 'This is the man who by his own mouth will not bring his children anywhere near this prison, yet expects you to all bring yours!' The whole room erupted. It seemed as if every single one of the seventy or eighty men and women in the room was screaming at me. The poor children looked frightened out of their wits, and I would guess that by my expression I could have passed for one of them but for my age and greying hair!

I knew I couldn't leave the room. I felt that if I did the whole room would pour out into the small annexe behind me. I also knew that the officer would not open the grille to let me out. He wouldn't have time before the crowd followed me and all his training would tell him to contain a potential situation. I just had to ride it out. My shirt was saturated with sweat. I could feel the beads forming on my forehead and trickling down my face. My heart was thumping. Then the alarm sounded. The officer outside must have heard the commotion and set it off. I am sure the shoppers in the nearby Marks & Spencer at Sprucefield roundabout outside Lisburn heard it as well.

Now I knew exactly what would be going on in the rest of the prison: the same set of responses that happened every time an alarm was sounded. All movement in and out of the prison would be stopped. The emergency reaction force would be on their way to the point of the alarm. The governor would be making his way to the command suite, where he would be briefed by the senior officer in the emergency Control Room. Depending on the level of the alert, Gold Command at Prison Service Headquarters would be informed. And finally, management staff from the Security department would be on their way to the point of the incident so as to determine definitively the reason for the alarm being sounded. (There had been an escape many years before when an alarm was pulled at the main gate entrance of the prison. Instead of an officer being sent to verify the cause of the alarm, a member of staff from the Control Room telephoned the main gate to ask why the alarm had been activated. Of course staff, under duress from the prisoners, who by this time were in full control of the area, replied that the alarm had been pulled by mistake, and the escape succeeded.)

The alarm seemed to distract the prisoners and their visitors and, seizing my opportunity, I left the room. Thankfully the officer realised quickly that he had enough time to unlock and relock the grille, and I was out. As I made my way through the hospital the staff thanked me for coming over. They were not used to certain other governors responding to their requests as I had that day, but I had once been an officer myself, and I understood the pressure they were under.

There was little point in trying to discuss the situation any further with Billy Wright that day, so I returned to the Administration building to brief the No 1 governor on the situation. In turn, he briefed Headquarters. The LVF Visits settled down and apart from a bit of abuse towards staff the prisoners returned to their block as normal.

In the prison at the time situations like the one I had just experienced were normal: most were perhaps not quite as heated but they were often just as challenging. That night, as I left the prison with my colleagues I was still shaken, but this was the Prison Service. No debriefing, no counselling, just 'see you in the morning'!

The following day the LVF totally wrecked their side of H Block 6, causing something like £50,000 of damage. There was a battle to take back the block. That is the only way to describe it; a raging, bloody battle. As was normal in this kind of situation, the area around H Block 6 was sealed. Other prisoners were locked down and all available control and restraint-trained staff were detailed to HMP Maze. The prisoners had barricaded themselves in. As staff in body armour approached the barricade they would be met by anything the prisoners could find to throw. Jars of coffee and snooker balls were the least dangerous missiles: coffee jars full of ignited lighter fuel were far more worrying. However, prison staff are a brave and resilient bunch and they slowly but surely disassembled the barricade.

Then the real battle began. It was hand-to-hand fighting and the LVF put up a fierce struggle. It is unusual for batons to be used to strike prisoners, but such was the ferocity of the battle that permission was sought and given to draw batons. After sustained fighting the block was eventually secure and the prisoners captured and relocated in an empty H Block.

My main recollection of that day was that when the prisoners were secured, the No 1 sent for me and asked what I had actually said to the prisoners the previous day in Visits. He was clearly trying to make a connection between my interaction with the LVF and their visitors and the destruction of half an H Block.

My duties at that stage of my career did not involve any supervisory role in connection with the H Blocks, so I was surprised to be summoned by the No 1 the following day and instructed to take responsibility for the LVF prisoners in their temporary accommodation.

When I approached the H Block that morning I was confronted by the IRF—the prison's Immediate Reaction Force. This was a special unit of dedicated officers fully competent in control and restraint techniques. (Control and restraint techniques are a way of restraining prisoners to reduce the chances of staff or the prisoner themselves being injured.) They wear black suits and have helmets with mirrored visors. Think of a platoon of storm troopers wearing black suits from the movie *Star Wars*.

I met with the senior officer in charge and he briefed me on the routine imposed by the No 1 governor. This was basically twenty-three-hour lock-up, meals in cell and one hour's exercise per day per prisoner, during which they would be escorted by three control and restraint staff.

According to the Prison Rules I was required to speak to each prisoner individually to listen to their requests. The first day went fine and the requests were as you might reasonably expect following a major wreck: 'When are we getting back to a normal regime?'; When can we have visits?'; 'I want to see my solicitor.'

The following morning I was briefed by the No 1 governor regarding withdrawn privileges for the LVF prisoners. These were basically as the senior officer had described the previous day—except for the children's parties.

It had become the norm in the prison to have children's parties on a couple of occasions per year. This entailed permitting the prisoners' wives, girlfriends and children to meet in the gymnasium in the prison where they could interact with their husbands/boyfriends/ fathers for a 'fun day'. Food and refreshments were supplied by the prison authorities. It was like a large indoor picnic. The governor had decided, in conjunction with Prison Service Headquarters, to refuse this privilege to the LVF prisoners. This devastating news was to be delivered to the LVF prisoners by me.

Can you imagine the situation? I am surrounded by three 'storm troopers' in black suits, with helmets and reflective visors (so that they can't be identified by the prisoners), and who only ever speak when issuing commands or instructions to the prisoners. (These particular staff might have to take up other duties, and if they could be identified they might be vulnerable to attacks from inmates with whom they had been involved in earlier incidents.) I am in my normal attire of a suit, shirt and tie, so the only person that the prisoners can identify and threaten is the guy in the suit—me.

It did not help the situation when I told Billy Wright and his not-so-merry men that they had lost their privilege of children's parties. They appeared not to hear the part where I said 'the governor has asked me to inform you', as when I had finished speaking they directed all their anger towards me. They exploded. Staff stepped in, placing a clear shield between the spitting prisoners and me.

'So you are hurting our wives and children now as well! You bastard!' The abuse was unbelievable. I still had to go to each cell and by the time I had finished seeing each prisoner the wing was 'bouncing'.

I was suffering from some familiar symptoms: shirt soaking with sweat, beads of sweat running off my forehead. I was pale and felt as though my heart was trying to escape from my chest. The staff must have led me out of the wing, but to this day I can't remember how I got out.

A short while later, having calmed down at least to the point where I had stopped shaking, I reported to the No 1.

'Don't let them get to you,' he said. 'Don't be going back near them today.' That implied that my attendance tomorrow was more than a possibility. I thought that was bad, but there was far worse to come: news that made me more frightened than I had ever been in my career in the Prison Service to date.

The senior officer and his staff would routinely slip quietly down the wing where the inmates were secured. The prisoners would not realise they were there, and this enabled them to pick up titbits of possibly useful intelligence. The intelligence that day related to me.

'I know that bastard from Maghaberry. Let's get him fucking sorted.'

'We know where he lives.'

'When?'

'Friday night!'

How did I feel when Security told me about this? Numb is the only word that comes even close to describing it. The now familiar sensations of acute stress returned. Hairs standing on the back of my neck, sweating, nervousness and fear. I don't know I drove home that night, I simply can't remember. I left the prison and then I was home. On automatic the whole way. As soon as I walked through my front door my wife started telling me something about the children's speech and drama. She cut off abruptly, obviously recognising that I was involved in some drama of my own.

'What is it? What's wrong now?' she asked in a concerned tone. She knew me well. I turned and walked upstairs. She rushed up after me and now demanded to know what the problem was.

I sat her down on the bed and closed the bedroom door and then slowly related the events of the day. She was in shock too. 'The children! What about the children?'

'I know, I know,' was all I could say. But I didn't know—that was the problem.

A couple of hours later we had got our heads straight and she was packing the children's school uniforms and whatever they would need for a couple of days. We decided that they—and my wife—would be safer in her mum's house for a few days until we could establish how real this current risk was. I knew the procedure: the RUC would be informed and they would contact their army of touts to see if the threat could be verified. When they found that the threat was real, the police visited and told me that they would be watching my house on Friday night, the night of the alleged murder bid.

Friday night came. The police were parked at the back of my home and I was in bed with my gun and my dog. Did I sleep? Do I need to answer that? I watched every minute of every hour pass on the clock at the side of my bed and it was not the dog snoring that kept me awake. The morning came, the night had passed, and nothing had happened.

Police intelligence must have produced something concrete, though. They called later that day, having asked to speak to me and my wife. They explained to us that as our home was close to the road we were prone to 'drive-by shots'. They talked about the angle the bullets would hit the house. We were numb. One of our daughters slept at the front of the house. The police advice was to move out. We took it. A Chief Constable's Certificate was issued verifying the threat and we were gone within a few days to rented accommodation in a house in Glengormley on the outskirts of Belfast.

We loved where we had lived before the threat. It was a large five-bedroomed house on the outskirts of Templepatrick, a house to which we had recently added an extension, a house where we had lived for seven years. The children had made friends there. We had decided that our children should get a first-class education and our son had been accepted into an excellent prep school, which was the feeder school for a fairly prestigious school in Belfast. When we moved into that house my son was eight years old, my daughter four, and a month after moving there my wife had had another beautiful daughter. By the time we had to leave, our second child had been accepted into the same school as our son. Life was good. We were happy.

The Housing Executive bought our house from us at market value under the SPED (Special Purchase of Evacuated Dwellings) system. Thankfully the kids didn't have to change schools. But did we feel safe? No, definitely not. I had never been so stressed in my life. I was genuinely fearful not only about my own life but also about the lives of my wife and children. Surely things couldn't get any worse? How wrong I was.

A tunnel had just been discovered in one of the PIRA H Blocks. The jail was locked down and a search was planned for the following few days. I wasn't too concerned about the search, just delighted for the No 1 that the tunnel had been discovered before thirty or forty prisoners had disappeared, not over the wall, as was normal with a prison escape, but under it.

I sat in at the morning meeting as an interested observer—simply to hear what the plans were for the search. The governors, in their role of bronze commander, were each allocated to a particular H Block. (The bronze commander is the governor at the coal face, in this case the governor in charge of each search.) Although the tunnel had been found in only one of the H Blocks, the No 1 had decided to search all PIRA H Blocks. Governor Ross was detailed to H Block 4 for the first day.

One of the basic rules of searching is that—for obvious reasons—prisoners are not moved from the area which is being searched (the dirty area) to an area that has already been searched (the clean area). The prisoner could conceal contraband on his person and transfer it to a 'clean area' without it being discovered by the search team. For some reason this rule had not been followed during Governor Ross's watch.

The following morning, to my surprise, the No 1 sent for me. I had the somewhat rose-tinted idea that he might want to know how my family and I were coping following the death threats from the LVF.

'Good morning, Billy,' he started. 'Need you to take over the search in H Block 4 for me.'

'Of course,' I replied, 'if those are your instructions, but may I ask why? It's just I am not a block governor and I respectfully suggest that they might be annoyed if I'm brought in and used instead of them.'

The No 1, obviously under major pressure from the politicians, snapped back, 'I don't care who is or isn't annoyed—speak to the Security governor and then get on with the search!'

'Will do, Governor,' I said and left the room to head on over to be briefed by the Security governor.

As I walked to Security my wife's words from earlier that morning were echoing in my head. 'Now don't you be volunteering for any-thing to do with this search, we have enough bloody trouble at our door without you bringing more home with you.' Sometimes she didn't understand. Sometimes she didn't try to understand. Sometimes she didn't want to understand. I enjoyed my job and always believed that I could make a difference, but I also recognised that the pressure that we as a family now found ourselves under was causing the first serious cracks to appear in my relationship with my wife.

The security briefing didn't take long. The search team were in place. I would be there to oversee and deal with any problems either locally or by referring them to Silver Command for their decision. (Silver Command was the title given to the Command Centre at prison level.) Even now I wasn't overly worried by my role. The search yesterday had gone okay, except for the movement of prisoners between wings. The staff wanted the search over. The prisoners wanted the search over. The governor wanted the search over. God, I wanted the search over.

I went to the block governor's office and let the staff get on with the search. The worst thing a governor can do is to be too visible when competent staff are trying to do their job.

Just before the search began there was a knock on my door and the principal officer came into my office.

'Yes, PO, what can I do for you?' I asked.

'Sorry to disturb you, Governor, it's just two of PIRA want a word.'

'Do you know what they want to discuss?' I enquired.

'It's something to do with the search, Governor,' he offered. 'Okay, Principal, show them in.'

One of the prisoners was serving a life sentence for his alleged involvement in the 'corporals' killings' in West Belfast. This had taken place in 1988 following Michael Stone's attack in Milltown Cemetery on mourners at the funeral of the three IRA members killed by British soldiers in Gibraltar. In the aftermath of the funeral two British Army corporals who were driving in the area were attacked by an angry crowd and driven at speed to another location where they were shot and stabbed several times. The following year two senior members of the IRA's Belfast brigade were jailed for life for their part in the corporals' murders.

This prisoner was a member of the PIRA army council in the prison, so we were well known to each other. I knew the other prisoner to see but had had little contact with him. He was from the Tyrone branch of the IRA and although he had a position near the top of the command structure of PIRA in the prison he did not sit on the army council.

I got up, walked round, and sat on the edge of the front of my desk. PIRA had a habit of standing while the governor sat so that they were talking down to him. In they came, looking businesslike.

'Governor, about this search,' one of them said. No pleasantries this morning, then.

'Yes, what is the problem?' I asked.

'We just want to make something clear to you before the search starts today,' he said in an intimidating tone.

'Go on,' I said.

'We don't want any of our men to be strip searched by the IRF [Immediate Reaction Force], and we don't want them in the block. If either of these two requests is not heeded we will hold you personally responsible.'

The other inmate had adopted an intimidating pose when he entered the office and now turned as if he was squaring up to me. This was something I had experienced a dozen times but it still made me feel threatened and pressurised.

'I understand what you're saying, but the only reason any of your men would be searched by the IRF is if they refuse to comply with the search procedures as explained to you yesterday. So it's the actions of your men that will dictate whether I call the IRF into the block,' I explained.

With that, the first prisoner looked me in the eye and said, 'You have been warned.'

This was the first time I had been threatened by the PIRA. We had had many heated arguments in the past, but these arguments had been about visits, transport or the catering budget. This was very, very different.

I understood that the PIRA were fuming about their tunnel being discovered. I still found it hard to understand how the tunnel had not been found earlier. When the tunnel was discovered it was found that three of the cells in the wing where the tunnel had been dug were filled nearly to the roof with soil. The prisoners had managed to cut through the thick concrete floors using drills powered by bastardised motors that they had removed from the washing machines in their H Block, and they had even installed electric light in the tunnel. A number of chairs had been dismantled and rebuilt to support the roof of the tunnel. Why hadn't someone in the stores questioned the huge number of chairs that were being delivered to the H Block? It was only when a vigilant dog handler noticed a disturbance in the ground near the exterior wall of the prison and raised the alarm that the tunnel was discovered. In the earlier days of Maze Compound a spotter plane would have been flying low over the prison taking pictures of the ground to identify tunnels. This practice must have ended following the prisoners' relocation to the H Blocks on the assumption that tunnelling out of an H Block was impossible. It was like a scene from *The Great Escape*!

The two prisoners then left the room. That bloody numb feeling again. The stress. Would I ever get through a single year, even a month, without it? At that moment I would have settled for a week. How was I going to break this latest twist to my wife over dinner tonight? I need not have worried about that: I didn't leave the block until after ten that night.

The search was going well and I was fairly relaxed as I could not see any reason to call in the IRF. Then the proverbial hit the fan. A prisoner in B Wing was refusing a full search.

A full search is undertaken by two search officers in a prisoner's cell. The prisoner would first remove his clothing above the waist—shirt, jumper, whatever—then raise his arms and turn around to demonstrate that he had nothing concealed on his person. One of the staff would check the shirt. The prisoner would then put his shirt back on and remove his lower garments. Finally he would be required to lower and shake out his underpants. Every attempt would be made to preserve his dignity during the search.

I had no choice but to call in the IRF. As I made the call the PIRA prisoner's words filled my mind: 'You will be held responsible.' I knew exactly how serious this threat was and exactly what it meant. I called the Command Suite to inform them what had happened and the decision that I had made.

The wings were located in the 'legs' of the H, so the prisoners could see from their cell windows the IRF enter the yard and head towards the block. The prisoners in the block went berserk, banging on their doors and yelling at the tops of their voices. 'Great!' I said sarcastically to myself.

When the IRF got to the block the senior officer in charge came to my office to meet myself and the principal officer in charge of the search. The PO gave us his assessment. 'I think that the PIRA have one prisoner in each of the three remaining wings who they've ordered not to comply with the search. What the idea behind this is I'm not sure. Perhaps something to do with prisoners' morale. And the IRF coming in gives them all a focus again.'

I agreed with his assessment and instructed the IRF senior officer to carry on and search any prisoner who refused to comply. I also accepted that this meant that the remainder of the search would take five times longer to complete.

The abuse went unabated for the remainder of the evening and by ten o'clock, with the search of two of the wings complete, I was told by the Command Suite to call it a day and finish the job tomorrow. I did not think the last part of the instruction applied to me. After all, in each of the other blocks that was being searched, a different governor was required to cover each day.

I was the last to leave the block, along with the Security principal officer, an individual who would play a crucial part in a major drama that was to come in the year ahead, a situation that would change at least two people's lives for ever. He suggested to me that as soon as we went out of the front door of the block we should look straight ahead and walk quickly down the yard to get clear of the block as fast as possible. I knew exactly why.

The night guard officer opened the door of the block and we stepped out into the night air. Looking back, I'm reminded of the film *Butch Cassidy and the Sundance Kid*, the scene where they open the door, make a dash for it and run straight into the Mexican ambush.

The abuse from both sides of the H Block was unimaginable. I was more focused on getting to the gate, a walk of some hundred and fifty yards, than trying to make out the abuse that was raining down on us. Certainly I heard my name and a mass of profanities and threats. We made it out of the gate and as we headed towards the Admin building the shouts died into the distance.

My old friend fear had returned now, complemented, as always, by stress, but this time the stress had reached a level that was pushing me closer to the edge of reason. Such a mixture. The PIRA's threatening words at the forefront of my mind; the LVF's threat on my life; my wife's warning about bringing more trouble to our door. I felt as if my head was going to explode.

I headed up to the Command Suite, but it was locked. Everyone had gone home. Thankfully my wife knew the search was going on and did not expect me home until late anyway. I decided not to mention anything significant about the day's events, thinking that what she doesn't know won't hurt her. How misguided I was.

I was exhausted by the time I fell into bed. I hadn't been able to eat and once in bed found my sleep was continually interrupted by a mixture of dreams. Billy Wright and the two PIRA prisoners had starring roles.

I was quite subdued over breakfast and passed it off to my family as tiredness. Off to work, thanking God that at least my turn was over with regard to the search. Wrong again. The No 1 had left a message for me at the gate to go straight to the Command Suite. A debrief after yesterday, I presumed. Wrong again.

'Billy, I need you to continue with the search in H Block 4 today,' he said.

'But, Governor,' I protested, 'I did H4 yesterday. Everyone else is in charge of the block for one day, so how come I'm doing two days? Besides, I'm not a residential governor.'

The governor was furious. 'Are you refusing?' he shouted.

I realised that I had overstepped the mark.

'Of course not, Governor, I'm on my way!' I said as I hastily left the room. That was so unlike me, I thought. I don't challenge orders. It must be down to the stress.

I headed on towards H Block 4 lost in my own thoughts. For probably the first time in my twenty years of service I was disillusioned with my job.

I was brought back to reality by a strange sound as I neared the link gates. 'What is it?' I asked the officer on the gate as he let me pass through.

'They're on the doors, Governor,' came the matter-of-fact reply. ('On the doors' was shorthand for disgruntled inmates banging on their cell doors. Another regular feature of life in the Maze Prison.)

I hurried on to the H Block, wondering why the block was still locked down at almost eight-thirty in the morning. As I neared the block the noise got louder and louder. Can you imagine the sound of a hundred irate prisoners banging on their cell doors?

The fear and stress from yesterday had still not left my body, but here I was getting it topped up again and it not yet nine o'clock the following morning. For the first time I started reluctantly to accept that the job was having a massive detrimental effect on both my mental and physical health.

I entered the block and was met by a collection of very frightened staff. 'Where is the principal officer?' I barked. The ashen-faced PO came out of his office into mine. I closed the door and asked him why the hell the prisoners were still locked.

'They're going mad, Governor, it's not safe to unlock!'

I could see that he had lost his nerve and there was little point in me chastising him at this point. There would be time enough for that later.

'Look, Principal, the reason they're on the doors is because we should have unlocked them half an hour ago,' I explained. 'Well, the staff won't unlock them now, Governor, they are genuinely frightened.'

I knew that I had to act quickly to defuse this dangerous situation.

'Okay, get on the telephone to the Command Suite. Tell them the situation and that I am going down to unlock one of the PIRA prisoners. Get me a set of cell keys, now!' I ordered.

A set of cell keys was thrust into my hand and the officer on the grille into A and B Wings let me pass. He was pale and clearly not impressed at finding found himself closest to the terrible racket that was pouring out of the wings. I moved down to the end of the leg and turned right into B Wing. I checked the cell cards as I moved quickly down the wing, looking for the name of one of the prisoners who had threatened me yesterday. Being so close to the racket of the cell door banging was unnerving, to say the least, but I had to take immediate action to prevent the H Block accommodation being completely destroyed.

Finally I came to the cell I was looking for and shouted through to the prisoner that it was Governor McKee and I needed to unlock him to talk. Without even waiting for a reply I quickly opened his cell door.

The prisoner came out of his cell like a greyhound hurtling out of the traps. He was already shouting and pointing at me.

'You were warned yesterday. You're a dead man walking. Whether it happens to you this year or next, you'll know why, when it does!'

'That's okay,' I said. (What a stupid thing to say—it was far from okay!) 'You and I both want this search finished today. Your men need to be showered and fed but before we do anything I need you to guarantee the safety of my staff.'

'Your staff's safety is guaranteed,' he said a little more calmly, waving his hand in a dismissive fashion.

'I also need your men off the doors,' I shouted over the noise.

The prisoner turned away from me and shouted out something in Irish. The same words were passed around the block prisoner to prisoner, cell to cell, wing to wing; and within minutes the block had gone deathly quiet. I then secured the prisoner in his cell and headed out to the 'circle', or the central area of the H Block. I entered the circle and the staff were all looking at me anxiously.

'Okay, lads, that's us ready to go,' I explained. 'Your safety is guaranteed but we need to get the search finished today. The prisoners need to be unlocked in a controlled manner, showered and fed, as quick as you can before they go back on the bloody doors again.'

I could see the relief in the officers' eyes, yet the fear was still there as well. Was there ever a time lately when that fear was not present? As they drew their keys I headed into the block governor's office.

I closed the door and collapsed into the chair, feeling more like a puppet that just had its strings cut than a member of the senior management team of the most infamous prison in the Western world. This was a prison that at times had filled the headlines with the likes of the 'dirty protest', 'the escape' and of course the 'hunger strike'. I reckoned we were right up there with Alcatraz or Colditz in terms of notoriety. My shirt was saturated and I was shaking. The principal officer was keeping out of my way and the rest of the staff were busy with the unlock, so thankfully no one saw me in the dreadful state I was now in.

The search continued quite slowly for the rest of the day and as it drew towards five o'clock I knew that we wouldn't complete the final wing until the next day. I spoke to the No 1 and he advised me to stand down the search when the current wing was finished. The staff were exhausted. From the time the tunnel was discovered they had been required to work twelve hours or more a day. Tired men, through no fault of their own, do not search effectively.

I left the block as soon as the staff had secured the prisoners for the night and headed up to the Command Suite. Surprise, surprise, this time there were actually other governors still there. I slipped into a seat in the corner, listening to the conversations taking place around the table. I half-expected the governor to say something resembling thanks, but no. I was emotionally drained and physically exhausted, not just because of the last couple of days: the past few months had taken their toll on me too.

I was just about to leave the room when the No 1 addressed me. 'Billy, if you head down to H4 first thing in the morning and we'll get the search wrapped up tomorrow.'

My tiredness, combined with the fear and stress of the past months, caught up with me. I stopped and turned to look round the room. 'I won't even be here tomorrow, Governor!' And with that I left the suite. The silence, as they say, was deafening.

———

Well, back to the present. No more wine tonight. I am duty governor tomorrow. Who would have thought *that* twenty years ago? William McKee in charge of HMP Prison Maze.

Thank God that this year was nearly over. There was not enough left of 1997 for it to get any worse. Wrong again. Tomorrow's date was 27 December 1997. The events that would take place tomorrow would change my life forever.

Chapter 13
Murder in the Maze

The following chapters outline the events as I remember them leading up to and following the death of Billy Wright. The other parties involved in the various conversations that took place both leading up to and around that time may well have a different recollection of these recorded events and conversations.

Well, that's Christmas as far away as ever, I thought as I made my way down the M1 towards Lisburn and the infamous Maze Prison. I was the duty governor today, Saturday 27 December 1997. Throughout my twenty years in the service I had managed to avoid working on Christmas Day, and this year was no different. During my thirteen years working in the administration side of the prison I never had to work bank holidays, but since becoming a governor I was expected to do my fair share. This year, as in previous years, I just got in first and volunteered to work on the day after Boxing Day. This ensured that I would be there as usual on Christmas morning for my three children and have the great pleasure of seeing their faces as they opened their presents.

We always had the same routine at Christmas. Round to my wife's parents on Christmas Eve, leaving and collecting Christmas presents, then a walk around the corner to her aunt's. My wife's aunt's home was always the scene of a Christmas family gathering that I thoroughly enjoyed. Friendly, down-to-earth people who, from the first day I came into their lives, had made me feel more than welcome. I laugh now when I remember the first time I met my wife's aunt. I had been wearing a T-shirt with 'Billy Boot' on the front of it. Jean had thought that that was my real name. I really liked Jean. We stayed at the party until nearly eleven and then headed home. Then, of course, we had to sit up and wait until the kids were fast asleep before sneaking up to the roof space to bring down the presents. I remember one night, or should I say morning, finishing putting the children's bicycles together at half past three and then getting up four hours later to see the absolute delight on their faces as they surveyed their respective chairs covered with presents.

We didn't allow the children downstairs until everyone was ready. They were led into the drawing room with their eyes closed and left facing their chairs where the presents were arranged. On the count of three they opened their eyes and just stared, feasting on the pile of gifts and surprises that lay before them, before diving in and ripping asunder the wrapping paper.

I realise now that I didn't appreciate and treasure those moments as much as I should have. But then they do say that you only really miss things when they are gone, and I was to discover how true that saying was over the months and years that followed. I could not have imagined that the chain of events that was to begin today would destroy and take from me all that I held dear.

So here I am again, driving in through the gate of Long Kesh. Well, that was one name for it. Back in the 1970s when the first of the new H Blocks was being built the prison was known by many names: the Cages, Maze Compound, the Kesh, Silver City, and many more.

I had been briefed by Deputy Governor Crompton before the Christmas break. These briefings took the form of a fairly informal chat between the deputy and whatever governor was detailed in charge of the Maze for the weekend. the instructions were almost always the same. 'Keep an eye on the Visits. Do your best to keep them running smoothly. If the prison is short of officers, stand down the Towers with the exception of H Block 6. Any complaints from the POA [Prison Officers' Association], tell them you are following my instructions.' And of course the add-on, which we were all well aware of: 'the number of staff on sick leave is over a hundred so the staffing situation will be tight. So do your best with what you've got.'

What happened later that day made the instructions issued to me by Governor Crompton particularly significant: 'Stand down the Towers with the exception of H6.'

I parked up in my designated car space, one of the few perks the governor grade still enjoyed, and which was particularly useful on a teeming wet day as it was only a hundred yards from the main gate of the prison. As I made my way through the prison—being searched, having my training bag scanned, having my ID checked—my mind drifted to the day ahead, and the kind of decisions that I might or might not be have to make.

I always made a point of checking which lower ranked governors were detailed with me at the weekend. I always liked to be prepared. Whether or nor we had a smooth weekend sometimes depended on who was paired with me. Most of the governors were good people to have with you but, as in all walks of life, there was the odd bad apple. At that time in my career I was an acting governor four filling a vacancy created by the redeployment of my boss from Inmate Services to Works. As I had been one of her governors in Inmate Services the governor nominated me to act up when she moved. I had been successful on the recent promotion board but as yet had not received a posting.

My two colleagues on the day were an ex-chief officer, now a governor five following the amalgamation of the chief officer rank with the newly created governor five rank, and an acting governor who was formally the Security principal officer. The chief officer was a uniformed grade, his uniform complemented by braid on the hat and a Sam Browne belt. The uniform meant authority, and the chiefs always gave me the impression that they were really the ones in charge of the jail. They carried the same kind of authority as a matron in a hospital. When the post of matron was removed from hospitals, standards of cleanliness dropped noticeably, and the job has now been reinstated in the management function: similarly, there was a fall in standards in the Prison Service when the chief's role was removed. This caused a vacuum in the service: neither principal officers nor governors took over their role. In the past, the very words 'the chief is doing his rounds' had everyone on their toes. Newspapers and books were hidden, ties were adjusted, caps were put on and the place tidied up. I firmly believe that it was a political decision to remove not just the rank but the uniform as well in order, for some misguided reason, to reduce the authority of the chief officer rank. I also believe that there was an underlying jealousy on the part of some people in governor grades, who would have given anything to have the staff respect them as much as the chiefs.

I have no doubt this particular individual was an effective chief officer, though I had few dealings with him when he fulfilled that role. I'm sure his efficient manner had the desired effect of keeping staff on their toes. My feeling is that he still saw himself in his previous role and his new responsibilities did not always sit comfortably with him.

Brian Barlow was a different kettle of fish. He was regarded as a very valued member of the management team and the fact that he was the principal officer in charge of the Security department in the Maze Prison spoke volumes. My promotion through the ranks had been quick and as a result there was understandable resentment in certain quarters. There were staff who had been in the job many years before me who felt they had been overlooked in favour of me. Was Brian Barlow one of them? Perhaps.

I base this assessment on my first night as duty governor in charge of HMP Maze. There was an incident in one of the H Blocks and I had to make a decision on how best to resolve it. Brian Barlow came to brief me on the incident. The details are insignificant—I cannot recall what the problem actually was. However, the man who was briefing me, a man with many years' experience, a man who should have been advising an inexperienced duty governor of the steps that would normally be taken in an incident such as this, simply said, 'so it's over to you, Governor'. I never forgot that moment, even though I had enough confidence in my own ability to make the appropriate decision, and never shied away from making decisions. I always remembered a piece of advice given to me by Dessie Stewart during my training in 1977. He said, 'Young McKee, the job is easy! Just apply common sense to your decision making and believe me you will get more right than you will wrong.' Twenty years later I was still heeding Dessie's advice.

I headed up to the Command Suite in the main Administration building. It was about ten to nine. I knew that Joe Helm was detailed for an eight o'clock start so he would have been in the prison for the numbers being returned and also to give his permission to go ahead with the unlock. (When staff came on duty in the morning, before the night guard staff were allowed to leave, the prisoners had to be counted first by the night guard and then by the officer who was relieving them. These numbers were returned to a central location where they were added together to ensure they matched the number of prisoners we were supposed to be holding.)

On that particular day the numbers had been returned correct so the governor had given permission to unlock (allowing the prisoners out of the wings into the 'circle'), the night guard staff had headed home to bed, and the prison day was under way. The staff would not have to unlock the prisoners' cells as they were now on twenty-four-hour unlock. A prison where the prisoners were not locked up at night, a prison where the Prison Rules may as well have been torn up, a prison that probably held more murderers than any other prison in Europe, and we did not lock them up at night. But then this was the Maze.

Breakfast would already have been left into each of the respective blocks, carried into the prison wings by the orderlies, and the prisoners would be getting ready for their visits. Saturday was the busiest day of the week for visits, with working mothers and girlfriends taking advantage of their day off to come to the prison to see their fathers, uncles, boyfriends or brothers.

I was relaxed. I headed up to my office on the top floor of the Administration building to catch up on some paperwork and was joined by acting governor Barlow. We chatted, partly about prison matters, then moved on to other idle conversation. We were actually just killing time until the duty principal officer had calculated how many staff we were short, where we were short and, most important, which staff we could move to fill the more important posts. This process was normally sorted by around ten past nine. The duty principal officer that day was a man with enough common sense and experience to carry out his role with the minimum of fuss.

He came to my office about ten past nine, as expected, and after the usual formalities began to brief us on the staffing situation. I was seated behind my desk and Brian Barlow was standing to my left. The duty principal officer explained, 'That's the prison up and running, Governor, I have done all I can but the Visits are still eight men short.' As I was the governor in charge of Visits I knew more than most the massive impact being short staffed could have in that area. But this was nothing new. The Prison Service worked a one weekend on, one weekend off staff detail system, but if sick numbers were particularly high at the weekend it made the system harder to manage. This was one of these weekends. I never understood why the numbers of staff standing in for people on long-term sick leave were not balanced over the two weekends so that instead of having one 'tight' weekend and one fully staffed weekend there could have been two reasonable weekends.

I could spend half this book questioning decisions and procedures that did not appear to make any sense. Perhaps the Maze and its prisoners were only another pawn in the political game that was being played long before I even thought of joining the Prison Service and that at that stage looked as if it would always be played.

The duty principal officer had a list of diminishing task lines agreed between the governor and the POA and he had the governor's authority to apply those that meant he could stand down certain posts and move staff to more important posts. By the time he had spoken to me he had already carried out that task. Now I had to issue the instructions that every governor in charge issued every Saturday when there was a staff shortfall; which of course meant every Saturday.

'Stand down the Towers but leave H6,' I instructed. He acknowledged my instructions and left the room.

Brian and I chatted for a little longer, then he went over to the Security Office, where he said he would be based if I needed him.

I assumed that the other governor would be in the kitchen sampling the prisoners' breakfast. This was part of his role as duty governor: a governor would sample each of the three meals on the prisoners' menu and record his comments in the kitchen log. That governor would meet Brian later in the morning and divide the prison in half, deciding and agreeing which sections each would visit. As the governor in charge of the prison I was required to stay in the Administration building just in case of an incident.

Around nine thirty John Blundell, a POA committee member, burst into my office. I could tell he was greatly annoyed about something. Before I could speak he launched into a tirade. 'You can't stand down H6!' he shouted. For a second I didn't know what he was talking about. Then it dawned on me. 'You mean the Tower at H6?' I responded.

'Yes, Governor: we have an agreement with the governor that that Tower is not allowed to be touched as the H Block houses two opposing factions,' he said, still shouting.

'John,' I said. 'I did not give any instructions to anyone to stand down H6 Tower and if H6 Tower is stood down get it manned again right away'.

John simply said, 'That's fine, Governor.' He left my office about four minutes after he came in. I made a mental note to speak to the governor covering H6 to find out how the Tower or Towers came to be stood down.

Just before ten o'clock the general alarm sounded and I was just about to head to the Command Suite when the telephone on my desk rang. I picked it up. I knew beyond doubt that the call had been triggered by the alarm being hit.

'Governor, there is an incident at H6,' the senior officer from the Control Room said. 'A shooting, but no further details at the moment.'

A shooting? Shit!

I was experienced enough to know that the last thing the senior officer needed was a dozen questions from me. He had a prepared and approved list of duties to carry out in the event of any emergency. He and his staff would be going down the list that was posted on the wall, positioned so that everyone could see it by just lifting their heads. As each task was completed a bulb would light up beside the task so that staff did not need to ask each other whether things had been done. It also meant that if I or any other governor came into the Control Room we could see at a glance where we were with regard to the task list.

I went to the Command Suite. When I arrived an officer was already writing various pieces of information on the whiteboard, detailing the time, the information and the source and location of the messages he was receiving.

This was all normal. Everything was extremely well organised, from the Command Suite room itself to the staff, who were trained to know just what to do when the alarm was sounded. I knew exactly what the senior officer in the Control Room was doing and was confident that when he had exhausted his list of tasks he would contact me again, to bring me up to speed and also to ask for any further instructions from me.

My radio crackled into life. It was acting governor Barlow calling to inform me that he was heading down to H Block 6 to get a first-hand view of the incident. I advised the log keeper of the conversation in case he had missed any of it, but as the radio system was on talk-through he had heard the full conversation.

The telephone beside me rang. It was the senior officer from the Control Room informing me that he had executed the approved task list. I knew from the log in the Command Suite everything that the senior officer knew—one of his colleagues was calling through at regular intervals, which allowed the log keeper to keep us all up to date without anyone having to stall the process by asking questions.

As I looked at the log I began to assess the various pieces of information in it, making decisions so that I was prepared to advise the senior officer of my instructions when his call eventually came through.

Another part of me, however, could not come to terms with what I was reading. 'Shooting in the air lock out of H6. Billy Wright believed to be mortally wounded. Two INLA prisoners believed to have come over the fence from their side of the H Block, opened the door of the van and shot Billy Wright. No other injuries or fatalities.'

As a matter of course the area around H Block 6 had been sealed. No one was allowed in or out without my permission, which would be relayed through the Control Room. The gates in and out of the H Block were now being electronically operated by the Control Room staff. All movement in and out of the prison and within the prison had also been stopped. Now it was time for me to earn my salary.

When an incident happens in any prison the rules state that the incident should be contained and the remainder of the prison brought back to normal as soon as possible. Once I was convinced that the incident was confined to one area of the prison I advised the senior officer to return the rest of the prison to normal. Doing this reduced the chances of pressure building elsewhere, which could have resulted in a second incident.

I knew that the police, the army and the coroner would already have been informed of events by the senior officer in the Control Room and that, following my instructions, the rest of the prison would be operating as normal.

The telephone beside me rang again. It was the other governor. 'Yes?' I said.

'I heard what's happened! What do you want me to do?' he asked.

'Okay,' I instructed, 'I want you to go to the LVF Visits in the prison hospital. Let them know there has been an incident at H6 and until it is resolved their visits have been suspended. Under no circumstances mention there has been a shooting. I also want you to get Billy Wright's visitors out of the Visits and take them to one of the spare rooms in the prison hospital. Once you have them isolated from the rest of the LVF and their visitors, explain that Billy Wright has been shot but that is all you know at present. Please remain with the visitors until I contact you again.'

I then rang the senior officer in the Control Room and instructed him to inform the visitors' entrance area that no further LVF or INLA visits would be taking place today due to the incident in H Block 6. If the visitors were going to create a fuss I would prefer it to be outside the prison wall.

More information was now coming in. Brian Barlow had performed a very courageous act. He knew that there was at least one gun, perhaps two, in the INLA side of the H Block. To get into the H Block he had to pass by one side of their wing. He could easily have been shot from the window as he walked towards the main door of the H Block. I had given my permission to allow him to enter the block and he had made his way into the 'bar' of the H where the staff and management were located.

(The H Block was divided into four wings, each wing holding twenty-five prisoners. These wings were located in the legs of the 'H'.)

I waited for Brian's call but I knew he would not come back to me until he had exhausted all his inquiries. As I waited, I thought about the standing down of the Tower in H6.

Thank God I had advised John Blundell at nine thirty to ensure that the Tower was not stood down. I could imagine the repercussions if the Tower was unmanned and prisoners came over the wire fence beside it. I gave the matter little thought after that, accepting that half an hour was more than ample time to have the officer detailed back to the Tower—if, indeed, he had left his post.

The telephone rang again. 'Brian here, Governor.' He quickly apprised me of the situation.

'Governor, apparently three INLA prisoners came over or through the fence while the van taking LVF prisoners, one of whom was Billy Wright, was in the air lock waiting to exit H6. They got the back of the van open and fired. At this stage it is believed that Billy Wright was the intended target. The LVF know Billy Wright is shot as they had a view of the yard from their side of the H Block and they're going berserk. And finally, Billy Wright is dead.'

'Okay, Brian, stay put and I'll get back to you,' I said, and hung up.

I accepted Brian's word that Billy Wright was dead but also realised that we could not confirm it officially until after the coroner had examined the body. By this time Governor Maguire, third in charge of the prison, had arrived, and, as he was senior to me, he took over the management of the incident. Governor Maguire knew that he had to give priority to getting the gun or guns out of the INLA wing. Almost immediately the name of the person who he knew would come to our aid sprang into Pat's mind. Father Murphy. The Control Room staff got Father Murphy on the telephone for me.

'John, good morning,' Pat started. 'Can you please make your way to the Maze at your earliest possible convenience? We've had a very serious incident and your help at this time would be very much appreciated.'

'Give me half an hour, Governor,' he said, and hung up. John had been involved with the Maze long enough to know that any questions he had would be answered when he arrived at the prison. He was as good as his word and arrived in the prison twenty minutes after receiving Pat's call. Pat quickly briefed him about the incident and explained that we believed there were one or more guns in the INLA wing.

I had already informed Brian Barlow, who was in H Block 6, that Father Murphy was willing to come into the prison to see if he could help us. Brian had already made contact with the prisoners and had advised them that we needed the gun or guns out, otherwise nothing and no one would go in or out of the wing.

The INLA told him that they were sending the guns out. Collecting the weapons was the job that we had envisaged Father Murphy carrying out for us. We knew, and Father Murphy knew, that he would not be at risk from the prisoners.

Father Murphy headed to the block and met Brian Barlow, who explained that he needed the prisoners to break up the gun or guns, put them in a box, along with any remaining bullets, and pass them to Father Murphy. Father Murphy readily agreed. Securing the gun and bullets in a box meant that any fingerprints would not be obliterated or smudged by Father Murphy's.

Pat suspected that there would be both an official and a public outcry about weapons having been smuggled into the prison, but that this had happened would not have surprised many of the members of staff and management. After all, the perpetrators of the murder of Billy Wright had already had two other weapons smuggled in for their use at HMP Maghaberry during the previous twelve months.

This was the Maze. A search of the prison in 1995 had yielded eleven mobile phones along with over £100 in cash. In 1995, mobile phones, unlike the pencil-thin varieties that are available today, were the size of bricks and, similarly, weapons could not be dismantled and smuggled into the prison in pieces. It is unlikely that they were smuggled in internally, and if management had known how they and other larger items were getting into the jail appropriate measures would have been introduced to end the practice. Staff also suspected that prisoners returning from home leave smuggled in contraband secreted internally and the searching regulations in force at the time forbade the prison authorities from carrying out internal searches. Metal detectors used during the searching of the prisoners did not register any of the secreted items and therefore the prison authorities' hands were tied. One prisoner was given the nickname 'the suitcase' by the other prisoners, such was his capacity to smuggle internally concealed illegal items into the jail.

As John Murphy made his way to H6, Pat turned to me looking for reassurance that the prisoners' telephones had been turned off in the prison. Was I struck dumb? I couldn't speak! I hadn't: it had never occurred to me. I hadn't thought of it, and obviously no one else had, as no one had brought it to my attention. Pat didn't have to ask again—he knew from my expression. He immediately phoned the Control Room to tell them to kill the inmates' phones. I apologised and we moved on.

Mistake number two was waiting just around the corner. I assumed that Billy Wright's girlfriend was his next of kin, but what I should have done was to get someone to check his file. (In the event of a prisoner's death the next of kin identified in his file is the person who is informed first.) Billy Wright's nominated next of kin was his father, David Wright. Because the phones had not being secured the media quickly got hold of the 'Murder in the Maze' story and David Wright found out about his son's death a short time later.

The rest of the day was taken up by the clean-up operation.

The forensic teams arrived, secured the van and removed the weapons, and the prison returned to normal, or as normal as could be expected, bearing in mind that a prisoner had been murdered by another prisoner and we had been unable to prevent it.

Brian Barlow and the other duty governor had been excellent in the way they had handled themselves and had dealt with the difficulties they had faced that day. I was disappointed by the two mistakes that I had made, though I knew I would get over it. I did not imagine that some ten years later Billy Wright's murder in the Maze would still be impacting on my life.

Chapter 14
Dealing with the Aftershock

The fallout from the shooting of Billy Wright was frightening. The media coverage was non-stop. Everyone seemed to have an opinion. The RUC were on high alert—it was a near certainty that there would be tit-for-tat shootings in the nationalist communities by Billy Wright's cronies seeking revenge for their leader's murder. Police surveillance of Catholic-owned bars had been intensified amid fears of retaliatory strikes by loyalists who had vowed to take revenge for Wright's death.

One man who was murdered at the time was Coalisland man Seamus Dillon, who was working as a doorman at the Glengannon Hotel in Dungannon when he was gunned down: over twenty bullets were fired at him. Another man and a fourteen-year-old boy were also injured in the attack. No one was ever charged with the murder, but since it took place on 27 December 1997 it was suspected that the responsibility lay with Billy Wright's followers.

The murder marked a volatile time in the peace process and there were genuine fears that the ceasefire might not hold.

In the days after Mr Dillon's death, politicians, clergymen and Mr Dillon's family pleaded that there should be no retaliation.

At the time of the murder of Billy Wright we were still living in the house we rented in Glengormley after our evacuation from our home outside Templepatrick following the LVF and PIRA death threats. We lived there while we were waiting for our new house on the outskirts of Belfast to be built. I arrived home just after six, having left Pat Maguire and Martin Mogg to deal with the fallout from the shooting.

My son had heard the news and although he knew I worked in the Maze he hadn't realised that I had been in charge of the prison that day. My wife knew the true position, naturally enough, and her state of mind, after all we had been through the previous year, is easy to imagine.

'Why is it always you?' she asked, not for the first time. 'Do you keep asking for all these high-risk, high-profile jobs? How come there are never any other governors' names mentioned? I can't take much more of this!'

There was nothing I could do, nothing I could say that could make any difference to how she felt.

I turned on the television to catch the six o'clock news. Once again it was Billy Wright, Billy Wright and more Billy Wright. Then an interview with Finlay Spratt, the POA chairman, caught my attention. I couldn't believe what he was saying, words that were being heard in the houses of thousands of people the length and breadth of Northern Ireland.

'These governors,' he began, 'they are always cutting posts in an effort to save money and today we can all see the true price of their cost-cutting efforts. A man lies dead and it is more by good fortune that we have not other fatalities on our hands today.'

He talked on but I had stopped listening.

The standing down of the Tower was attracting attention as a significant reason why the murder had taken place. I just knew, as I reflected on my conversation with the POA's John Blundell earlier that morning, that somehow I was going to be implicated.

'Did you stand the Tower down?' my wife asked.

'Of course I didn't,' I snapped. If she didn't believe me, what chance did I have of others accepting my version of events?

I didn't sleep that night. My mind was turning over the events of the day.

The following morning I was into work first and waited anxiously to find out what was happening. What was being said? What was being alleged? I had met with the other two people who had been present at the time I gave the instructions to stand down the Towers.

The principal officer detail manager (Donald McCallum), Brian Barlow and I had discussed the issue.

'No, Governor, you definitely instructed me to stand down H6 and leave the rest,' began the detail manager.

'No, you're wrong. You told me that we were eight staff short and how would dropping one Tower have helped to solve that problem?' I replied. 'Besides, why would I ask you to stand down a Tower that everyone knows is sacrosanct?'

'Yes, that's right,' Brian interrupted, 'if Billy had said, "Stand down H6", I would have said, "Fuck sake, Billy, you can't touch H6."'

The detail manager, however, was still adamant that his version of events was correct. He refused to accept Brian's or my version of events and has stuck to his story ever since.

I was immensely thankful that I had a witness and was pleased to learn that an English governor, Martin Neary, had been appointed to conduct an inquiry into the murder. Martin Neary had carried out an inquiry into an escape from Parkhurst, where I was seconded during my governor training.

The newspapers were full of every theory under the sun, but every piece of coverage included the claim that 'standing down the Tower by the governor [me, of course] was crucial to the success of the murder attempt'. The comments that Finlay Spratt had made on television had drawn attention to the issue of the Tower, and the media had latched on to it.

The RUC took statements from everyone who could contribute to the police inquiry. Of course I was unaware of the content of the other statements.

Over the coming weeks the prison settled down and some semblance of order was restored.

––––

The children's parties had gone ahead, without the LVF of course, and everything appeared to go as planned. Even Mr Mogg attended and had a go on the children's trampoline. This also found its way into the papers. I am sure that he would have preferred his trampolining to fill the papers for a couple of weeks rather than the headline that actually appeared: 'Escape from Maze'.

The children's parties had gone better than expected and the staff responsible for arranging them were giving themselves a well-deserved pat on the back when the news came through.

It was bad enough that a prisoner had escaped from the Maze but the fact that the prison authorities were still unaware of it until later that evening, when the PIRA informed the governor that they had planned and executed another escape from his prison, was deeply embarrassing.

Liam Averill, a PIRA prisoner, was one of the prisoners who had attended one of the children's parties. When the parties were over the prisoners were required to return to their respective H Blocks where a head count would be carried out.

Unfortunately, when the inmates arrived back at the block where Averill was housed they all rushed through the grilles together and the staff on the grilles committed the cardinal sin: they assumed that all the prisoners had returned.

Averill had dressed as a woman using articles of clothing donated by some of the female visitors. One or more of the women put make-up on him to complete the disguise, and the prisoner slipped on to the bus transporting the visitors back to the car park. The head count of the visitors leaving the prison was obviously incorrect as well.

After the governor was informed of the escape the embarrassment was further compounded by staff having to take a head count of all the prisoners in all the accommodation in the prison so that we could confirm that the information given to us by the PIRA was correct.

I feared for Martin Mogg's future: the murder of Billy Wright, following hot on the heels of the Averill escape, was causing our political masters untold embarrassment. But he seemed to be riding out the storm and the Neary Inquiry was given the additional remit of investigating the murder of Billy Wright as well.

The prison was still on edge following the murder of Billy Wright and there was a genuine fear of reprisals in the prison. The No 1 called a meeting to discuss this potential problem and to seek the views of the prison management staff. The meeting was particularly relevant to me as the only place in the prison where the different factions could and did meet was Visits. The PIRA and the loyalists shared the same toilet on both sides of the Visits block. INLA had already managed to have two guns smuggled into two separate prisons so there was nothing to stop the other factions following suit.

The Visits could therefore provide the opportunity for the loyalists to take out one of the 'opposition' in a revenge killing. I thought this unlikely—all the other factions in the prison, Protestant and nationalist alike, had little or no time for the infamous Billy Wright. The consensus of opinion at the meeting, however, was that any opportunity that could be identified as a possible avenue for another murder should be removed at all costs. This of course meant that the Visits would have to be rearranged in such a way as to keep opposing factions separate from one another.

When I had taken over the responsibility for Visits I had never considered the physical make-up of the Visits blocks. I had inherited the areas from the previous managers and I had seen no need to make changes. The old phrase 'if it ain't broke, don't fix it' came to mind. The rooms on the right-hand side of the Visits block were the biggest and the decision of who should be allocated there was based on numbers. As the PIRA and UDA had the biggest numbers of prisoners in the jail they were given access to the biggest rooms. The other side of the Visits block was used for prisoners from the UDA and PIRA factions, along with the smaller number of UVF prisoners. I could understand the method in this madness: on quiet days during the week the spillover visiting rooms were not used, allowing staff to be deployed to other duties.

In a normal prison, if there was a problem like this the prisoners would be told that their visiting arrangements were being changed, they would be moved and that would be the end of the matter. But this was the Maze and nothing happened without the agreement of the prisoners.

The conversations around the table dragged on for over an hour and they were leading precisely nowhere.

'Governor,' I said.

'Yes, Billy,' came the reply as I got his attention. 'Governor,' I said again, 'why don't we just ask the prisoners to move?'

Laughter filled the room. Everyone was so wound up it probably helped relieve the tension. One of the older governors, Alan McMullan, led the laughter—I should have known. I thought he might have learnt his lesson after the last time he made derogatory comments about my aspirations to solve the budget deficit in Inmates Catering. On that occasion he had suggested two bowls of stew a day as the solution to the problem. He had been wrong then and had only succeeded in providing me with extra motivation to succeed. He could well be committing the same mistake again. Some people never learn.

'Sure, why don't *you* go and ask them, then?' he suggested between bursts of laughter. As before, the other governors were smiling, but this time I knew there were some who shared the older governor's view that my idea was ludicrous. Others, who had respected my problem-solving skills in the past, were smiling because they knew the sort of determination I possessed and that he could well be proved wrong again. I was ignoring him and he knew it.

'Do you think that you could talk them into moving, Billy?' asked the governor.

'I don't know, Governor, but with respect there is nothing I have heard this morning that is offering a solution anyway,' I replied.

'Okay, Billy, give it a go; but, as always, tread carefully,' he warned me.

I had already begun formulating my strategy and decided that it might be easier to switch the spillover of PIRA from the left-hand side to the right-hand side of the Visits block. The other part of the equation was to relocate the loyalists to the left-hand side, filling the space vacated by PIRA.

The theory was fine. Putting it into practice might prove just a little more difficult. I remembered what Ken Crompton had said after my success with Inmates Catering: 'It's better that senior management aren't aware of the methods you used—had we known we might not have approved!' Of course he had been right on that occasion, and here I was again, scheming and stretching the rules: whatever it took to sort the Visits but, most important, to prevent any more 'Murder in Maze' headlines. How I had come to hate those three words.

The UDA inner council at that time included Michael Stone, Skelly McCrory, an inmate called Philpot and a fourth man whose name escapes me. All I remember about him is he ran about the H Block bare-chested, long hair unkempt, and generally leaving a trail of mayhem in his wake.

I decided that Michael Stone, the UFF gunman, was the most likely of the loyalists to listen to my proposals.

I'm often asked what he was really like. Like most people I remember him as a long-haired lunatic running amok in Milltown Cemetery, hurling hand grenades and firing indiscriminately during a republican funeral. He received a severe beating that day at the hands of some of the mourners who captured him after his getaway driver drove off without him. Perhaps as a result of that beating, he is now crippled with arthritis and on occasions confined to a wheelchair. I once spoke to Michael about that incident, and he admits that he underestimated the response of the mourners at the funeral. He fully expected them all to run for cover once the first shots were fired and grenades thrown. The fact that many of the mourners put their fears for their personal safety to one side and chased and captured him, I believe, earned them Stone's admiration. He would not, of course, openly admit any admiration for his sworn enemy, but there was something in the way he told the story that gave me that impression.

Michael also told the story of going to Londonderry to assassinate Martin McGuinness but refusing to carry out the murder because when the now Deputy First Minister left his home he had his small daughter by the hand. I think Michael used this tale to demonstrate that although involved in a 'war' he did have some scruples.

I was surprised when Michael Stone appeared in the headlines again after allegedly attempting to murder or cause explosions at Stormont. He knew, I am sure, that this was an ill-conceived plot and that the only possible outcome was a trip back to prison—not the Maze, of course, but Maghaberry—and that his life sentence licence would almost certainly be revoked, which meant he would remain in prison for many, many years to come. There is, as usual, much speculation as to the real reason behind Michael's actions. Many people seem to agree that he wanted to return to custody. But why? Protective custody, perhaps? Access to expensive drugs for his arthritis? Publicity? Only one man can provide the answer, but whether he will ever share it with any of us is quite another matter.

———

I had established a fair bit of credibility with Michael Stone a year earlier during and after a rooftop protest by the UDA/UFF prisoners in one of the loyalist H Blocks at the Maze. I can't recall exactly what they were protesting about: there were so many protests and they happened so often that they were almost routine.

At the time of the protest I was still involved in Inmate Services and I was surprised to be selected as a negotiator to attempt to talk Michael Stone and the ninety or so other inmates off the roof and back into their cells. I was surprised on two counts: first, I had not attended any negotiating training courses; and second, as with the tunnel and the LVF wreck-up, the blocks were nothing to do with me. But my prison bosses had complimented me on my ability to talk to the prisoners in such a way as not to make matters worse and bring confrontations to a satisfactory conclusion without bloodshed. Sometimes I enjoyed the plaudits; but at other times I just wished they would pick someone else!

On this occasion the negotiating team was made up of two governors. I was joined by one of the former senior officers from Visits, who I had always believed would reach the governor grade. He was almost there, having been selected to fill a vacancy in the governor five grade. We were set up in the back of a van on the outside of the wall separating us from the rooftop protest. One of the governors from Research and Development had bravely approached the block and put in a telephone line, which allowed the prisoners to have direct contact with the negotiators. The protest ran into the next day, with constant conversations between us in the back of the van and the prisoners in the block. My colleague and I were working split shifts as it was too much to ask both of us to be there day and night.

When a protest begins, whether or not it involves a hostage, the procedure followed is standard practice all over the world. The services to the area are turned off so that the protesters are denied the creature comforts of heat, light and water. This is carried out in an attempt to unsettle those involved and damage their collective morale if at all possible. It also leaves the door open for give and take between the negotiator and the perpetrators.

This particular protest demonstrated that solving one problem can exacerbate a different one. The new procedure, to which I had agreed, of allowing the prisoners to stockpile food had helped solve the catering problem, but the stockpiled food was a factor that prevented the swift conclusion of this latest protest.

We discovered how easy it is for a negotiator to become selfish when dealing with a crisis. It becomes 'one's own' protest, and the feeling of wanting to be the one to end it grows more intense the longer the negotiations continue. If we had been trained appropriately I am sure we would have been made aware of this tendency and advised how to control it.

By the second day the other acting governor and I felt the end was in sight. Michael Stone was doing most of the talking, but that was typical of him.

It was time for the changeover between the negotiators and I was due to take over the talking. I recognised my colleague's reluctance to leave me to it. He felt it. I felt it. He didn't want to hand over the reins: I was desperate to grab them. We had agreed that all our talking over the past thirty-six hours was close to paying dividends.

The radio—our link to the Command Suite—crackled into life. The message was simple. 'Governor McKee, please relieve your colleague and send him home to bed.' My colleague's look of despondency was immense. I couldn't offer sympathy—I didn't have any. It was my turn, my protest and I was going to bring the drama of the last couple of days to an end.

Although the end was in sight the minutes grew into hours and I started to become prey to negative thoughts that my colleague could yet have the final say. Now I had to be careful. I was torn between winning my negotiations and pushing so hard that I ended up making the situation worse and prolonging the protest. Two further issues could then easily present themselves. The other two loyalist blocks could lend their support to the protest and there could be three rooftop protests to deal with. Or the governor in the Command Suite might feel I was pushing too hard or being stonewalled by Stone, which meant I would be replaced with a fresh face. No ifs, buts or maybes: the order to stand down would be given and that would be that.

I forced myself to relax. It took another hour to end the protest and the feeling of punching-the-air elation was quickly replaced by the realisation that although the prisoners were now off the roof there was still the small matter of getting one hundred terrorists back under lock and key so that the fabric of the interior of the block could be checked. Well, someone else can do that, I thought as I confirmed to the Command Suite that the protest was over and that Michael Stone had given his guarantee that the UFF/UDA would discuss their problems with management in an attempt to resolve them by peaceful means.

Just as I was about to leave the cramped back of the vehicle to stretch my legs, Michael Stone was back on the field telephone, just to inform me that his men were going back on the roof to clear the debris and collect whatever of their possessions remained there. I asked Michael to give me a few moments to inform the Command Suite so that they didn't go into a panic when they saw prisoners returning to the roof.

In the service decisions are sometimes taken that defy logic. The answer I now got to a question that I hadn't asked was one of them.

'Don't give them permission to return to the roof!'

'What?' I hadn't asked for permission for the inmates to go back on the roof, I had just told the Command Suite, for their information, why the inmates were going back to the roof.

Whether it was the build-up of pressure over the past forty hours I don't know, but I exploded down the radio.

'Don't let them back on the roof? Jesus Christ, the whole bloody block will be back on the roof if I try to deny access to one or two of them. Wise up!' Silence.

I picked up the field telephone and spoke to Michael.

'Go for it, Michael, but do me a favour; no more than three, please, or you'll give somebody a bit higher up the ladder than me a bloody heart attack if they see more than three of you going back on the roof.'

Michael laughed. 'Got that, Governor, thanks!'

I went back on the radio. 'I've given Michael Stone permission to allow three prisoners on the roof to clear the debris and to bring all their personal possessions down. Besides, it will save us the trouble.'

'Message received,' came the reply.

I climbed out of the van, stretched my legs and glanced around the corner to get a view of the H Block. Sure enough, Michael had been as good as his word and three prisoners were clearing the roof.

I was joined a little later by two of the senior management team who had arrived to discuss the final push to return the block to normal. God, what *was* normal in the Maze Prison? I had given up trying to answer that question long ago.

Before the protest the prisoners had warned the staff what was going to happen and the decision had been taken to evacuate the block. We didn't want a hostage situation to deal with as well as the protest. The problem now was that there were a hundred terrorists running wild inside the H Block, all high on the euphoria of what they felt had been a successful protest.

There was no chance that the staff would return to the block while the prisoners remained unlocked. Why did I have that unpleasant feeling in the pit of my stomach again? There were three of us involved in the discussion and I knew that neither of the others, just like the prison officers, had any intention of entering the block. That, of course, left me!

Shit, I thought, my wife's right. Why is it always me?

I entered the H Block, allowed through the small wicker gate by the one remaining officer still on duty from the H Block staff. 'Good luck, Governor,' he said as I passed through.

What am I letting myself in for now? I wondered as I almost strolled up the yard to whatever was waiting for me on the other side of the open door to the block.

The silence was ghostly as I entered the circle using the keys I had been issued with before I set off on this ridiculous journey. I didn't even have a radio with me because the boss was concerned that it could fall into the hands of the prisoners and they could block the network or listen in to the communications between staff.

There was still not a sound as I turned left to walk towards A and B Wings.

Still the silence. I felt quite spooked by it. I hadn't known what to expect, but silence was definitely not something I had contemplated.

'Hello!' I shouted. My own voice echoed back. 'Hello!' I shouted again, raising my voice a little.

I turned down the wing and as I turned the corner the dining room grille opened, which made me jump. Michael Stone came out of the dining room and I was relieved when he gently closed the grille behind him. It had been a few years since I had been surrounded by paramilitary prisoners firing questions at me and I had lost some of my appetite for that.

Michael approached me. 'Where are the staff, Governor? I can guarantee their safety and to be honest the lads want some grub.'

So they hadn't even bothered to open the tins that were stockpiled, but maybe peas, carrots or baked beans are not that appetising without something else to go with them.

'Look, Michael, the staff won't come anywhere near the block unless you and your men are locked in your cells,' I explained.

Michael started to laugh. 'We can all return to our cells if you want but we have all the locks fucked. So what do you want to do now?'

Great! I was going to have to think about that one.

'Okay, Michael. Please tell all your men that I need them back in their cells to start with. While you're doing that I'll check with the kitchen to make sure that your lunch is being prepared and I'll check to see what we can do to secure the doors of the cells.'

Leaving Michael to get on with his task, I headed out to advise the two senior governors, who were waiting outside the block, of the position, especially with regard to the inoperable cell doors.

This was not the first occasion when cells had had to be secured without the aid of damaged locks. The Works staff arrived in the block with a load of wooden planks. The planks were called 'dwangs'. Wherever that name came from I have no idea, but they solved the problem with the cell doors. The 'dwangs' were cut to the exact width of the distance between opposite cell doors. The idea was to hammer the 'dwangs' into position so that each pair of doors could be secured.

It took a good hour and a half to secure all the prisoners in their cells, during which time the prisoners' lunch arrived in thermos boxes, which would keep the food warm until the prisoners could eat.

On my way out I met the staff returning to the H Block, and there were quite a few appreciative comments from them: 'Thanks, Governor'; 'Well done, Governor'; 'Nice one, Bill.' It was a lot more than I got from the two senior governors who were still waiting on me as I left the block.

'Happy enough. Block okay? No damage?' they said as I approached.

'Yeah, we're fine. Apart from the locks on the cell doors I couldn't see anything else. I have asked the tradesmen to check where they went on the roof to see if there's anything needs repairing. But everything else appears normal.'

'Right.'

That was it. The two members of senior management turned on their heel and, absorbed in each other's conversation, left me standing outside the block. No thanks. No 'well done'. Exactly nothing!

———

If nothing else, the successful conclusion of the rooftop protest gave me a good basis for having a discussion with Michael Stone about the prison's concern to avert another murder in the Maze.

I arranged to speak to Michael the next day he had a visitor. I asked the member of staff escorting him back to his H Block to leave him with me in one of the Legal Visit boxes for a few minutes.

'Well, Michael, how are you? No more rooftop protests planned, then?'

'No, Governor, all is sweet. What can I do for you?' He knew fine well that I had a reason for asking to speak to him out of sight in Legal Visits.

I adopted the sternest look that I could muster and left it a moment before I spoke. This prepared Michael for bad news.

'What is it, Governor? What's wrong?'

'Look, Michael, we're very worried in the jail that after the murder of Billy Wright someone might be next,' I said before pausing again to allow my words to sink in. Michael knew well that of all the loyalist paramilitary inmates in the jail his name would be at the top of any hit list.

'What are you going to do about it?' he asked, with a touch of anxiety in his voice.

God, that was so easy, I thought, as I smiled inwardly.

'Look, don't worry—I have it sorted. I'm going to move the loyalists to the other side of Visits, which will keep your side and you in
particular out of harm's way,' I explained.

There was definite relief in his eyes. He knew that the PIRA still
remembered the 'madman' running through Milltown Cemetery,
hurling grenades and shooting at will, taking life after life during his
attack on a PIRA funeral. (Stone has always maintained that PIRA have
the gun he used on that day and that some day he will die from a
bullet fired from it.)

I continued. 'Look, Michael, before I do anything I need to meet
with the UDA inner council and explain my intentions. Obviously, to
avoid my proposal being delayed because of conflict, it would be
better if we discuss and get agreement first.'

'Great, Governor! Look, I appreciate you doing this for us,' he said
as he turned and left the room.

Later that afternoon I received a call from the principal officer in
one of the H Blocks inviting me to meet with the UDA inner council
to discuss my proposals regarding the Visits move.

I was already in the governor's office in the H Block when the
members of the UDA inner council arrived for our meeting. Michael
Stone first, followed by Skelly McCrory, then Philpot and the 'wild
man of Borneo' lookalike. Skelly was the most boisterous of the quar-
tet, so I was not surprised when he spoke first. He was a bodybuilder
and had the height to go with his physique. The skinhead haircut and
a plethora of tattoos gave the finishing touches to this larger-than-life
character, who now addressed me in a threatening tone.

'What the fuck are you scheming at now, McKee?' he shouted.

Sometimes I think he was so used to bringing his troops to order
in the wing that he never adjusted his volume when he moved into
normal conversational conditions. I also felt that when I had been negotiating with the UDA over the Visits and Inmates Catering problems,
now long since resolved, Skelly was one of the few who had had the
gut feeling that I was 'stroking' the prisoners. It was clear that thought
was at the forefront of his mind as he came to my latest proposals.

'No fucking stroking this time either,' he said as if reading my
thoughts.

I had to force myself to refrain from asking, 'Now, would I do that?'

Skelly and I had a reasonable working relationship now, but he had an explosive temper, and a heated discussion had once led to a bruised neck—mine, not his. I touched my neck as if remembering our last encounter.

'The governor is responsible for all the prisoners, regardless of persuasion, in the Maze and, following the murder of Billy Wright,' (I shuddered as I remembered the unfinished business in connection with that subject) 'he asked me to have a look at the only place in the prison where opposing factions come into contact. The Visits.'

'So what are you thinking of doing?' Skelly said as he leant over the desk to stare at me.

This wasn't comfortable at all. I chose my words carefully: I did not want to rile this giant of a man or provoke him to reach for my throat again at some remark I might make that annoyed him. I found myself moving back, almost subconsciously, in an effort to stay just over an arm's length away from him.

'What I would like to do is move you and your men's visits to one side of the Visits block so that the opportunities for violent acts between opposing paramilitaries when you meet in the toilets are diminished,' I replied.

Before anyone else could speak, Michael said enthusiastically, 'Great, we'll go for that. Okay?'

Skelly fell into the classic trap of believing that Michael had grasped the opportunity of what was on offer a little faster than he had, so he started nodding in agreement. So far, so good, I thought. I was already imagining the look on Alan McMullan's face as I relayed the news to the boss at the next morning meeting.

Getting the UDA's agreement to move was only the beginning of a long road to achieving the objective of splitting the Visits. The next stage would prove more difficult: before we next met they would have had time to discuss my proposals, dissect them and come up with their own ideas. It was much too early to even consider sharing my ideas with anyone—my plan could easily fall flat and leave me with the proverbial egg on my face.

The next step was to meet the UDA inner council on site at the Visits and begin to put pen to paper on the structural changes that I had in mind for the new loyalist Visits. I was correct in my assumption that my proposals would be closely scrutinised before this next meeting, and Skelly and company turned up well versed to challenge me as we discussed the practicality of the move.

The area that required conversion was actually two visiting rooms, one used by PIRA and the other by a loyalist faction.

By taking down the central wall and making a few other minor changes we would end up with a reasonably sized new Visits block for use by the loyalist prisoners.

We argued about bits and pieces as we made our way through this second meeting, but the longer the meeting went on the more confident I was that we would reach an acceptable conclusion. I was right, and at four o'clock on that Monday afternoon we shook hands on a final agreement that the move would take place as soon as the structural changes were complete. We shook hands: what other prison in the Western world was forced to deal with their inmates in such a manner? But, as I have said many times, this was the Maze.

'I need you to think about something else for me before you go,' I suggested.

'You're getting fuck all else,' came the terse reply—from Skelly, of course.

I thought 'leave it for now' and dismissed my proposed request as if it was not that important anyway. I had only wanted to point out to Skelly and the rest that while the work was being carried out the number of visits they would be allowed would obviously be curtailed.

Now for the No 1 governor, and Pat of course.

'What have you done now?' Pat asked when I explained that we needed a meeting with the boss and that it would probably be a good idea if the Works governor was present as well.

I quickly briefed Pat on the agreement I had reached with the UDA inner council, omitting to fill him in on the words of persuasion I had fed to Michael Stone prior to our meeting.

The meeting with the boss went exceptionally well and all the questions that I would have expected were asked and answered. But there was one question that I wasn't prepared for: 'So what do PIRA have to say about your proposals?'

'Well, sir, I thought it was important to get the loyalists to accept the proposals first. The PIRA will benefit more out of the move as they will end up with more visiting tables than the UDA and to be honest I am confident that they will have little difficulty with what I am proposing.'

'Even so,' said the governor, 'before we rubber stamp your proposals I want two things to happen. First, before you go anywhere near PIRA I want you to run through the proposed structural changes with the Works people and make sure that what you are suggesting is possible. Finance to cover the project should not be a problem—like ourselves, Headquarters can't afford another 'Murder in Maze!' Second, if the Works people can't envisage any problems then you can speak to PIRA.'

The Works staff found nothing in my proposals that would be a problem. There were no supporting walls to come down and the remainder of the work was fairly insignificant on the grand scale of things.

So to the PIRA. I contacted the principal officer of the H Block where Padraig Wilson, the PIRA OC, was housed and arranged a meeting with the army council. I explained my proposals without mentioning the real reason for the move and sold it to them on the strength of the extra accommodation that such a move would provide. As I expected, there were no objections and the only additional request they made was to have the visiting rooms repainted.

I informed the boss later that day of the outcome of my discussion with PIRA and he gave the go-ahead for both the work and the move. As I got up to leave the office he looked up from his desk: 'By the way, well done again!' A little appreciation makes all the difference.

At the next morning meeting the older governor who had tried to criticise me did not have a great deal to say.

Chapter 15
Enough is Enough

I was glad to have the distraction of dealing with the redistribution of the visiting rooms: it had put the Neary Inquiry to the back of my mind for a while. But now that the Visits issue had been resolved the events of 27 December 1997 again forced themselves to the forefront of my mind.

I was surprised that the inquiry team had taken so long to get around to interviewing me and I had been made aware that the inquiry into the two incidents was close to being wrapped up. It worried me that as one of the central characters on the day in question I had not been approached for interview.

I contacted the inquiry team and explained who I was and the role that I had played on the day of the murder. The person I spoke to gave the distinct impression that the team weren't really that interested in hearing what I had to say, and I found this very confusing. Nonetheless, I persevered and demanded to be interviewed so that I could give my account of what had happened that day before the inquiry ended.

Finally I was interviewed in Rosepark House by a member of the inquiry team, but the same lack of interest was apparent from when I entered the room until I left.

I was interested in the conclusion the inquiry had reached with regard to the standing down of the Tower. The individual who was interviewing me flicked through what I imagined was a draft copy of the inquiry's report and paused before reading me the section of the document that I was most concerned with.

'The standing down of the Tower in H Block occurred due through a misinterpretation of the governor's instructions.'

I explained that the statement was incorrect and that I wanted it altered to give an accurate record of events. I explained that the orders given on the day in question were both clear and concise and that I had a witness who could confirm my version of events. I added that the instructions given on the day were the exact same as the orders given on any Saturday when the Visits were short-staffed: 'Stand down the Towers but leave H6.' If the duty manager knew that the H6 Towers were never to be stood down and believed that the instruction I had given him was to stand down H6 Tower, why did he not raise the matter with me?

I ran through the rest of the day's events, missing nothing out. I highlighted the full conversation that I had had with the detail duty manager and pointed out that another of the duty governors had been present at the time and that he would be able to confirm my version of events. It felt good to have my recollection of the day's events listened to, especially the fact that I had a witness who had already verified my story.

I was surprised that, although I had been speaking for almost fifteen minutes, the individual interviewing me did not feel it necessary to record one single word of what I said. He did, however, say that he would contact the other duty governor with a view to confirming my version of events.

I left the meeting feeling confused, to say the least. I felt that the inquiry team had made up their minds about the direction the inquiry was going and that, despite my contribution, the wording of the report as read to me that day would not be altered.

When the inquiry's report was published my worst fears were confirmed. The relevant section was exactly, word for word, as the inquiry team member had read to me on the day of our interview.

I immediately asked for a meeting with Martin Mogg, who now had a dual role as governor of the Maze and Prison Service director. I asked Martin what was going on with regard to the inquiry. He was well aware of the conversation that had taken place between myself and the detail duty manager. Martin explained that that section of the report was worded in the way it was to prevent the finger of blame being pointed at any one person. I was very annoyed and Martin knew it. For God's sake: the detail duty manager who actually issued the orders to stand down the Tower at H6 was never even referred to in the report, but I was! Martin admitted as much, but we both knew that irreversible damage had been done.

By this stage the new McKee family home had been finished and in April 1998 we moved in. This house, we had decided, was to be our final family home; and so it was. But not for the reasons that we had intended.

Just as we had when we moved to Coleraine, we were involved in the planning from the very beginning so we were able to have the inside of the house built to our exact specification. Internal walls were positioned so that the rooms were the size we wanted. We were able to fit our own choice of kitchen, bathrooms and fireplaces, so all in all the finished house was as close to perfection as we could get it. The area where the house was located was excellent from a number of perspectives: the view, nice neighbours, reasonable commuting distance to the children's' school. We loved it. But as usual my career interfered again.

The word 'collusion' in relation to the murder had started to be mentioned more and more, and the findings of the Neary Inquiry were not well received by either Billy Wright's father, David, or Wright's former colleagues in the LVF.

The Coroner's Court was held in Downpatrick and again I was surprised that I was not called to give evidence. The Security governor at the time of the murder was chosen to appear, I assumed so that he could explain the murder and the events leading up to it from a security perspective.

It was common knowledge that the camera that overlooked the area where the prisoners came over the fence in the H Block to perpetrate the murder was broken and that this had been reported a few days earlier. An explanation was also required as to how the hole in the fence had gone undetected, and the Security governor was the best man to answer that question.

The other controversial event that required an explanation was how the LVF visits list had ended up in the INLA wing in the prison: this meant that the INLA prisoners knew exactly what time Billy Wright's visit was scheduled. I was the governor responsible for the department that issued the list, but again I was not consulted about how this might have happened.

The matter of the duty governor and the standing down of the Tower on the day of the murder attracted much unwanted attention, so much so that Geoffrey Donaldson, a local MP, in a question in the House of Commons asked why the name of the governor in charge of the prison on the day of Billy Wright's murder had not been disclosed. This was followed by a meeting between David Wright and the Northern Ireland Secretary of State, in which Mr Wright also asked her to reveal my identity. The Secretary of State explained that she could not, in the interests of security, reveal my name, to which Mr Wright responded, 'Personal security or state security?'

The vagueness of the Neary Inquiry and the subsequent non-disclosure of my identity only added to the collusion theory.

I also discovered that my name had been passed to David Wright by one of the officers on duty that day, perhaps in an effort to deflect responsibility or blame from his door. The continuing speculation surrounding my role on the day of the murder was making me highly stressed, and I knew it was only a matter of time before the LVF also discovered my identity.

We had been in our new house for about three months and it was now completely decorated and furnished. I had been sad to move from our previous home, but we had accepted the move was necessary, and now that we were settled a degree of normality had returned to our home life.

Then the phone call came. A governor from Headquarters called to advise me that because of my involvement in the events of 27 December 1997 I should apply for the Key Persons Protection Scheme. I didn't know where to start to explain to my wife the latest twist in the security implications of my chosen career. I just didn't know!

I applied for the package, which was of course approved, and within weeks our beautiful home became a mini-fortress. Bulletproof glass was fitted to windows at the front of the house; cameras, linked to all the televisions in the house, were installed to give full coverage of all views and angles of approach to the house. There were also light sensors which lit up the house like the Blackpool illuminations whenever someone even looked as if they were about to step on the drive. Sensors were positioned at various points around the house that emitted one of two different tones to alert us to an approach from either the front or the back of the house. Finally, an alarm was installed, linked to the telephone line, which when activated registered as an emergency call to the RUC, which would produce an immediate response.

Our home was now equipped to level one of the Key Persons Protection Scheme, the same package that was used for leading judges throughout the Troubles.

I was still working in the Maze, dealing with the PIRA, who had told me I was a dead man walking; and of course the LVF, who were just waiting to discover the identity of the governor who had somehow been implicated in the murder of their leader.

The stress that I was under at that time was wearing me down both at work and at home. Even though my home, my beautiful home, had been turned into Fort Knox I still didn't feel safe. I wasn't sleeping, and the odd cat or dog crossing the garden in the middle of the night and activating the sensors did nothing to help.

Of course I also had my personal weapon as added protection, and a couple of car thieves who stole my six-week-old BMW just before the new security measures were installed can count themselves lucky that they are still alive today. The RUC were able to confirm that the car thieves were a team from West Belfast. They had forced my patio doors open and retrieved my keys from the hall table before opening the front door, getting into my car and roaring off into the distance. Had the sensors been installed and had the burglars activated them, I don't suppose I would have been asking, 'Excuse me, are you terrorists here to assassinate me or do you just want to steal my car?' Given the extreme stress I was under, combined with the unimaginable levels of anxiety caused by almost every aspect of my life being affected by the security implications of the ongoing threats, I know what action I would have taken to protect my family and myself. The two intruders would have been shot dead—of that I have no doubt. I also know that even if I had been aware in the heat of the moment of the devastating consequences that such an act would have had on my life and career, there would still have been two bodies lying waiting for the coroner at the bottom of the stairs.

There are no words to describe how I felt at that particular time in my life. I was exhausted, both physically and mentally, and yet still expected to turn in for work each day.

Martin Mogg had started to include me in his monthly meetings with both the UDA inner council and PIRA army council. I realised that he required my presence there to deal with questions raised in relation to my area of responsibility in the prison. Many times in those meet-ings a question would be asked and Martin would say, 'Perhaps, Billy, you want to deal with this one?'

I was losing weight, my complexion was drained of all colour and I felt that I was just existing as opposed to living. My relationship with my wife was at an all-time low, and that did not surprise me in the least. I had had enough.

One morning I went to see Pat. 'Pat, I've had enough. I've completed four tours of duty at the Maze Prison. There are governors in the service who you and I both know have yet to set their foot through the gates of the Maze and that's not fair. I'm both physically and mentally at the end of my tether. I used to enjoy my work here. You more than most know the immense pleasure I got from taking on the challenges at Maze and I believe that I did make a difference.

'I enjoy working with you more than any other line manager, mainly because of the belief and support that you have continually displayed towards me. But, like I say, I've had enough!

'According to PIRA I'm a dead man walking and I fully expect the LVF to discover at any moment that I was the governor in charge of the Maze the day Billy Wright died. My marriage is hanging by a thread. Please get me a transfer.'

Pat said exactly what I expected him to say. He didn't want to lose me, but a transfer from the Maze was not his decision to make. He asked me to put my transfer request in writing and he would forward it to Headquarters as soon as he received it.

As I left Pat's office I felt an overwhelming sense of relief. I was leaving. I didn't care where they posted me, I just wanted out!

Two weeks passed. Nothing. No posting, no letter or telephone call even giving me any indication of a decision. I telephoned Headquarters to ask how far they had got with getting me out of the Maze.

'Yes, we received your written request through your line manager just over two weeks ago and we are still dealing with it.'

'Look, it can't be that hard. I have done more than my fair share of time in the Maze.' God, I've done more time than some of the bloody prisoners, I thought.

'Well, the problem which is holding us up is just, well, we can't get any of the other governors to agree to transfer there!'

I exploded. 'Listen to me. I have been posted in and out of the Maze many times during my career and I have now completed four tours of duty. Never once have I refused to go anywhere I was posted. The other governors signed the exact same piece of paper that I did, agreeing to go to whatever prison they are sent. If I do not receive a posting by four thirty today my solicitor will deal with this matter from tomorrow on.'

I slammed down the telephone and realised I was shaking with anger. Used and abused. It was only now that I fully accepted that fact, a fact that my wife had continually pointed out to me over the previous few years.

My office telephone rang at four twenty-five. 'Report to HMP Maghaberry from next Monday morning.'

Chapter 16

Budgie

I had as good a weekend as I had had in a long time following my departure from the Maze that Friday night. I knew without doubt that I was passing through the gates for the last time. There wasn't much chance that I would be posted there again anyway, but if I was I would just adopt the stance of the other governors and refuse to go!

I was detailed as governor five in charge of Lagan House at HMP Maghaberry. (Although I had been successful at the last governor four board I had not yet received my posting.) Most of the prisoners in Lagan House were serving life sentences and there was a reasonable group of staff employed there. At last I was back to working in a proper prison and I found I was enjoying myself in my role as prison governor. Over the following weeks my health slowly returned to normal, or perhaps to a new kind of normality: I knew that my life would never again be normal in the true sense of the word.

One of my duties was again to fill the role of duty governor at night and over weekends. On one such evening I received a call from the assistant chief constable. He explained that Johnny Adair had been arrested and was on his way to Maghaberry *by helicopter!* Well, this was going to be a committal with a difference. I had known the infamous Johnny Adair when I served at the Maze and I still smile when I recall the first day I met him.

I had to meet with Michael Stone over some potential problem with Visits. Michael turned up for our meeting with a small, insignificant-looking prisoner with neatly groomed curly hair. I asked Michael who the young prisoner was. Michael looked surprised. 'You mean you don't know?' he laughed. 'It's Johnny Adair!' Over the next few years I got to know Johnny Adair well as he had become a member of the UDA inner council in the Maze Prison.

The helicopter landed on the outskirts of the prison and Johnny Adair was escorted from the helicopter into the reception area. The escorting police officers were in overalls but also wore balaclavas to protect their identity. As soon as Johnny Adair saw me he obviously remembered me from the Maze and greeted me with, 'What about you, Billy, is this where you are now?' The police didn't understand how Johnny Adair could be so informal with me. They didn't know how it used to be in the Maze.

I find it amusing now to read that the prison authorities in mainland UK want the staff to call the prisoners by their first names. That has been the norm in Northern Ireland prisons for many years. Individuals on the outside who do not understand prisons would probably not realise how essential it is to have good working relations between staff and prisoners, and calling each other by our first name is very much part and parcel of that process.

While he was being escorted from the helicopter to the reception area of Maghaberry Johnny Adair told me that he didn't want to be segregated at Maghaberry but preferred to be mixed with 'the men'. I explained that this was not the Maze and in this prison he would do what the governor directed.

As it happened, the governor decided to integrate Johnny with the other prisoners: he knew that this was what Johnny wanted, but that played no part in his decision.

The following day I was walking through Visits and noticed Johnny Adair on a visit with Gina his wife. As soon as he saw me he jumped to his feet, gave me the thumbs up and shouted, 'Thanks, Governor. Thanks.' He obviously thought I had somehow fixed it so that he had been integrated with the men as he wanted. I shook my head. Johnny still thinks he is in the Maze, I thought.

Johnny Adair was a sentenced prisoner who had had his release on licence revoked. He was just one of many categories of prisoner secured at HMP Maghaberry.

The majority of life sentence prisoners housed at Maghaberry were there for non-terrorism-related crimes and a vast amount of work was involved in dealing with their various reports. In completing the 'lifer' reports I had read some gruesome details of crimes perpetrated by civilian criminals. Several of the inmates had been convicted of murdering small children, and that was probably the hardest thing to set aside when one of these individuals was sitting across the table from me requesting some insignificant item that the Prison Rules and Governor's Orders prevented them from having. I always prided myself in not becoming warped by the contents of their files, which revealed some truly horrendous crimes: I could not allow their past actions to influence my decisions.

I didn't have a problem with the majority of the lifers, and after interviewing the first few of them about their crimes I quickly became able to isolate my personal feelings from the job in hand. There was one lifer, however, with whom I didn't have a comfortable relationship, and despite repeated attempts at 'wiping the slate clean' for him we were destined never to enjoy the type of working relationship that I had established with the other prisoners.

My introduction to the prisoner came one day when I was waiting to interview him at Governor's Requests. He entered my office with a smirk on his face. He appeared to have his hair secured at the back with a bright yellow ribbon, but it turned out to be not a ribbon but a budgie perched on the back of his neck. At that time, prisoners serving a life sentence were permitted to have birds as pets in the prison.

The prisoner was showing blatant disrespect to my rank and to me personally, so I decided to nip his insolence in the bud. 'Get out of my office now, and should you ever return to my office with your budgie on your shoulder let me assure you that only one of you will leave the office alive!' My comments had the desired effect and the smirk was wiped from the prisoner's face as he, complete with budgie, flew from my office. That initial conversation set the tone for our future relationship.

In order to get any prisoner to discuss their crime a level of trust has to be established so that he feels comfortable enough to open up and discuss his crime, his feelings at the time of the crime and, most important, for the interviewer to ascertain whether the prisoner displays remorse about his crime or sympathy for his victim. This was not a problem with most of the prisoners. There were a few who were so ashamed of their crimes that they went one of two ways: either they refused to admit their guilt; or they withdrew so much into themselves that it took months of individual work with them to draw any type of response to the preset questions that I was obliged to ask.

Before a lifer can be considered for release there are two main criteria that must be satisfied. First, he must have served an acceptable amount of time for the crime he has committed; and second, he must be judged as not being a further threat to society. Remorse, admitting to the crime and participating in recommended prevention awareness courses also played a major part in the decision to release the prisoner back into the community.

This particular prisoner (now without his budgie, of course) was due to be considered for release and I had to interview him in order to get the information I needed to complete his life sentence report. As a matter of course I also read his 'house' file, security file and his main file, which covered details of the crime, so that I was well prepared before interviewing him.

In cases such as these I would set up the interview with the prisoner, during which I would cover all aspects of the crime and make a judgement as to the level of remorse he demonstrated. After the interview I would review all the material and then prepare and complete the full life sentence report, which I would present to the board at a time to be set in the near future. Once I had prepared the final draft, the prisoner would be allowed to read the report so that he would have all the information that would be heard by the board.

On this occasion the report was quite contentious and since I knew that the inmate could be quite volatile I decided to take precautions. I put a three-man control and restraint team in place just outside my office but positioned so that they would only be visible after the prisoner had entered my office. I advised the prisoner that before he started to look at the report I had prepared he should be aware that there were parts I had no doubt he would not be happy with. I suggested that when he reached those parts of the report he should stop, count to ten and then read on. I told him that if he was to react in any other way I would have him removed from my office immediately and he would not be allowed to read the remainder of the report.

He just gave me one of his customary glares, sat down and began reading the report. He was a very intimidating prisoner and used both his eyes and his body language in a threatening manner. As he reached a sentence that he resented he would glare at the offending words, eyes bulging, and then turn his gaze to me. I would just return his stare and silently point back to the report. By the time he had reached the end of the report he was fuming, and I had to give him some credit for the absolute control that he had to exercise to keep his emotions in check. Perhaps he had accepted that to react the way he wanted to would merely have confirmed one particular comment contained in the report.

He stood up, leaned across the table and poked me gently in the chest with his finger. 'Are you frightened of me?' he asked in his best effort at a threatening voice. The three control and restraint staff were ready to enter my office. I raised my hand to indicate that they were not needed for the moment.

'No, I am not frightened by you, but if you poke me again with that finger you will need medical assistance to have it strapped,' I assured him.

He was obviously not expecting my response and was no doubt annoyed with himself when he returned to his seat.

It was my turn now. 'Are you afraid of me?' I asked.

He almost exploded with anger. He clearly wanted to respond violently, but somehow he contained himself. Credit where credit is due.

I stood up and pointed towards the door. 'I think it better if you return to your cell now, don't you?' ·

As he got to his feet he was shaking with anger. His eyes were bulging. His complexion was scarlet. I thought better to err on the side of caution and signalled to the control and restraint team. They entered the office, calmly fell in behind and to each side of the prisoner and escorted him to his cell in the wing.

As he left the office I called the class officer in the wing where the prisoner was housed. 'Word of warning, lads, you have an extremely annoyed prisoner on his way back to your wing. Watch yourselves.'

There was laughter at the other end of the phone. 'Thanks for the warning, Governor, we'll keep an eye on him'.

The board date was set and the prisoner, his solicitor and anyone who had prepared a report on the prisoner were required to attend.

Before the board, however, this particular prisoner and I were to find ourselves at loggerheads once again. The prisoner, who had been allowed compassionate leave from the prison to visit his dying father, had gone absent without leave and had remained at large for a considerable period of time. He had eventually been rearrested, but not before several police constables had been seriously assaulted.

Despite this serious offence, Prison Service Headquarters had granted a further period of parole to the prisoner over 12 July. I was the duty governor on 10 July and took a call from a concerned police sergeant who was objecting in the strongest possible terms to the prisoner's release, even though it was only for a few days. Once the sergeant had explained the possible life-threatening reasons for his objection I had no alternative but to cancel the prisoner's parole.

I explained to the senior officer at the residential house where the prisoner was housed that I required him to speak to the prisoner on my behalf and inform him that his parole had been cancelled due to police objections. Prison Service Headquarters were informed of my recommendations and supported my decision.

The senior officer sent for the prisoner and told him the governor had cancelled his parole. The prisoner's response was almost predictable.

'Governor cancelled my parole? Must have been that bastard McKee!'

The Parole Board meeting was held several weeks later and all the interested parties were present. Following the presentation of my report the board were asking me about my recommendation not to consider the prisoner for release yet. I had made this recommendation because I believed that he would reoffend and that his volatile nature could not be trusted.

Halfway through my explanation the prisoner jumped to his feet, complaining angrily about my comments. His solicitor was pulling at his client, trying to get him to calm down and sit down, but the prisoner continued shouting and gesturing towards me. I had been standing to present my report when the prisoner's onslaught began, and now the members of the board were glancing from the prisoner to me. I simply opened my arms as if to say 'Now do you understand what I mean?' I didn't need to say another word.

This was just one example of how different prisons can produce different problems, but after all the difficulties that the Maze had thrown at me this little altercation was not even a spit in the bucket when I compared it to some of the trials and tribulations that I had had to deal with during my career as a governor in the Northern Ireland Prison Service.

Chapter 17

The Final Straw

The Good Friday Agreement had been implemented and as a result the Maze Prison was emptied of both staff and prisoners. There were pluses and minuses, of course.

The cost of running the prison—estimated at £40 million—was saved, and for the first time since the 1970s there was a surplus of prison staff of all grades. But some five hundred terrorists, some of whom had committed mass murder, were back on the streets.

The surplus of staff was a concern to me as I was still on a list waiting for my promotion to governor four. Of course, all the governor fours from the Maze had to be found positions before anyone new would be promoted. An early retirement package was hastily put together and because of the generous terms on offer, staff were applying from the first day the notice was released.

I knew that the time had come to give honest consideration not just to my future career but also to my family. My marriage had settled a little since I was transferred to Maghaberry but I still had a feeling that all was not as it used to be.

Before making any decision I felt it important to have all the necessary information available in order to make an informed decision and this was what prompted me to apply to ascertain just how much an early retirement package would be worth in financial terms. I was stunned to learn that my package would be in excess of £200,000. This figure was of course taxable; and a further concern was that my pension would be frozen until I reached sixty years of age. I accepted that although £200,000 was a sizeable amount of money, once my mortgage was redeemed, what was left would be used quickly, within a few years if I was unfortunate enough not to find alternative employment. I realised that I wouldn't be able to retire if I accepted the package and that I really would need to find another career.

After much soul searching I concluded that the deciding factor would be my governor four promotion. I contacted Prison Service

Headquarters to have the position clarified with regard to my promotion and they assured me that there were ample spare governor four grades in the service and there was no intention at this stage of promoting other governor fours who remained on the list. Well, that was that. I discussed with my wife whether to take advantage of the package, and she agreed that I should take it and get out of this environment that had brought us both so much heartache and pain. So that was it. Decision made, forms submitted: all I needed now was my leaving date. But yet again the Prison Service interfered with my plans.

Two weeks after I had submitted the forms to accept retirement a notice was issued from Prison Service Headquarters inviting qualified governor fives to submit their names for a governor four board that would be held shortly. I was livid! I had based my decision to leave the service on at best a half truth, at worst a downright lie.

Before I did anything I tried to discuss the issue again with my wife, who I think saw the chance of an escape route from this environment that she had come to detest fading. She knew me well enough to realise that the light of ambition, despite everything that I had been through in the Maze, still burned brightly.

'Do what you want,' was her response, 'because you always do!'

There was a message there that I choose to ignore; a message that if I had picked up at the time just might have made a difference to the way my personal life turned out.

I wrote to Headquarters asking to rescind my application for the early retirement package. The answer was curt, referring me to a note on the application form that stated applications, once submitted, could not be rescinded. I wrote another letter explaining that my decision to leave had been based on misinformation from their department. They refused to budge. The next letter they received on the subject was from my solicitor, and I was prepared to have my day in court if necessary.

During the negotiations I had occasion to visit Prison Service Headquarters on a totally unrelated matter and while waiting for my appointment I bumped into Robin Halward, the then chief executive of the Prison Service. Robin knew me well as he had hosted a ceremony at Stormont Castle in recognition of the Butler Trust award I had received earlier in my career. I wasn't sure whether or not to speak to him, but he took that decision out of my hands by approaching me and shaking hands. 'Look, Billy,' he said, 'what is happening between my department and you at present I regard as just as a bit of business. You may win or we may win, but either way I refuse to fall out with you personally over it. You have given the service a great number of years' outstanding service and I and many of the senior managers in the service have appreciated your contribution. Let's just see how the situation works itself out over the following few weeks.' With that he shook my hand and bade me farewell.

This was the measure of that great man. He always made time for staff. In my opinion he was the best chief executive the service ever had and I, perhaps more than most, regretted his departure from the Northern Ireland Prison Service.

There was a lot of bad feeling caused by my decision to withdraw my application for retirement, no more so than from other governor fives who realised that if I was allowed to stay there would be one less governor four post available for them to apply for. Some of those same governors were attending a meeting at Prison Service Headquarters about an entirely different matter when the subject of my current position with regard to leaving or staying in the service was discussed.

The general consensus of opinion was that I should not be allowed to remain in the service, but a good friend who was at the meeting asked those present how well they knew Billy McKee. They looked puzzled by his question, but he continued, 'If you know Billy McKee as well as I do you'd know that if he says he will be back, believe me he will be back!' My friend knew me well and also knew that if I believed I was in the right I would persevere to the end with a dogged determination.

The week after my meeting with Robin Halward, I received a call from my solicitor confirming that good sense had prevailed and that I was to be allowed to rescind my application for the retirement package. I was later told how the department had got around the rules. They wrote to all the governor fives who were taking the package advising them of a shortfall and inviting them to reconsider their position. Of course, I was the only one who wished to alter my position and that was that.

I was subsequently promoted to governor four and given the responsibility of the residential houses at HMP Maghaberry. Three of the governor fives at Maghaberry had worked with me before. One was the highly rated principal officer from A Wing in Belfast and the other two were once two extremely enthusiastic senior officers who had approached me many years earlier to seek my support in addressing the problems they had in the Visits at HMP Maze.

Each governor five had the responsibility for one of the residential houses at Maghaberry, and my responsibility was to ensure the houses ran smoothly and along the lines laid down by the governor. I was also the countersigning officer for all lifer reports. From time to time I was required to carry out investigations both at Maghaberry and, on the odd occasion, at other prisons. These ranged from, for example, an inquiry into a prisoner collapsing while being restrained by prison staff to another regarding a prison officer found sleeping in a cell one Sunday morning.

However, of all the inquiries that I carried out the one that I remember most vividly was an inquiry into the suicide of a prisoner called Kenny Loke.

Kenny was an illegal immigrant and was due to be deported back to his country of origin. He had been moved to the prison hospital because it was believed that he had attempted to cut his own throat, perhaps because of the depth of depression into which he had sunk. He was secured in a special observation ward where he could be watched constantly, so that staff could react immediately to any attempt to harm himself.

One evening after the prison was locked for the night Kenny was in his ward as normal but left his bed to visit the ablutions area at the bottom of his ward—he was at that time the only prisoner in the ward. One of the nurses on duty saw Kenny head to the toilet and thought little more about it. The psychologist had made a note in Kenny's file that he could be returned to normal prison accommodation from the following Monday, which implied that Kenny had recovered from his acute depression.

However, after a short time the nurse became concerned that the prisoner had not returned from the ablutions area and she walked to the bottom of the corridor where there was a viewing window that gave a clear view of the toilet area. As she raised the flap she screamed. The sight that met her was not Kenny washing his hands but his body, secured by a ligature, hanging from a vent in the ceiling.

A second member of staff heard the nurse scream and ran to help. The first priority was to cut the prisoner down. A special knife called a Hoffman should be used for this procedure: this is a knife shaped so that a ligature can be cut without causing further injury to the casualty's neck. The knife would normally be kept behind breakable glass in the secure pod in the hospital.

The first problem the hospital staff encountered was that the key for the door to the prisoners' accommodation was on a key board which was held by the night guard senior officer, who was located in a central part of the prison. Precious minutes were lost while the senior officer was contacted and instructed to make his way to the prison hospital. When the senior officer arrived with the keys the door was opened to allow the nursing staff to enter the area where the prisoner was hanging.

A video should have recorded the time the senior officer entered the hospital, but during the course of my inquiry I discovered that the video tape had either disappeared or had been taped over.

While waiting for the senior officer to arrive with the keys, the nurse entered the pod to break the glass and get the Hoffman knife. There was no knife there. The night guard senior officer was, however, able to cut the prisoner down and somehow relieve the pressure of the ligature on his neck. The next step was to try to resuscitate him, but in order to obtain access to the required equipment the nurse had to run to her office at the other end of the hospital to get the keys to the cupboard where the resuscitation equipment was stored. When she returned with the keys she found the lock on the cupboard was faulty, and further precious minutes were lost before the equipment could be released. Despite the nursing staff's best efforts, Kenny Loke could not be revived and a short time later was pronounced dead by the coroner.

I was tasked with the role of investigating officer. Some weeks later, after numerous interviews, I produced a report containing my findings and a total of thirty-four recommendations. Every one of my recommendations was accepted and implemented, and thankfully that was the last suicide in the prison hospital.

I was summoned to the Coroner's Court a few years later to answer questions on my investigation. Kenny Loke's family were present in the court: they needed to attend that day to attempt to get closure on the death of their son. I tried to be as careful with my wording as possible so as not to add to their emotional pain; for example, I never used the word 'prisoner' but always referred to Kenny by his first name.

I was in a poor mental state at the time of my Coroner's Court appearance and could easily have submitted a letter from my psychiatrist to ask to be excused from attending, but during the inquiry I felt

I had somehow got to know Kenny, and I felt it my responsibility both to him and to his parents to try to help bring them to a place that would help them move on with their lives without their son.

A few weeks after the Coroner's Court I was both surprised and pleased to receive a letter sent from Kenny's parents through Prison Service Headquarters thanking me for what they described as the delicate way in which I had discussed their son's death and the complete and thorough way in which I had carried out the inquiry and presented my findings and recommendations.

The real satisfaction for me, however, lay in the fact that my report resulted in changes to both physical layout and written instructions in the prison hospital. I hoped that after these changes other parents would not suffer the way Kenny's parents had suffered, not just from the tragic death of their son but also being left with that terrible feeling of 'what if?'

––––

Of course now that the Maze had closed there would be no prizes for guessing the identity of my line manager, now a governor two and deputy governor at Maghaberry. Pat Maguire, of course.

Maghaberry Prison residential houses were all called after rivers in Northern Ireland: Bann, Erne, Foyle and Lagan. Two new houses which were under construction were to be called Bush and Roe. The female prison, which was totally separate from the male houses, was called Mourne.

Mourne House was a small prison set in its own grounds within Maghaberry estate and over the years it had attracted a certain amount of unwanted publicity. Several staff had been dismissed in recent years for a number of serious indiscretions. There was on one occasion speculation regarding the finding of used condoms in the workshops; and at least one former prison officer is now living with a female prisoner whom he used to guard. There were approximately forty female prisoners secured in Mourne: and at one time, like the Maze, it had its own wing of female terrorists.

Young male offenders within the Northern Ireland penal system were held at the Young Offenders' Centre at Hydebank Wood on the outskirts of South Belfast, but there were so few female young offenders in the system it was not financially viable to have a separate unit for them. These young women were housed along with the adult women prisoners in Mourne House. Although it would have been preferable to keep them in separate accommodation, it was felt from a psychological perspective that it was better to let the young girls have company rather than to keep them isolated: at times there might have been only one of them in the system.

The one young female prisoner who stands out in my mind more than any other was a young girl from Strabane called Annie Kelly. Annie was a big strong girl and was responsible for many assaults on staff. To give an indication of her violent behaviour, on more than one occasion when she was being transported to the prison by the police the prison would be informed that the police car was on its way back to Strabane because Annie had wrecked the inside of the car! Annie was an extremely resourceful girl and she managed to wreak horrendous damage on the fabric of her prison cell. On one occasion she broke almost through the wall and on another she managed to dig a huge hole in the floor. The equipment she used was plastic eating utensils that she had secreted in her cell. I suppose when one considers what one girl armed with plastic cutlery was able to do to the fabric of her cell we should not have been surprised by the tunnel that twenty-five PIRA had dug out of a cell in the Maze several years earlier.

Annie also self-harmed in a horrific way that I honestly felt was her way of asking for help. On one occasion we discovered that she had screwed bedsprings into her flesh. At one stage a straitjacket was used to try to prevent her self-harming but Annie gave it back to staff removed and shredded!

Martin Mogg, who was governor of Maghaberry at the time, was at his wits' end as to what to do or how he could help her. In the end he resorted to having her handcuffed to the wall in her cell so that her hands were secured in such a way as to prevent her hurting herself. This course of action, which was probably born out of frustration, only lasted two days. A member of staff informed the papers what was being done, providing them with a copy of Martin's instructions as to how and when Annie should be handcuffed. Such was the public outcry that this procedure was abandoned. Annie was released on bail shortly afterwards, which provided me with some thinking time before her next period of incarceration, which, knowing Annie, wouldn't be long coming.

Annie had been in and out of the system many times before I got to know her through prisoner adjudications which came about when she was charged with assaulting staff. Although I would not for a moment condone violence towards staff there was a part of me that felt sorry for Annie. During my time in Maghaberry I got to know her quite well and tried, with the help of the probation department in the prison, to provide her with the help and support she obviously needed to address her offending behaviour.

Annie explained to me on one occasion that she only hated the police when she was drunk. I explored this emotion with her and discovered that Annie had had an older brother who enjoyed a drink and was well known to the local police. When he was making his way home from the pub, and depending on how drunk he was, the police would sometimes pick him up and put him in a cell for a while to sober up, dropping him off close to his home later in the evening. Unfortunately, on one such evening, after the police had dropped Annie's brother off he was knocked down by a lorry and killed. Annie told me she knew that the police had been trying to help her brother but yet when she was drunk she blamed them for his death. This was just another example of the complicated mind that was Annie.

Annie was a big girl, tall and carrying a fair bit of weight. She was annoyed by her excess weight and this was brought to my attention one day as I sat chatting to her just after she had been committed for a short sentence.

'Governor,' she began. She was always respectful to me. 'You know my cell card?'

'Yes, Annie,' I replied. 'Why, what's wrong with it?' (There was a cell card on the wall outside each prisoner's cell giving details of the prisoner: name, date of birth, complexion, height, build, etc.)

Annie continued, 'It's just, Governor, my build on my cell card says large and I'm not large, Governor, sure I'm not?'

I felt a lump rise in my throat. Poor Annie: we forget because of the other issues that she is still a young girl with the same insecurities as any teenager.

'No, Annie, you're not large,' I said. 'It says large because you are so tall that's all.'

Annie was too sharp to swallow my explanation. 'Governor,' she began. 'If it was because I am tall it would say tall!'

I just had to try to laugh the matter off as I couldn't change the cell card. Annie was, unfortunately, of 'large build' and that was that! I couldn't do it for Annie or for any of the other 'large build' prisoners. That approach gave me a certain credibility with all the prisoners: they knew I applied the same rules to them all. Everyone knew where they stood and it made managing them easier.

(I didn't realise at that time but my relaxed manner and fair treatment of the prisoners, especially the women, would soon help to make me aware of an attempt on my life as a result of the events of 27 December 1997.)

Now there were two sides to Annie Kelly: the violent, aggressive side and the mischievous side. Annie was brighter than most staff gave her credit for and the manager of the Education Department told me on one occasion that Annie had the necessary spark to excel at writing stories. It was perhaps this conversation more than any other that inspired me to try to sort out Annie's life, in prison at least.

Because of her destructive and violent behaviour Annie was the one young female prisoner who was not permitted to mix with the other female prisoners. Indeed, when the prison was informed that she was on her way the cell where she was to be housed was cleared of all furniture apart from a specially adapted bed that the authorities hoped she could not destroy.

I believed that by adopting this stance we were pre-judging her behaviour before she had even got through the prison gates. I decided to change this style of managing our 'problem child' and introduced what I believed to be a more appropriate way of dealing with Annie Kelly. The next time Annie was sent to Maghaberry I instructed the staff to secure her in a normal cell with normal furniture and await my instructions. I met Annie at the reception area of the prison and took it as a positive sign that the police car arrived at and left the prison in one piece.

I explained to Annie that I wanted to help her have a more enjoyable experience in prison than she had had in the past and that I also wanted her to get involved with the prison departments that could help her come to terms with her continuing offending behaviour and enable her to build a future that would be prison-free. Annie had a younger sister who was very special to her, and I stressed the importance of Annie setting the right example to her so that she would not end up like Annie and her older sisters, in and out of prison for a large part of her teenage years. Annie appeared to be receptive to what I was saying and assured me that she would try harder this time to behave. Although I wanted to give her the benefit of the doubt I knew her too well to allow my staff to lower their guard when she was around.

I devoted most of my time during the next few weeks to Annie and the new regime that I had put in place for her. It was a carrot and stick approach. I set out the plan week by week and explained to her that if she behaved well for a certain period she would move up to the next level, and so on.

I met with the staff who were responsible for Annie first thing each day, both to find out how she had behaved the previous day and evening and to take on board their views and comments on Annie's new regime. Not all staff were receptive to the new approach. This was understandable as most of them had suffered at Annie's hands, or rather her fists. According to staff who had been assaulted she could punch like a man. There were other staff, however, who were great with Annie. They would help her to fix her hair and apply a little make-up, which I believe helped Annie to feel more like the young girl hidden underneath her rough exterior. These particular staff never suffered any assaults from Annie and, like myself, although they were wary of her, they felt comfortable enough to sit in her cell and interact with her.

I often think that the mistake the authorities made with Annie—perhaps because of her 'large build'—was treating her like an adult prisoner instead of remembering that she was really a troubled and troublesome teenager. I also heard of staff winding Annie up, especially during the night guard when management were not in the building. I was never able to prove this or I would have had the guilty parties charged and relocated.

Annie had bought into her new regime and after I finished my meeting with the staff each day I would have them open Annie's cell so that I could chat with her, under their supervision, and encourage her to keep up her good behaviour. She was, like a child, definitely responding to praise and I had started to believe that maybe, just maybe, we had turned a corner.

The probation department in the prison were a great support at this time and recognised a change in Annie. After the first few weeks Annie had gone from being locked up twenty-three hours a day to having her cell door locked back in the morning and only closed during the lunch and tea periods each day. This gave her the freedom to walk about her wing and spend time in the recreation room watching television or listening to music. She had also started to interact with staff in a positive manner, and I couldn't have been more pleased.

The next stage of Annie's rehabilitation was to have her interact with other female prisoners in the evenings with the long-term aim of having her housed with them full time to enable her to enjoy female company. I met with the female prisoners in one of the other landings and explained to both them and to the staff that Annie's behaviour had improved and that I wanted their agreement to permit her to join them for evening association as the next step in her rehabilitation.

The prisoners were more receptive to my request than the staff, but since Annie had spent her two weeks in Mourne without incident I did agree to permit her to associate with the other female prisoners.

The agreement was that Annie would visit the other occupied landing from six to eight o'clock each evening. She would be called back to her own landing at eight o'clock and I warned Annie that she must leave immediately she was called. All went as planned for the first few days and the other female prisoners became quite relaxed with Annie. I believed that the interaction with the other women was proving to be a crucial part of her rehabilitation.

But all good things come to an end and as Annie and the prisoners became more familiar with each other the older prisoners, I suppose in an attempt to make Annie feel welcome, invited her to help herself to the odd choc ice from their fridge. Unfortunately, one evening Annie ate the lot! The association with the other prisoners had to stop but Annie continued to stick to the rules of the new regime and succeeded in getting to the end of her sentence without major incident.

As a consequence of Annie's change in behaviour a member of the probation staff identified a special unit in Donegal that she believed could take Annie to the next level of her rehabilitation. She accompanied me to Coleraine Probation Service where I made an impassioned presentation recommending Annie for a place at the unit. The Probation Service, having had sight of Annie's prison and criminal record, were reluctant to afford her the place that we felt she desperately needed and perhaps deserved. Somehow we convinced them of Annie's merits and she was awarded a place in the unit subject to good behaviour between then and the beginning of the course. Unfortunately, after Annie was released from prison she attempted a robbery armed with a toy gun. This meant that she could not go on the course, which might have made a big difference to her future life.

Annie once more fell into her old ways, but this time, instead of self-harming, she began to pretend to commit suicide. She would apply a ligature to her neck and play dead. Staff would rush to her cell, cut her down and frantically attempt to revive her. Annie would then burst into fits of laughter.

Just before Christmas Annie seemed to have done her usual trick with the ligature. Staff, as usual, rushed to her cell to cut her down, waiting as always for Annie to burst into laughter. Annie didn't laugh, or breathe. She was dead.

Did Annie overstep her acting or had she had enough of life? The only one who knew that was Annie. Annie's death affected staff deeply. Male prison officers shed tears—I did myself. I was stunned. Poor Annie did not deserve to leave this world in such a lonely, undignified fashion. Just another prisoner that the system was ill-equipped to deal with. I felt the system had let Annie down. Although I had tried my best I felt I had let her down too. Has her death made a difference? No. If a new 'Annie Kelly' were to enter the system tomorrow I can imagine the prison staff already moving the furniture from her cell.

_____

Another part of my new role involved the additional responsibility of prisoner adjudications. These were akin to an internal court set in place to deal with indiscretions and offences against Prison Rules. The adjudications were run along similar lines to a normal court, and the prisoner had many of the same rights. The adjudicating governor had the power to issue a variety of punishments should a prisoner be found guilty of the offence he was charged with. These ranged from loss of tobacco, for example, for the more trivial offences, to the top end of the scale, which gave him the authority to extend the prisoner's stay in prison.

The Billy Wright murder was rarely mentioned by now, but there had been talk of a Canadian judge being appointed to review several murders committed during the course of the Troubles.

I had managed to bury the whole affair and was back on top of my game and extremely content with my career. It is strange how when things are going well a bolt from the blue can suddenly reawaken old fears and return you to a place that you no longer wish to visit.

On one particular morning I had ten adjudications to preside over, and the first few had been fairly straightforward. The staff escorted in the next prisoner and handed me the documentation relating to the charge. This adjudication also ran smoothly. The prisoner understood the charge. I heard the charging officer's statement, then listened to the witnesses, and followed up by giving the prisoner the opportunity to answer the charges. The evidence was substantial and the prisoner, despite his best efforts, was unable to convince me that he was not guilty of the offence with which he was charged. After announcing the verdict I asked the prisoner if he wished to say anything in mitigation prior to me awarding a punishment. The prisoner stared at me and his words chilled me to the bone.

'You have made a mistake today, Governor McKee, and you made another more serious mistake on 27 December 1997; only on that day a good man died.'

The staff looked at me for instruction, concern and puzzlement evident in their gaze.

I continued with the adjudication and made the award that I decided was commensurate with the offence. As soon as I had made the award the staff escorted the prisoner from the room. There were several staff present who had worked in the Maze and were well aware of the implications of the prisoner's remarks.

'The bastards know it was you now, Governor!' The bastards being, of course, the LVF. Although I had a suspicion that they knew I had been in charge on the day of the murder I had tried to convince myself that they didn't. I asked the staff present when the prisoner made the remarks to submit a report to the Security department confirming the substance of what the prisoner had said.

I wasn't sure what to do now, but the obvious first step was to have my security reviewed and upgraded if appropriate. The result of the security upgrade was that the rear of our house, including the sun-room, was fitted out with bulletproof glass to match the front. This raised my stress levels again: I knew that the Prison Service didn't throw thousands of pounds away without reason, and a considerable amount had been spent on my home. It was a reminder that my life was really in danger. I also had to advise my wife of the frightening new circumstances.

A few weeks later a Canadian judge was appointed to review several murders that had occurred in the province, murders in which the security forces were rumoured to have colluded. One of these murders was that of Billy Wright in the Maze Prison on 27 December 1997.

My solicitor and I had a meeting with Judge Cory in Belfast. He was quite an elderly gentleman, courteous and extremely sharp. I gave him my full account of the events of 27 December 1997 and highlighted my concerns, especially about the Neary Inquiry. Judge Cory thanked me for my time and I felt that at last I had been interviewed by an man who had listened, made notes and actually gave me the impression that he was concerned for my position and believed my version of events.

Was there collusion? Why were two directly opposed paramilitary factions housed in the same H Block when there were other empty H Blocks in the Maze? Why did the warnings of MI5 go unheeded? Why did the then security minister decide not to relocate Billy Wright to the Maze from Maghaberry only to change his mind two days later? How did two guns get into the prison? Why was the camera overlooking the H Block Yard not repaired when it had been reported broken? How did the visits list, for the first time ever, end up down the INLA wing? Why did the hole in the wire fence go undetected? Who really gave the instruction to stand down the Tower at H Block 6? Why did my witness allegedly change his story? Why was Neary's team reluctant to interview me? So many questions, so few answers. I just didn't know what to think any more.

My health had begun to deteriorate again. I was permanently stressed. I was taking four diazepam a day, which appeared to dull the edge of the stress, and also forty milligrams of fluoxetine to treat my depression. Then things suddenly took another turn for the worse. Security sent for me and told me that they had received intelligence that a female prisoner well known for her LVF sympathies had stolen a letter opener with the intention of stabbing me in reprisal for my suspected involvement in the murder of Billy Wright.

Was there to be no end to this? No escape from this relentless stress that felt as if it was growing by the day? After all, the murder had occurred five years ago. What really shocked me was that Security had intelligence that a letter opener had been stolen and that it was to be used in a murder bid, yet the prison was not locked down to facilitate a search to find and recover the weapon.

The women's prison fell under my area of responsibility and among other issues I had to attend that part of the prison to carry out adjudications. I was right in my assumption that there was to be no end to my stress. Things went from bad to worse when I received a phone call from the Security principal officer late one Wednesday afternoon. This time the call related to another female prisoner with LVF sympathies, and the news gave me enormous concern for my family.

The female prisoner had asked to see the principal officer from Security urgently because she had some life-threatening information. The principal officer visited the women's prison and interviewed the prisoner. She explained that the LVF now knew for sure that Governor William McKee was in charge of the Maze on the day of the murder of Billy Wright. The LVF also had Governor McKee's home address and had passed it to the LVF unit in Ballysillan in Belfast. The governor would be murdered.

I was shaking! I needed to think! What should I do?

I realised that the Principal Officer was still on the telephone waiting for an answer.

'Okay, Principal! Did you believe her?' My heart was thumping and I was sweating.

'My gut reaction is that she was telling the truth.' The principal officer went on, 'She says that you have always been more than fair with the female prisoners and with her in particular and that she didn't want your death on her conscience.'

When I heard those words, 'your death on her conscience', a shiver ran down my spine. I was trying to take in the information I had been given and at the same time think what decisions I needed to make to protect my family and myself—I felt my head was about to explode.

'Principal, I need to know if the LVF have my address. What I would like you to do is to interview the prisoner again and tell her that Governor McKee has moved house within the past few weeks and the address the LVF hold may well be that of an innocent family.'

'Okay, Governor,' came the reply. 'I'll go straight away to see the prisoner and you head on home. I'll call you as soon as I've spoken to her.'

I was still shaking as I left Maghaberry. I just couldn't deal with this latest information.

When I arrived home I parked on the drive hoping that the telephone call I was expecting would come before I went into the house.

I didn't want to discuss the threat in front of my wife and certainly not in front of my children.

The call didn't come so I locked the car and reluctantly went inside.

I went into the kitchen, where my wife was preparing dinner. 'What is it now?' she asked, seeing the stress on my face.

Before I could even try to answer her the telephone rang. It was the call I was waiting for, but I was afraid of what I was about to be told. The Security principal officer had checked my address before he spoke to the female prisoner again.

'Billy, they have your address,' he began.

'God, they have my address,' I interrupted him, the panic evident in my voice.

'Billy, look: this could happen tonight. I just don't know!' the PO continued. 'My advice is get out of the house. Take your family and get the hell out of your house now!'

My wife had been listening to only one side of the conversation but it was still clear to her how serious the situation was.

'Who has our address?' she screamed at me across the kitchen. I had to tell her that we needed to get the children and leave the house now.

'The Portadown LVF has it. They know I was the governor in charge of the Maze the day of the Billy Wright murder and they have passed my details to the LVF in Ballysillan to have me shot!' I replied, still shaking.

My wife was screaming and crying and my two daughters rushed downstairs to see what was wrong. The principal officer was shouting down the telephone at me, which took my attention temporarily away from the mayhem around me.

'Get out of the house now!' the principal officer was shouting again, trying to make himself heard over the pandemonium at my end. 'I will stay here in the Security office until I hear from you. I have informed the RUC and they will try to get a car in the area to allow you time to get out!'

My wife had stopped crying, probably in an effort to calm the children, but her stubbornness had kicked in. 'I am not letting those bastards drive me out of this home as well. I have had enough of this! I can't do this any more!'

I wasn't really concentrating that much on what she was saying; I was thinking ahead, thinking that I needed to get us all out of the house now. I knew that once my wife had dug her heels in she would prove virtually impossible to shift. I rang her parents and quickly explained the situation. They were there in twenty minutes and between us we half carried, half dragged my wife into her parents' car.

I threw the children's school uniforms and school bags into the boot of their grandparents' car and locked the house. My son was working at the time and was unaware of what was happening until he was collected at eleven o'clock that night by his grandfather. My wife and children stayed with her parents for a few days and I stayed in two different hotels so as to keep on the move.

I got in the car and headed off towards Bangor. I don't know why I chose Bangor: I didn't have family there. I was just so confused. My close friend and colleague from the training college lived in Bangor—perhaps I was subconsciously thinking of him. Once I had booked into the hotel, using a false name, I rang him. He gave me directions to his home and I was there in ten minutes. I needed his measured responses to my panicky ramblings to help calm me down and think more rationally about my predicament.

I had called the Security principal officer to update him on the current position and tell him the location of my family, and he agreed to get the RUC to determine through their many informers if there was anything 'on the go' regarding a murder of a member of the security services.

This was another anomaly that I could never get my head around. The prison Security department had definite, irrefutable intelligence from a female prisoner that the LVF had my home address, knew I was the governor in charge of Maze on the day of murder and had asked the Ballysillan end of their organisation to kill me! What more did they need? Police procedure, however, incredible as it may sound, dictates that unless they can obtain verification of a threat through their own sources the threat is regarded as invalid.

I stayed in a different hotel the following night, again using a different name and address. A meeting had been arranged for the following morning with a senior manager from Prison Service Headquarters to establish what further protection could and would be offered. Exactly nothing. That was what came out of the meeting. Tea and sympathy—that is what we received at Headquarters, and that was all. Because the police could not verify the threat, that was that. The threat mustn't be real: that's really what they were saying. My wife was crying, I was shouting. Still nothing. I had thought that since the Prison Service had spent over £30,000 protecting my home, moving me at enormous expense from my previous house, again because of threats from the LVF, that this latest threat just might have been taken a little more seriously.

They reluctantly offered us a temporary house move to the Prison Service college at Millisle. Everyone and his brother knew that staff evacuated from their home following terrorist threats were relocated in abysmal accommodation at the college. The security there was a joke and I would have felt more vulnerable living there than in my bulletproof house on the outskirts of Belfast. So we were left with no alternative but to move home again.

Christmas was only a week away and we tried to make the best of things for the sake of the children, but the holidays were flat. My wife refused even to put up the Christmas cards. Our lives were miserable. My relationship with my wife was now non-existent and that didn't surprise me at all. But there was nothing that I could do or say that could make things even remotely better.

I knew a part of her understood that our problems were not directly my fault, yet she also believed that my ambitious nature, combined with my 'moth to a flame' attitude to the challenges of the Prison Service, had played a significant part in the predicament we now found ourselves in.

We loved where we lived. The new house was perfect. I had just spent a small fortune landscaping the gardens. This was our home. This was the children's home.

I was now off work ill with stress and it took tremendous effort to force myself to go back to work. When I did eventually return to work I was sent to the Prison Standards Office based at the Young Offenders' Centre Hydebank Wood to give me a break from the sharp end of the Prison Service.

An English governor was in charge of preparing the 'standards' for the Northern Ireland Prison Service. His posting was temporary, though he made it clear to anyone who would listen that he wanted to transfer to our service. He was the most unlikeable person I have ever come into contact with in my whole life and after discovering that he was constantly undermining me while I was adapting to my new role I told Headquarters to get me back into the prisons.

I was moved back to Maghaberry on detached duty and ended up filling a temporary governor three role in the prison. When I returned to Maghaberry I found a new man at the helm, but it came as no surprise to discover the name Pat Maguire on the name plate on the door of the No 1 governor's office.

Although back at work and happy to be among friends at Maghaberry I was still ill. I was on heavy medication just to help me through the day and had become very withdrawn. I wasn't sleeping and we were still living under the shadow of the LVF death threat. My girls had settled down, but I had to check that all windows and doors were secured before they went to bed every night. My son is a very deep individual and it was hard to determine how much he had been affected by the past few years' events. He spent much too long in his room, which added to my stress: I felt that I had let him down and that I was continuing to let them all down. My wife, who may have been on the brink of a nervous breakdown at this stage, was more or less ignoring me. I did not resent this: how could I after the year that she had just had?

We were nearing Christmas again and I was determined to shake off the gloom that had descended on our home and our lives.

There was a lot of media speculation at that time regarding the recovery of a computer, possibly containing Prison Service staff details, allegedly recovered from the home of a person who had sympathies towards PIRA. But I had enough to worry about without thinking about something that did not concern me. Wrong again!

The computer's hard drive was analysed and the experts were able to ascertain what information the computer had actually contained. I was still so absorbed in my own problems I still had not even considered how I might be affected by the information recovered from the hard drive.

Then I received a call asking me to report to the No 1 governor's office. I had got used to that over the years and it no longer caused me the same anxiety that it once had when I was the 'new kid on the block' as an inexperienced governor working in the H Blocks at the Maze Prison. I had also over the years stopped trying to second-guess the reason why I might be summoned to the No 1's office and had all but ceased to imagine that I had done something wrong.

When I arrived at Pat's office I found two men in civilian clothes sitting at the boss's desk. Pat was there, as was the Security governor.

'Sorry to interrupt you, but I received a pager call to report to your office,' I said to Pat.

'Yes, Billy, that's correct, but it wasn't me who was looking for you; it was these two gentlemen.' He turned towards the two men at his desk and introduced them as policemen involved in the computer recovery story that had appeared recently in the media. The hairs lifted on the back of my neck, my mouth dried up, my heart started to beat faster. Please, no! I thought. Please, God, no more trouble! Not me again!

The policemen on Pat's right started to speak and I had to refocus to pick up what he was saying.

'Yes, Governor McKee, a bit of bad news for you. The first layer of information has been recovered from the hard drive of the computer that was recovered from a house in West Belfast over a week ago. Contained on the first layer are the names, ranks, establishment employed at and home address of seventy officers and governors. Among those seventy names and personal details were yours.'

I stopped listening at that point and turned to leave. The police officer called after me but I couldn't stop. This latest piece of information had pushed me over the edge. As I left the governor's office I noticed his secretary's office was empty. I headed straight in, and as I tried to close the door behind me two staff, a governor and a senior officer, came in behind me. The governor was my highly rated ex-principal officer from Belfast, now working with me as a governor in Residential. The senior officer coincidentally had exactly the same name as the governor. He had also worked with me in the officer grade in A Wing in Belfast.

They could tell by my body language and expression that I had just had some devastating news. The governor placed his hand on my shoulder as I explained the latest security information the police had just passed to me. 'Look, you have got through worse than this and you'll get through this as well,' he tried to reassure me. The tears were running down my face. The senior officer, embarrassed for me, excused himself and left the room. I only found out when I left the room myself that he had stationed himself outside the door so that he could stop anyone coming in and seeing me in this state. The other governor stayed with me until I had recovered my composure, and we left the office together.

I just walked out of the prison and drove home.

Chapter 18

The Long Road to Recovery

I had been here before. Under threat from two paramilitary organisations at the same time. Although the PIRA threat to my life had been issued a while ago I couldn't dare to presume that they had forgotten about me. If that organisation was still targeting prison staff and taking the kind of risk that had recently become apparent with the theft of the computer, I could only presume that my life was still in danger.

The LVF threat definitely remained live and within the next twelve months I would be reminded of that in the strongest possible terms.

I arrived home earlier than usual, and my wife immediately looked for an explanation. She probably didn't see any difference in my appearance—for the past twelve months I had looked wretched, pale and red-eyed, stress and lack of sleep having taken its toll. How was I going to begin to explain this latest 'paramilitary interest' in my personal and career details?

'We need to talk,' I began.

We walked through to the sunroom and I looked out of the windows at our lovely garden. We were halfway through autumn and the leaves had turned that beautiful golden brown, the colour that signalled they would soon shrivel and fall on to the neatly manicured lawns and pond.

As I looked, an immeasurable feeling of sadness came over me as I thought of the conversation that I was about to have with my wife, a conversation that would probably end with yet another 'For Sale' board appearing in the garden, that would end five years of happiness, sadness and fear: fear having been the predominant feeling, at least over the past two years.

Our conversation lasted for over two hours. No blame was directed at me any more. It was a time to look forward, putting especially the safety and happiness of the children first, and trying to decide where to relocate to this time. Neither of us could come up with an answer to that question. There was sadness and devastation, tinged with a degree of relief, as we finally prioritised what was important in our lives.

The position we now found ourselves in was that our home address was in the hands of two different paramilitary factions, and that, combined with the death threats against me, left us with no choice but to sell our home and start all over again. How many times was this now? I didn't want to even think about it. Because we couldn't come up with a new area to move to we decided that after Christmas we would place the house on the market and move into rented accommodation that would allow us time to plan for the future.

Little did I know that this future would not include me. This Christmas was to be the last Christmas Day I would spend with my children and would herald the start of what was to be the worst chapter in the book of my life.

My son was now seventeen years old and had lived in a total of seven different houses during his short life. That simply wasn't fair. No sooner had he made a new friend than a promotion or threat would come along and you could bet that it would be closely followed by the removals lorry.

I had never known my wife to be so calm over a terrorist threat before. She seemed to have an air of resignation and to have accepted that yet another house move was inevitable.

Christmas came and went. Even though I didn't realise that it was to be our last family Christmas together, when I look back I know that I couldn't have enjoyed it any more if I had. Despite the death threats, because we had reached a decision with regard to the future I had a new-found contentment about me and a misplaced optimism for the future.

The other good or bad news—depending on which perspective you viewed it from—was that the security risk assessment carried out by the RUC had resulted in a Chief Constable's Certificate. This confirmed that the level of threat on my life was serious but it also meant that the Northern Ireland Office would meet the majority of our relocation expenses.

We rented a three-storey terraced house and put the furniture we didn't need into storage until we had found and bought a new house.

I lasted just under six weeks in our rented accommodation. My relationship with my wife had deteriorated past the point of no return. I telephoned from Maghaberry one afternoon and during the conversation she admitted that she 'could not do this any more'. What could I say? Nothing. I packed my bags and moved out. This was just the start of another twelve months of hell for me. The end of my marriage didn't surprise or shock me when I thought about it: I was just numb.

It was devastating for the children but I knew myself that in the long term it was for the best. I still continued to see them as much as possible and my relationship with them now, although different, is probably stronger than ever.

My health continued to deteriorate and one Saturday afternoon I was rushed from Maghaberry to Lagan Valley Hospital with a suspected heart attack. I had felt ill on Thursday and had to go home early. Friday was no better. On Saturday I didn't make it into the prison until ten o'clock and by lunchtime my condition had deteriorated. I was in the Security department and they were so concerned that they sent for a hospital officer, who immediately phoned for an ambulance.

That Saturday turned out to be my last day as a governor on duty in the Northern Ireland Prison Service.

Although the doctor's initial diagnosis was that I had had a heart attack, he later concluded that in fact I had suffered an anxiety attack brought on by the enormous stress I had been under. I returned from hospital to the rented apartment in Templepatrick that I now called home, but my health continued to cause concern. I approached TMR, the trauma and stress management company that had a contract with the Prison Service at that time. The company offered psychological support for staff who had mental health problems caused by their employment.

I was referred to a psychiatrist who diagnosed my illness as post-traumatic stress disorder and he set in place a course of remedial help which was provided by the counsellors from TMR. Some six sessions later the Prison Service decided that I had had enough and refused to pay for any more sessions. Fortunately, a telephone call from Finlay Spratt, the POA Chairman, encouraged the Prison Service to review that decision. I remember parts of the conversation: 'You don't understand,' Finlay was saying, 'Billy McKee is like a gypsy, he has to keep moving all the time trying to keep one step ahead of these bastards that want him dead! He is an emotional wreck and a qualified psychiatrist has diagnosed him as suffering from post-traumatic stress disorder.

Not only does he need the continuing support of the trauma and stress management company, he deserves it!' With that Finlay slammed down the phone and assured me he would call me later. Later that afternoon, as good as his word, Finlay called and confirmed that I could again attend TMR and receive the ongoing support that I so obviously required. I was of course so ill and in need of TMR's support that I had continued to see Mike, my therapist, anyway and had paid for each session myself.

I have now had over sixty sessions and although I still suffer from PTSD the counselling sessions have enabled me to live with and manage my illness most of the time. In the early sessions of my treatment the counsellor arrived at the conclusion that I was displaying suicidal tendencies and recommended that I should not be on my own, especially in the evening. As a result, my brother insisted that I come and live with him in his home in Dromore, County Down.

The Prison Service also called to my home and removed my personal weapon. It was typical of the Prison Service that despite the urgent circumstances—a governor suffering from post-traumatic stress disorder and believed to be suicidal—it took three days after they were notified to come out and collect the weapon. That, more than anything, reinforced how far I had fallen.

I appreciated my brother's gesture and his company in the evenings had a positive effect on my health, although our arrangement turned out to be short-lived. As I was living with my brother I had put his address on my latest sick line, which I posted to Maghaberry Prison. Several days later I had just arrived home at my brother's house when the phone rang. It was the Security department from Maghaberry repeating the words I had heard some two years earlier: 'Get out of the house now, there is a joint team of UFF/LVF gunmen on their way to murder you. Get out of the house now!'

I threw down the phone and it rang again immediately. This time it was the RUC, who confirmed the information that I had just received from the Security department at Maghaberry. As I rushed from the house I am sure that I cut a tragic figure. I certainly felt like a tragic figure!

I was an absolute mess both mentally and physically. I felt that on top of my PTSD I was close to a nervous breakdown. The psychiatrist recommended stronger medication and with six diazepam and forty milligrams of fluoxetine per day I was just about able to cope.

Now I had nowhere to go, and the totally dilapidated accommodation at the Prison Service college became my only option. I couldn't risk the personal security or health and safety of any more family or friends so I reluctantly agreed to move there. I missed the company of my brother in the evenings and my medication became my friend. I would wake in the morning, take a couple of tablets and sleep until lunchtime. I took more tablets just before ten at night, which knocked me out until morning. This made my days very short, but it was the only way I could escape from the pain and stress that had taken over my life. The tablets, combined with my sessions with Mike, my counsellor, helped me to get through that year.

In May of the following year the Prison Service, after consulting with my psychiatrist, and after I had had a medical with the Northern Ireland Office doctor, decided to retire me on medical grounds. My career was over after just under twenty-seven years' service. This felt like another loss on top of those I had already suffered. I had now lost everything: my wife and children, my home, my health and now my career. I felt that my mind was all that was left to go.

A few days later I was pleasantly surprised to receive a call from my good friend Alfie. I explained that my depression had not been helped by retirement and listened as Alfie put his slant on my predicament.

'Listen, Billy, have you not considered how lucky you are? You have had a great career in the service. You have now been given your freedom to do what you want in life and what's more you *will* have your health back and you're still young enough to enjoy many more happy years ahead of you. How many of us would wish we could swap places with you?'

Even as he spoke I felt as if every line of pain that had built up over the stressful times was falling from my face and for the first time in ages I began to look forward to my future. Hearing Alfie's voice made me feel better, as it always did, but the words he spoke turned my interpretation of my position on its head. I don't think Alfie realised just what he had done for me that day. Those words of support and advice altered my perspective, and had such a dramatic impact on me that the following day became the first step on my long road back to normality.

As my new life took shape over the coming months, in the odd dark moment that still surfaced Alfie was only a phone call away and to this day his continued support and gentle words are enough to sustain me and keep me looking forward, in the direction my life is now headed.

Almost two years after that life-changing conversation with my good friend Alfie, someone new came into my life. That friendship has since developed and grown into something that three years ago I did not think possible. Like Alfie, she is helping me to adjust to life after the Prison Service, a life in which stress and threats of murder have been replaced by absolute love and total commitment. I have found happiness again.

The first inquiry into the death of Billy Wright was suspended, along with investigations into several other high-profile murders around which there was a suspicion of state collusion. A new inquiry was put in place under the Prison Act, but subsequent government legislation changed the terms of the inquiry by introducing the Inquiries Act, which will enable the government to keep the findings of any of the 'collusion inquiries' confidential. I wonder why?

Chapter 19
The MacLean Inquiry

Following the announcement of the MacLean Inquiry into Billy Wright's death it was decided that the issue of legal representation should be dealt with first.

I was concerned that I might find myself in a vulnerable position in the unfortunate event that evidence presented during the proceedings should go against me. After a lengthy discussion with my solicitor and barrister I decided to apply for my own personal legal representation instead of using the Prison Service legal team. In order to make this application my solicitor and I were required to appear before the inquiry, where my solicitor made a formal request on my behalf for separate legal representation and explained the reasons why my application should be approved. Lord MacLean, the chairman of the inquiry panel, arrived quite quickly at an answer, and I was relieved to hear him say that he would look favourably at the application.

The only downside of the day came when I heard the news on Ulster Television at six o'clock that evening. Ivan Little was reporting on the day's proceedings from the Europa Hotel in Belfast, where the inquiry was dealing with the preliminaries before the full inquiry (which was to be held at the courthouse in Banbridge, County Down) was opened. During the course of Ivan Little's report he mentioned that 'William McKee, the governor in charge on the day of the murder, has applied, among others, for individual legal representation.' That was really the first time my name had appeared in the public domain and it unsettled me.

The preliminaries took much longer than expected, with writs being issued by the inquiry against both the Northern Ireland police and the Prison Service for failing to produce various pieces of documentation within the stipulated deadline. Then came the news that the Prison Service had destroyed much of the material that had been requested, and this of course only encouraged the collusion theorists.

A few weeks later my solicitor was informed that my application for individual legal representation had been successful, and yet another waiting game began.

The phone call finally came. I was required to attend, accompanied by my solicitor, for interview with the Billy Wright inquiry solicitor.

I had mixed feelings. On the one hand I welcomed the opportunity to tell my side of the story, which just might be believed and therefore absolve me of any responsibility in connection with the assassination of Billy Wright. On the other, I was concerned that there could be inconsistencies or disparities in the evidence presented that would paint me as a villain and support false information, already widely published, about my involvement with regard to the standing down of the Tower, which was still viewed by many as crucial to the success of the murder of Billy Wright.

The day of the meeting finally arrived and as I made my way to Belfast to meet my solicitor my mind was full of thoughts about the forthcoming meeting, its contents and conclusion. My solicitor advised me to answer all questions with complete honesty as he fully believed that I was an innocent party and therefore had nothing to hide. He did, however, add that if I was asked to offer an opinion or indeed draw a conclusion based on the events of 27 December 1997 he would interject, advising that in his legal opinion such a question was unfair; he also recommended that I should not answer such a question.

We were met in the foyer of the building where the meeting was scheduled to take place and were taken up a few flights of stairs to the interview room. We were led into the room by a former murder squad detective from Scotland who then introduced us to the solicitor who was representing the inquiry team.

It quickly became apparent that the former detective and the solicitor comprised the interview team, and the solicitor quickly explained the format the interview was to take. It was not what I had expected. I had imagined that the questioning would be similar to that of a police interview, an impression that had been reinforced by the presence of an ex-murder squad detective on the interview team. I couldn't have been more wrong. The two parties on the opposing sides of the desk were more than civil and most courteous throughout the duration of the interview, which lasted some four hours from beginning to end.

As we made our way through the proceedings, on a couple of occasions my solicitor did interrupt to stop me answering a question that he deemed inappropriate, but apart from this there was very little asked that either surprised or concerned me. The surprise came at the end of the summing up by the solicitor representing the inquiry.

'Are you aware of the fact that there are four other people who were on duty on 27 December 1997 whose statements contradict your evidence?' the solicitor asked.

'Actually, I am probably a little surprised, but not as much as you might have expected,' I explained. 'Several years ago, around the time when it was announced that there would be a further inquiry to establish the facts with regard to the murder, a fellow prison officer had been involved in conversation with a member of the Prison Officers' Association. My colleague had explained that I welcomed an inquiry as I believed and hoped that a full, impartial inquiry would absolve me of any claims of involvement or collusion in the events of 27 December 1997.

'My colleague also mentioned that as I had a witness I believed this would support my claim of innocence and was confident the truth would finally be told.

'The answer that my colleague received from the POA representative was a major cause of anxiety to me; he replied that if I were to check I would find that I did not have a witness as I had thought.

'This confused me to say the least. What could he mean? Brian Barlow had been standing beside me when I issued the orders with regard to the standing down of the Towers and was also present at the follow-up meeting between the duty principal officer Don McCallum (who actually passed my instructions to the managers in the H Blocks with regard to the standing down of the officers in the Towers) and myself.

'After being informed by my colleague of the content of the conversation and, more important, of the possible and probable ramifications for me, I immediately decided to contact Brian Barlow, my witness, and ascertain exactly what was going on. By this time Brian had already retired from the service and was employed in a security role with a private company that looked after the new Laganside Court Complex in Belfast.

'I telephoned the court and was quickly put through to speak to Brian. "Brian," I said, getting straight to the point, "do you recall when the duty principal officer entered my office on the morning of 27 December 1997 with regard to the staff shortage in Visits?" Without waiting for him to answer I continued, "The duty principal officer had told me he had the jail up and running but that he was still eight staff short in Visits. I then instructed him to stand down the Towers but to leave H6 and to send the 'stood down staff' to Visits." I kept talking. "The day following the murder the three of us had a further meeting when we discussed the instructions given and when the duty principal insisted that I told him to stand down H6 Tower and leave the rest you interjected and said, 'Look, Don, I'm a PO, the same rank as you, and if anything I should be supporting you, but I can't tell a lie. If Billy had said, "Stand down H6", I would have said, "Fuck sake, Billy, you can't stand down H6!"'

'"No," began Brian. "That did not happen and I won't be telling lies for anyone!"

'I challenged Brian one final time, but he again denied that he was present when I spoke to the duty manager. I didn't know what to say. I just said, "That's fine, Brian" and hung up. But it was far from fine.

'I couldn't understand why this latest episode was happening. What I did understand, however, was what the POA representative was getting at when he said that if I were to check I would find that I did not have a witness!'

What was behind this turn of events? Why were individuals changing their stories? An almost crazy thought crossed my mind. If people change their stories and tell—in my opinion—blatant lies it is because they have something to hide. What was there to conceal? Security force involvement? Collusion?

I could think of no other reason. But as quickly as the thought entered my mind I dismissed it. I neither could nor would believe it.

During the course of the questioning I explained to the solicitor that standing down one Tower would not help to alleviate the problem of being eight staff down in Visits. The duty manager was also aware that the Tower at H6 was not to be stood down, so if he thought I had issued instructions to stand down this particular Tower, why did he not remind me that the Tower should not be stood down and confirm that he had indeed understood the instructions issued?

At this point the solicitor excused herself and her colleague and left me with my solicitor for a few moments. Presumably they were discussing the parts of my statement that contradicted the statements of my former colleagues.

I could not begin to explain the overwhelming sense of relief when they returned and the solicitor informed us that they had arrived at the conclusion that my evidence had more than a hint of truth about it. Hopefully the inquiry team will feel the same, I thought, as my solicitor and I made our way downstairs after the meeting.

The inquiry opened a few months later and I was pleased to discover that each day's proceedings were to be posted on the Internet a few days later, which enabled me to keep abreast of what was being said and, perhaps more important, what was not being said.

It was clear from the very outset that the inquiry was to be organised in chronological order. It began with Billy Wright's initial incarceration at HMP Maghaberry, dealing in particular with the decision-making processes that resulted in him being transferred to H Block 6 in the Maze Prison, an H Block that would eventualy also house another paramilitary organisation which was not only directly opposed to the LVF but had also, as we were to learn during the course of the inquiry, vowed to murder Wright at the first available opportunity.

The inquiry examined in great detail the other firearms incident in Maghaberry that had been perpetrated by the two assassins of Billy Wright around the time of Wright's transfer to the Maze. On this occasion 'Crip' McWilliams and John Kennaway, two inmates with INLA affiliations, had two weapons smuggled into the prison and had gained access to the residential accommodation where they believed Billy Wright had been secured. Fortunately they got no further than the entrance hall into the house, and they were relieved of their weapons and secured in the prison cell block.

It was generally believed at the time that the target of the two terrorists had been Kevin McAlorum, another INLA inmate, who was believed to be responsible for the murder of the then INLA leader Gino Gallagher, who had also been secured in the same house as Wright. However, at the inquiry another suggestion was put forward for the first time: that the intended target on that occasion was in fact Billy Wright.

Many of the other statements made to the inquiry were basically background information and it was only when the news that three MI5 agents had been summoned to appear that the media's interest was really piqued.

The agents called were the head of MI5 operations in Northern Ireland at the time of the Wright murder, and two desk officers whose responsibility it was to keep both the RUC and ministers updated with relevant and important security information. Imagine the surprise when it was revealed that the MI5 desk officers had passed on to the RUC, and allegedly to ministers, that there was a death threat against Billy Wright, a death threat that had been issued by the INLA, some of whose members were, of course, to end up in the same H Block at the Maze as Billy Wright. A few days later I also discovered through the media that a former No 1 governor had met unofficially with the political wing of the INLA, who had revealed to him that the guns had been smuggled into Maghaberry and had been intended to be used in the murder of Billy Wright.

When the security minister took the stand and was presented with the information that had allegedly been forwarded by MI5 to both the police and to ministers, he responded with shock and horror. He explained that this was the first time he had been made aware of this information, and that had he known of it at the time it would most likely have been decided to take Billy Wright to a different prison.

The MI5 officers were mystified as to why the intelligence they had obtained and passed on had been ignored.

Surprisingly, lessons were not learnt from this rather serious over-sight, an oversight that left Billy Wright dead and all but ruined my life. A chance to stop the 7/7 bombers in the UK may also have been missed when yet another fax from MI5 to the police went missing. A report due to be released towards the end of 2008 is expected to reveal that an MI5 document, sent to West Yorkshire police by fax, which raised suspicions about ringleader Mohammed Sidique Khan and his accomplice Shehzad Tanweer, either did not arrive or was not acted on by the police. It is believed MI5 did not follow up their fax. When I read this story I felt a strong sense of déjà vu.

Further controversy followed when it was also revealed that the decision to relocate Wright to the Maze was initially rescinded, only to be changed back again two days later. The transfer was dragged further down the collusion road by a statement made by Peter Robinson MP in which he said that he had received information during a meeting with the then Prime Minister John Major that a loyalist politician had allegedly stated that something needed to be done about Billy Wright.

Mr Robinson's evidence also revealed that during a meeting with Billy Wright, Wright had informed him that, although he had done many bad things in his life, he was not guilty of the crime for which he had been convicted. Wright's second disclosure was perhaps viewed as being of greater significance: he had stated that he believed he would be murdered by soldiers of the state.

Controversy continued over the years, and perhaps the most controversial event was the sudden departure of a senior lawyer, Derek Batchelor QC, from the inquiry. There was no warning or even rumours of the resignation and it appeared to happen quite suddenly.

A different barrister was appointed to replace Mr Batchelor and began working with the inquiry in early September 2008.

As the days of the inquiry stretched into weeks and then into months I became more and more frustrated. My stress levels had begun to rise again and there were more sleepless nights. I needed more counselling sessions to help me to maintain some sense of perspective.

I was due to be called to present my evidence at the end of June, but the departure of Mr Batchelor meant more delays.

Brian Barlow was called to give his evidence, as was Duty Principal Officer Don McCallum.

Brian Barlow insisted in his evidence that he was not present at the meeting during which I had issued the instructions to Don McCallum to stand down the Towers. To his credit, however, he did state that he would have been surprised if I had asked Don to stand down the Tower at H Block 6. I was confused, to say the least. I was one hundred per cent certain that Brian was at the meeting, and because I could remember the exact conversation that had taken place I was mystified as to why my recollection and Brian's were so different.

My confusion over Brian's stance in his evidence paled into insignificance when I followed over the Internet the evidence presented by Don McCallum, the duty principal officer on the day of the murder. He couldn't remember who was present at the meetings on the morning of the murder.

However, as I read through his evidence on the second day of his testimony, I was shocked to discover that he made remarks to the effect that Governor McKee had a reputation for telling porkies.

I could see from the transcript on the Internet that a barrister immediately sought and received permission to cross-examine the witness. He asked Don McCallum to give other examples of the 'lies' that Governor McKee had told in the past and also to identify witnesses who could support his assertions. Of course Don McCallum was unable to do either. My barrister then went on to point out to Don McCallum that this was the first occasion relating to 27 December 1997 on which such a detrimental accusation with regard to Governor McKee's character had come before the inquiry. The barrister furthermore suggested to Mr McCallum that the true reason for his assertion was to shift blame from his mistakes on the day of the murder onto the shoulders of Governor McKee.

I was disappointed by the evidence presented by both Don McCallum and Brian Barlow and dumbfounded by most of it.

Now the inquiry had heard from two of the witnesses out of the four who would be providing it with a version of the events of 27 December 1997 that would differ from my account. The other two sets of evidence, the content of which I did not yet know, would come from John Blundell, the Prison Officers' Association representative, and from a fellow governor on duty on the day of the murder, Joe Helm.

During the course of the latter months of the inquiry two key witnesses lost their lives: John Kennaway, by alleged suicide while on remand in Maghaberry Prison; and Crip McWilliams, who died after a seven-year battle against cancer. McWilliams and Kennaway were, along with John Glennon, part of the three-man murder team who killed Billy Wright on 27 December 1997.

The inquiry had now heard conflicting evidence pertaining to the day of the murder and they contacted my solicitor to obtain my permission to have an up-to-date report prepared by my psychiatrist. I suspect they were seeking to find out whether I had suffered any confusion or loss of memory as a result of post-traumatic stress.

The next letter that I received raised my stress levels still higher. It confirmed that the inquiry would reconvene on Monday 8 September and that the first witness of the day would be a certain Governor William McKee.

Chapter 20
Towards Closure

I couldn't decide if I was glad or sorry about this latest development. While one part of me wanted closure, another was frightened about what other, perhaps life-threatening, circumstances that closure might bring.

My barrister requested that I meet with him on the Thursday before my court appearance, so that he could go over a few points with me and brief me on what questions I could expect from the other legal representatives who would be present in the court.

Even though it was now over ten years since the murder, I had still to meet formally with David Wright, Billy's father. While I was attending the inquest in Downpatrick in an unofficial capacity I happened to be in the toilets at the same time as Mr Wright, but I did not recognise him. It was only later that evening when I saw his picture on television that I realised the identity of that pleasant gentleman who made polite conversation with me while we washed our hands in the toilets of the court. I often wonder how the conversation might have gone had Mr Wright known my identity that morning, and that I was the governor responsible for the Maze on the morning of his son's death.

After the murder of his son, David Wright had asked the security minister if he could meet with me, but permission had been refused. I was never asked if I would meet Mr Wright; I merely read in the *Daily Mirror* about his request, which I felt was justified, and that it had been refused. To this day I still have not been officially told of the request. Mr Wright had also asked for me to be identified at the time of the murder of his son, and this request was answered by the Northern Ireland Office with the standard reply, 'We are unable to provide an answer to this request on security grounds'. Of course this reply simply fed further ammunition to the collusion theorists, who obviously wondered why, if I was innocent of any wrongdoing, my identity was being concealed. David Wright had asked whether it was national security or my personal security that would be threatened by the disclosure of my identity. The implication was of course that if state security was at issue, there must have been state involvement in the murder. Again, to this day I have never been informed what response, if any, Mr Wright received to his question.

At the time of Billy Wright's murder, Geoffrey Donaldson, a union-ist MP, also asked for 'the governor in charge of the Maze on the day of the murder of Billy Wright' to be named in parliament. This was of course long before my name was eventually leaked to both Mr Wright and, more crucially from my perspective, to the Loyalist Volunteer Force.

As Thursday and my meeting with my barrister approached I found myself becoming quite agitated. I knew of course that this state of mind was caused not by the prospect of the meeting with my barrister but by my appearance at the inquiry, scheduled for the fol-lowing Monday.

The meeting was actually both short and fairly relaxed. My barrister ran through my statements: the first, the statement I had made to the police in 1997; and the second, which I gave the solicitors representing the inquiry early in 2008. The only real concern I had was the fact that I would have to face questioning from six or seven barristers in addition to questions from the three-person inquiry panel. In addi-tion to the barrister and junior counsel for the inquiry, there were also barristers representing the interested parties: the Northern Ireland Office; David Wright; the police service; myself; and various other members of the prison service who were implicated in the inquiry.

By this time I was aware of some of the contents of the statements made by prison staff whose versions of events were at odds with mine and I was naturally concerned about the possible implications for myself once the questioning commenced on Monday 8 September.

As I could no longer drive—I had had two major road rage incidents brought on by my post-traumatic stress disorder—I had to stay overnight with my brother, who lived within a short drive from Banbridge Courthouse, where the inquiry was sitting. My brother collected me and brought me to his home on Sunday evening so that I would be well rested before my appearance before the inquiry. As we neared his house I felt the hairs rise on the back of my neck as I recalled the last time I had stayed with him, when I had narrowly avoided being assassinated by a joint team of LVF and UDA gunmen. I felt a shiver run up my spine as we parked and walked the short distance to his home.

Not unnaturally, I had difficulty sleeping and read over my statement, just to familiarise myself once again with its contents. My barrister had advised me of the importance of sticking to the facts as outlined in my statement—to do otherwise would present the other barristers with the opportunity to challenge me. Suddenly I spotted a date mentioned near the beginning of my statement. The date was incorrect! How on earth had I missed that? And why did I have to discover the error a few hours before I was due to appear in court?

I had stated that Ken Crompton had briefed me on 26 December 1997 (the day before Billy Wright was killed) about standing down the H Block Towers in the event of staff shortages. Of course neither Ken nor I were even in the prison that day: the briefing had actually happened just before the Christmas break. Great, I thought, the one thing that my barrister had stressed—keeping strictly to the facts of my statement—was now at least partly out of the window. I had given the opposing legal counsel the opportunity to challenge me on a mistake and I just knew the direction in which this oversight would allow their questioning to lead. 'Is there any other part of your statement that is incorrect? Why has it taken until the morning of the inquiry for us to be told that there is an error in your statement?'

Any hope of a few hours' restful sleep was now gone. I tossed and turned until morning and as I was getting dressed I couldn't help but feel like an innocent man being brought to court to face charges resulting from a conspiracy. The only difference thankfully was that as this was an inquiry and not a proper court appearance I knew that regardless of whom the inquiry believed I would still be going home that night.

I arrived at the court just before nine o'clock and was shown to a small waiting room. I would be able to return to this room during the day if there were any breaks permitted by the panel. My solicitor joined me a short time later and tried to reassure me that the mistake over the date was of minor significance. We were then joined by Mr Macleod, counsel for the inquiry, who explained how the day would run and in what order I would be questioned and by whom.

I was comfortable with all of this and was actually starting to relax a little when Mr Macleod produced a document for me to look at. The document was a report, allegedly prepared by me, which was addressed to the Chief Executive of the Prison Service, Alan Shannon. But I had never seen the document before. I was stunned! My mind seemed to grind to a halt and I literally couldn't marshal a single thought. I simply couldn't speak.

Mr Macleod asked me again to consider the document, which seemed to kick-start my mental functions again. 'No!' I almost shouted. 'That is the first time I have ever seen this document.' The document was a report that covered, first, the background to the transfer of the LVF prisoners from Maghaberry Prison to the Maze and, second, the events relating to my role and the chronological order of what happened on the day of the murder of Billy Wright. Although I was not responsible for typing the report the second part outlining the sequence of events on the 27th December were accurate to the letter.

This was certainly not something that I had expected to be greeted with on the morning of my appearance at the inquiry, and I was knocked for six. Mr Macleod tried to reassure me that we would get to the bottom of this, which was a real concern to him as well as to me, and invited me to try to relax as it was nearly time to go into court.

My solicitor shook my hand and wished me luck. He also told me that neither he nor my barrister was permitted to speak to me or give me any advice until I had finished giving evidence, which added even more to my stress. I had a terrible feeling of isolation as he closed the door and I was once again on my own. Earlier that morning I had felt like a wronged innocent, but now I felt more like a condemned man about to go the gallows. I started to shake uncontrollably. At that point I probably looked more like a man who had just woken naked in the middle of winter than a former senior member of the prison service about to give evidence to an inquiry.

I was then, much to my relief, joined by two lovely young women seconded from the Scottish Civil Service who were there as support staff for the inquiry. They led me into the court and directed me to my seat before advising me that I was required to stand until the panel had entered and were seated.

The three members of the panel entered the chamber and took their seats. After a short introduction to the day's events by Lord MacLean I was asked to take the oath. I wondered what chance I had of the inquiry believing my version of events when there was only one of me but four of the other witnesses whose stories would conflict with mine but more or less support each other's.

All I could do was to follow my barrister's advice and tell the truth as I remembered it and answer all questions asked of me as clearly and accurately as possible.

Mr Macleod was the first to stand and, perhaps in an effort to relax me, he ran through my career history as a member of the Northern Ireland Prison Service from the time I joined to the date of my retirement on medical grounds. He stopped at various points during his presentation to ask me to confirm certain facts. I was forced to apologise to the panel when Mr Macleod reminded me of the threat to my life from the LVF when I was the governor responsible for the LVF prisoners following their wreck-up of H Block 6 and their subsequent transfer to H Block 2. It took me unawares and the sudden rush of emotion that followed left me close to tears. The panel was extremely understanding and gave me time to compose myself.

Mr Macleod highlighted my posting back to the Maze, my subsequent promotion to acting governor four, my success in resolving most of the problems with the Visits in Maze, and the eradication of the overspend in Inmates Catering. He also teased from me the background to the award with which I was presented by HRH Princess Anne at Buckingham Palace.

So far, so good, I thought. Mr Macleod's words were certainly building up into a respectable character reference for me and when he mentioned that Martin Mogg, the then governing governor of the Maze, had told Alan Shannon, the chief executive of the service, that Governor McKee was making a difference in the Maze, especially in the problematic area of Visits, I was particularly pleased.

I was quickly brought down to earth however when he mentioned the discrepancy with regard to the date of my alleged briefing from Governor Crompton that was contained in my statement, a genuine mistake that I had pointed out to Mr Macleod earlier that morning.

We now came to the matters that were pertinent to the murder of Billy Wright. Through a series of prepared questions Mr Macleod drew out my version of events. As I was telling the truth the questions were easy to answer and I had managed to bring my shaking just about under control.

The standing down of the Towers was of course eventually introduced into the proceedings and gone through in great detail. Don McCallum had given two versions of my instruction with regard to the standing down of the Towers. In his statement to the police he had initially said that I had instructed him to stand down just the Tower at H6; but in his evidence to the inquiry he said that I had ordered him to stand down all the Towers.

I remember being involved in two significant meetings on the day of 27 December 1997. The first was when Don McCallum came to advise me that an additional eight staff were needed to bring the Visits group up to minimum staffing levels. The controversy that arose from this meeting was that I was saying that Brian Barlow was present while the instructions were given with regard to the standing down of the Towers while Brian Barlow was denying that he was there. Don McCallum however couldn't remember if Brian Barlow was present or not.

The second significant meeting on that day was between myself and John Blundell, the POA representative, who as I recall, burst into my office just before nine thirty that morning to object about the Tower at H6 being stood down. My evidence to the inquiry was clear: the only people at the meeting were John Blundell and myself. However the evidence of the four other pertinent witnesses ranged from all five of us being present, that is Joe Helm, Brian Barlow, John Blundell, Don McCallum and myself to (according to Don McCallum's evidence for example) that it was just himself, myself, John Blundell and perhaps Jim Duffy another POA representative. Due to the disparity in the statements of the four other witnesses I hoped for the second time that day that their credibility as reliable witnesses was diminishing in the eyes, and more importantly the ears, of the panel.

I also told Mr Macleod about another meeting that I recalled taking place in the days after the murder of Billy Wright. This meeting had been at my request and it involved Brian Barlow, Don McCallum and myself. I had wanted to get to the bottom of how the Tower at H6 came to be stood down, as that particular Tower was excluded from my instruction to stand down the Towers. At that meeting, and again from memory, Don McCallum was adamant that I had instructed him to stand down the Tower at H Block 6 and leave the rest, but I asked Don how standing down one Tower would help to address the shortage of eight staff in Visits, and why I would stand down a Tower I believed to be sacrosanct. At this point in our conversation Brian Barlow interjected, assuring Don that if I had said 'Stand down H6', he would have said, 'Fuck sake, Billy, you can't touch H6!'

At this stage I should stress that I am not accusing anyone of telling lies. The entire incident happened almost eleven years ago and undoubtedly peoples' memory lapses will create confusion in their minds. However, I must also stress that my memory of the day of the murder of Billy Wright is as clear as if it happened yesterday.

Mr Macleod was concerned that this was the first time this evidence had been brought before the inquiry, and that it had not been mentioned in any of my previous statements. I assured Mr Macleod that I had discussed the meeting between myself, Brian Barlow and Don McCallum with the inquiry solicitors and respectfully suggested that if the notes of that meeting could be obtained then this fact could be proven.

The only other issue that caused me concern during Mr Macleod's questioning was the document that had been prepared in my name and forwarded to the chief executive of the Prison Service. Mr Macleod did not labour the point and finished his questioning before passing me on to David Wright's barrister, Mr Kane.

Mr Kane seized on the 'falsified document', as he termed it, and adopted a 'dog with a bone' approach, saying that some four days after the murder of Billy Wright there were 'falsified documents' passing between the prison and Prison Service headquarters. Eventually he moved on and, as was the focus of many of the other barristers present, concentrated on the issuing of the orders to stand down the Towers and the two meetings that had taken place on the day of the murder.

Again and again the issue of the conflicting versions of events was raised, and again and again I was forced to argue that I believed myself to be correct.

The questioning moved on around the other barristers and because of my introduction of the fact that I had said in my interview with Neary (who had originally carried out the investigation into the murder of Billy Wright in 1998) that Brian Barlow was present when I both issued the order with regard to the tower and at the subsequent second meeting with Don McCallum when the misunderstanding of my orders were raised, the barrister seized again on as he put it, 'yet another fact that was not contained in your statement'.

Again I reassured the barrister that the matter had been discussed with the inquiry solicitors at interview and suggested that if a copy of the interview notes with Neary and the inquiry solicitors could be made available that this would confirm I was telling the truth. I wondered what response the Neary investigating officer would have received if he had spoken to Brian Barlow to seek verification that he was present at both the initial meeting with Don McCallum and also the later one, as I had asked him too at that time.

In my opinion the barrister poured scorn on my suggestion and almost reluctantly directed me onto the next in line.

It was now almost three o'clock in the afternoon and I still had three barristers to go. My throat was raw, my shirt, as it had been many times in the past, was sticking to my back, I was shaking again and my stress levels had shot up, close to the point that in the past had required both medication and counselling. Still another legal eagle would fly to their feet, introduce themselves, assure me that they were not trying to trick me and then proceed, in my opinion, to do exactly that!

I had been told that if I needed a break at any point outside the official break times I just had to ask. I felt that I had reached and passed the need for a break much earlier in the day, but the thought of walking out at four thirty having presented my evidence and dealt with the resulting questions was the motivation that gave me the strength to force myself to carry on.

The next barrister was representing some of the prison staff, including the four other witnesses so his questioning was much more challenging than that of any of his predecessors. He did his best to pick holes in my evidence and continually reminded me that the evidence of his four clients was directly opposed to mine. I misunderstood one of his questions and gave him an answer that probably provoked him as much as his earlier questions had tried unsuccessfully to provoke me. I said something like: 'I can think of no reason why these four individuals' evidence is so far divorced from my version of events, and the only common denominator that I can come up with is that they are all members of the Prison Officers' Association and I am not!'

Mr Beer, the barrister, seized on my comments. 'That's a loaded statement: what are you implying?' he asked.

I assured the barrister that I was not trying to imply anything and was merely making the point that the only thing the four staff with the opposing version of events had in common was that they were members of the POA, while I was not. He was clearly not aware of that fact and queried it with me. I was able to confirm that this was indeed the case.

Mr Beer was handed a piece of paper and this seemed to distract him. Addressing the chairman, he confirmed that he had a copy of the mysterious document that was prepared in my name and put before the panel earlier that morning. All parties at the inquiry each had a monitor in front of them which could be used to show documentation to everyone. Mr Beer asked for the final page of the document to be put on screen and to the surprise of myself and others present, the document was not signed by me but 'pped' by Martin Mogg.

I was relieved for two reasons; first I was worried that I had not been believed when I assured the panel that morning that I had never seen the document before, and of course I would have been extremely embarrassed if the document had turned up with my signature on it! Second, Mr Mogg's signature supported, to some degree, my claim that I had never seen the document.

Now that that particular matter had been resolved, at least to my satisfaction, the wheel turned again and I found myself now facing questioning from Mr McHenry, a barrister representing Raymond Hill, the officer who may or may not—depending on the time of day—have been in the Tower on 27 December 1997.

Mr McHenry did not dwell on too much background information, moving quickly to the matter that concerned Officer Hill. Mr McHenry explained that his client would insist that he was stood down from the Tower on two occasions that morning, the first being ten minutes before I commenced duty, and then again at approximately nine thirty.

I was extremely surprised when Mr McHenry asked for a copy of the po/so journal from H Block 6 on the day of the murder to be displayed on the monitor. He invited me to read out the particular entry that he had highlighted: '8.50hrs From AMIS Office. Drop c/d Tower. ECR and SIR informed.' (ECR was the control room and SIR the security department.)

I was amazed, as no doubt were other people in the room, at this new twist in the proceedings. This on the face of it meant that the AMIS Office personnel had stood down a Tower which they had no authority to stand down and also, and more importantly, had failed to inform me of this when I reported for duty some ten minutes later.

I started to hope and believe that the chink in the armour of lies was beginning to widen into something more significant, and that it would lead to the inquiry accepting that my account of the standing down of the Tower at H Block 6 was the correct version.

Mr McHenry continued. 'There appears to be a disparity between the time that you have stated you believed you had resolved the Tower issue with Mr Blundell and that of my client, Raymond Hill.'

Raymond Hill was alleging that the second time he had been called from the Tower was at nine thirty, but I was confident that it was at that time that the matter had actually been resolved. If my times were correct, that would leave Mr Hill having to explain why it had taken him around thirty minutes to return to the Tower when it would normally take only six or seven minutes.

This was another matter for the panel. Who would they believe?

(By now I had come to believe that the Tower was actually a red herring, and there seemed to be a consensus of opinion that the standing down of the Tower did not and would not have made any difference to the final tragic outcome of the day's events.)

As the day grew finally to a close I was delighted when Mr Macleod rose to produce two important pieces of documentation that he had recovered. These were shown on the monitors.

The first document was the handwritten notes of my interview with Neary's representative. They confirmed that in early 1998 I had informed Neary that Brian Barlow was also present at the initial meeting when standing down the Towers was discussed. Although perhaps not as significant to others as it was to me, it proved that from the very beginning I had insisted Brian Barlow was present and this was not just something that I had claimed in an attempt to deflect blame for the standing down of the Tower.

The second document was the notes from my interview with the inquiry solicitors. Again, as I had assured the barrister earlier in the day, I had reported to the solicitors the matter of the second meeting between Brian Barlow, Don McCallum and myself, though the inquiry solicitors had omitted that part of my evidence from my statement. There were a few more questions to be asked of me and then a glance at my watch told me that my time was up. My ordeal was over.

The chairman thanked me for my attendance and apologised for the length of time I had been required to remain on the stand.

As I left the courtroom my throat felt raw. I had been talking for near enough five hours. However, a feeling of contentment suddenly came over me. A final conclusion to the murder of Billy Wright had just moved a step closer.

——

Of course there were other witnesses who were yet to appear before the inquiry. I was only really interested in hearing the evidence of five of them. Joe Helm, one of the governors who were on duty with me that fateful day; John Blundell, the POA representative; Arthur Gallagher and Brian Molloy, the two senior officers who were on duty in H Block 6 on the day of the murder; and finally Ken Crompton, the deputy governor who, just before Christmas, had briefed me on standing down the Towers.

Joe Helm was called to appear on 9 September, the day after me. I do not say this to cast disparity on any part of Governor Helm's evidence but I was surprised, on reading Joe's evidence on the Internet that night, that his evidence on the standing down of the Towers was quite vague in parts. Joe discussed two meetings that he believed had occurred. He said he had been outside my office when he had heard me arguing with Officer Blundell. The second meeting, he stated, had occurred in the AMIS Office, which was on the bottom floor of Administration. According to Joe, Brian Barlow, John Blundell and Don McCallum and myself were present at this meeting, which followed my initial interaction with Officer Blundell. Despite different approaches by the various barristers, Governor Helm stuck fairly firmly to his story. I smiled to myself as I read Joe's testimony. Although the evidence presented by Joe was very different from my own it was also different in parts from the other main players.

The next man called by the inquiry was John Blundell the POA representative and again his evidence was fairly similar to Brian Barlow's, yet was not even close to my recall of the meeting.

At one point Officer Blundell denied that I had instructed him to put the Tower on again, using the excuse that as a basic grade officer he did not have the authority to pass on such an instruction.

I smiled again the following day when Senior Officer Gallagher confirmed during his evidence that the phone call he received instructing him to put the officer back in the Tower was from none other than the POA representative John Blundell.

The following day I had the opportunity to review the presentation of my evidence with my solicitor and to discuss the evidence of the other interested parties. I believe, and that belief was supported by my solicitor, that I came across as a credible witness despite the fact that four other witnesses contradicted my views.

Ken Crompton was called a few days later but his evidence neither supported nor denied my version of events as he was unable to recall whether he had briefed me before the fateful day or not. I would have been happier if Ken had recalled our conversation where he advised me not to stand down the Tower at H Block 6, but nevertheless I was satisfied that his evidence at least did not contradict my version of events.

––––

The stress I had felt over the weeks following the presentation of my evidence gradually subsided again as I made my way back into the new life that I had cultivated for myself, life after the prison service. I accepted that the inquiry would probably be wound up around Christmas and realised that its findings would probably take a great deal longer to be delivered.

However as so many times before just when you think it is safe to go back in the water yet another piece of information slithers its way into the public domain and once again the collusion theorists are thrown a few more crumbs.

This latest information concerned a meeting that had taken place on 15 December 1997 attended by seven members of the INLA. Documentary evidence shown to the inquiry confirmed that the RUC Special Branch was informed of the meeting by the close of play that same evening. There had been an Army team watching the INLA as part of a general surveillance venture known as Operation Jaw. This operation was overseen by the RUC Special Branch. However The RUC could not produce any record of the meeting nor any kind of master log for Operation Jaw at that time.

Other records suggest that the Security Forces knew that at sometime during this INLA meeting the murder of Billy Wright was discussed. The waters were furthered muddied when neither the RUC, the Army nor indeed MI5 were able to confirm where this information actually materialised from. The only facts that they were prepared to present to the inquiry was their denial that the intelligence had been reported from any of their own sources.

This latest episode of absent information will be explored in some depth by the inquiry in the near future and comes fast on the heels of previous criticism regarding information missing from both police and prison files. In this case the inquiry were not aware of Operation Jaw until it was brought to their attention by another security agency which had produced two brief extracts of an Army log detailing their surveillance operation. The PSNI had already been asked to respond to questions put forward in relation to Operation Jaw but had failed to do so. This resulted in the inquiry suddenly being halted in September 2007 when they ordered a special report on police failings to produce evidence.

I suppose I wasn't unduly either surprised or concerned about this latest event but was quickly reminded of the possible implications for me when, once again, the standing down of the Tower was mentioned. The inquiry revealed that information from other security agencies had led them to believe that discussions at the December meeting had a distinct bearing on the gun used to kill Billy Wright, timing of the attack and the standing down of the guard in the watchtower who could have seen the killers on their way to murder Billy Wright! There was also a suggestion that the Army may have had the meeting bugged or even had an informer present in the room at the time of the meeting. This suspicion was all but confirmed when a PSNI lawyer told the inquiry 'The means by which it came was not disclosed and we would be anxious that that should not be disclosed.'

Following this latest discovery I reluctantly accepted that the inquiry would not be wound up around Christmas as I and many others had come to expect and therefore also realised that the findings would take considerably longer to be delivered. Although I knew that I would not achieve total closure until the findings of the inquiry were published, perhaps because I had my day in court and had emptied my mind of all the facts in relation to the murder of Billy Wright it had given me freedom, freedom to finally let go of that part of my life and to refocus on what is actually important to me here and now.

There were many different witnesses called to appear following my appearance on the 8 September 2008 and as usual I kept myself abreast of anyone evidence that affected me or contradicted my version of events.

Duncan McLaughlin, who was a former governor one at HMP Maghaberry was called on 21 October and the information revealed during questions from Mr MacLeod and answers given by Governor McLaughlin opened the proverbial can of worms with regard to the murder of Billy Wright.

Mr McLaughlin had been in contact with IRSP, the political wing of the INLA and had actually been in telephone contact on the very day of the firearm incident in Maghaberry. It was further revealed that he had met with them in person at the Quakers centre in Belfast. These meetings, Mr McLaughlin assured the inquiry, were done with the approval of the then chief executive Alan Shannon and Martin Mogg the director of Prison Operations. Intelligence reports also came to light which reported that Billy Wright had been the original target in the Maghaberry incident but following his transfer to Maze the target was changed to Kevin McAlorum. There was other contemporaneous information originating from outside the prison that INLA had indeed smuggled in the gun originally with the purpose of killing Billy Wright.

The most serious allegation to be made was that Mr McLaughlin had been informed by a member of the IRSP known as Ard Chamairle Member one (for the purpose of the inquiry) that the gun had been smuggled into Maghaberry to kill Wright. This supported the intelligence reports already presented. Steven Davis, the governor in charge of security at Maghaberry, had also listed this suspicion as one of three options that he highlighted in the investigation he had prepared into the incident at Maghaberry.

It was also obvious that the decision-makers at Prison Service Headquarters were not in receipt of this information, otherwise why were Billy Wright's would be assassins transferred to the Maze and to the same H Block that Wright was housed in so soon after the earlier incident?

Mr McLaughlin stated that he was sure that he had passed the information on to Martin Mogg, who was now deceased and could therefore not confirm or deny that he had been in receipt of the clear threat to the life of Billy Wright.

Had this information been passed on to the proper authorities the source of any threat to Billy Wright's life would have been removed and he would, in all liklihood still be alive today. As well as this my life would not have wrecked by the devastation that followed that fateful day on 27 December, 1997.

In my opinion it is unimaginable that a No.1 governor was permitted to meet the political wing of the INLA on his own. In doing so he would not only compromise his own personal security but also leave himself open to ridicule and worse. This was brought home in the starkest possible terms in the witness box on the 21, 22, and 23 October 2008 in Banbridge Court House as he was questioned by the various legal personalities that were present.

This latest development forced me to accept that the inquiry was now far from over and who knew what other incredulous information was going to make its way into the public domain before the final decision was arrived at by Lord MacLean and his team. I again, was forced to reluctantly accept that there was still no opportunity to finally draw a line under this whole sorry situation. However my day in court had helped and I knew that eventually there would be closure.

———

Looking back over my career and indeed my life there are, of course, regrets. I regret letting my job as a prison governor in the infamous Maze Prison get to the top of my list of priorities to the detriment of my family. I regret not spending more time with my children as they were growing up. I regret not picking up on the subtle hints that were delivered by my ex-wife as our marriage disintegrated around us.

But these regrets just like the Prison Service and the murder of Billy Wright belong in the past and my previous life.

I have a new life now devoid of the problems from the past, a life that is filled with love and laughter, a life that has given me the time I never had in the past for my children and now grandchildren, a different life that has given me a renewed optimism for my future. You know, I think my good friend Alfie just may have been right after all!